DON'T MISS OUT

The Ambitious Student's Guide to Financial Aid

33RD EDITION
ANNA AND ROBERT LEIDER

OCTAMERON
ASSOCIATES

Confused? Strangled by Loopholes and Red Tape?

If you run into snags or get confused by all the techniques we cover in this book, request our free brochure *We Can Help* (Octameron, 1900 Mount Vernon Avenue, Alexandria, VA 22301). It describes our college admission and financial aid services. Neither cost very much and both can save you a bundle—in money and in time.

Our Tuesday Special

We keep an experienced counselor by the phone nearly every Tuesday from 10am to 4pm EST to answer questions you may have about college financing (selection or admission). The conversation will cost you $40 which you may charge against your VISA, MasterCard or American Express. Call 703/836-5480.

Address editorial correspondence to:

Octameron Associates
PO Box 2748
Alexandria, VA 22301

703/836-5480 (voice)
703/836-5650 (fax)
octameron@aol..com (e-mail)
www.octameron.com

ISBN 1-57509-125-9

PRINTED IN THE UNITED STATES OF AMERICA

TABLE OF CONTENTS

CHAPTER 1

■ ■ ■ ■ ■ ■ ■ ■ ■ ■ ■ ■ ■ ■ ■ ■ ■ ■ ■ ■

USING THIS GUIDE

The sequence of topics in this guide parallels the steps you should take in your quest to finance college. First, you must define your monetary need and second, you must learn how to finance that need. Please don't skip straight to the scholarship resource chapters. For most people, equating the financial aid process with an isolated search for scholarships is an unproductive way to spend time, and the time of the kind organizations offering assistance. Instead, start at the beginning.

Organization of Guide

In Part I of this guide you'll explore the larger trends in higher education finance, and learn to separate fact from fiction.

In Part II you'll meet the players in the financial aid game. You'll learn how to calculate your family contribution—the amount of money your family will be judged capable of contributing to college costs. And you'll learn to take charge of the entire aid application process so you don't end up paying more for college than you should, or can afford (or make a frantic last-minute college choice that is not in your best interest).

In Part III, you move from fundamentals to more advanced topics. You become a master of the financial aid game—college selection, personal finance and tax strategies. You learn the best moves for two different situations: when college entrance is approaching fast and when college is still years away.

In Part IV, you meet the major money sources—the colleges, Uncle Sam, and the states. They dispense billions of dollars. By getting to know their programs well, you will not overlook a single penny that is due you.

Part V reviews two major alternatives for financing college—your boss, and the military. You might not like the suggestions, but you should know about them, and consider or reject them at this point in the process.

Part VI groups special opportunities. You've had the meat and potatoes. Now you are looking for the cake, or maybe just the frosting. You'll find sections here for the bright, the career-oriented, the athlete, the graduate student, and for minorities and women. The tips at the end of Part VI bring together ideas developed earlier at greater length. Review these tips, and when you're done, we'll award you the title of "Financial Aid Guru."

Chapter 2

■ ■

Paying for College
in the Year 2009

It Takes Special Knowledge

Families consistently overestimate the cost of college and underestimate the availability of financial aid. They are convinced college is essential to a prosperous future, yet terrified they won't be able to afford it for their kids. In truth, college can be expensive; however, don't throw up your hands and walk away. Financial help is available—plenty of it. But there is more to getting aid than matching a list of scholarship leads to a pile of stationary. It takes special knowledge. For instance:

Knowing the Written (and Unwritten) Rules. Thanks to tax code changes, and new infusions of financial aid dollars at the federal, state and college level, students should find ample help in paying their college bills; the process of getting all this money, however, continues to grow more complicated, and families who don't know the rules, will pay more for college than their savvier peers.

Knowing How to Apply. Student aid used to go to those who needed it most. Now it goes to those who know how, when and where to apply.

Knowing About the Buyer's Market. At many schools, competition for good students is intense. This competition creates opportunities—opportunities you can maximize.

Knowing Basic Personal Finance Techniques. Investments, gifts, low-interest loans, education bonds, lines of credit... When properly used, these techniques can help your cash flow and reinforce the availability of student aid. When improperly used, they cancel your eligibility for aid. You want to achieve the former and prevent the latter.

Knowing How to Tell Good Advice From Bad. Advice on college planning is plentiful. But not all of it is good. Some is dated. Some is wrong. And some is tainted by the self-interest of those who offer it.

Special knowledge is what this guide is all about. *Don't Miss Out* will teach you and your family how to formulate your own financial aid strategy—one that will lead you to a good, affordable higher education.

The Big Picture

Merit-based aid programs continue to flourish, while record-low interest rates have fueled an increase in student borrowing. As a result, there is now around $176 billion available to help families (at all income levels) pay their tuition bills. And, there is more money to be had. Uncle's biggest student aid effort, the Stafford Loan, is an entitlement program—everyone who is eligible for a loan can get a loan. But it takes an application. As the great Confucius might have said: "Apply forget—no loan you get."

Unfortunately, student expenses (tuition, room, board, books, fees, and transportation) will total nearly $286 billion, so families must still be prepared to pick up around 38% of the total tab, about $110 billion.

Take a good look at the following pie chart. Note that Federal, State, and Collegiate plans are the main sources of student aid. Not private scholarships. Our advice: When you look for financial aid, head for the biggest piece. Don't make the search for crumbs—that small percent of the Student Aid Pie which represents private scholarships—your number one priority. NOT SMART!

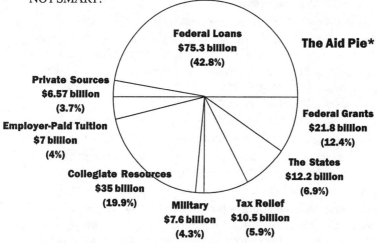

The Aid Pie*

Federal Loans
$75.3 billion
(42.8%)

Private Sources
$6.57 billion
(3.7%)

Employer-Paid Tuition
$7 billion
(4%)

Collegiate Resources
$35 billion
(19.9%)

Military
$7.6 billion
(4.3%)

Tax Relief
$10.5 billion
(5.9%)

The States
$12.2 billion
(6.9%)

Federal Grants
$21.8 billion
(12.4%)

Notes to Pie Chart

Federal Loans include amounts awarded under the Stafford, PLUS and Perkins programs.

Tax Relief for Education Expenses include the Hope and Lifetime credits, the deduction for tuition expenses and student loan interest payments, and the benefits realized through tax-advantaged education savings accounts.

Employer-paid Tuition includes company-based scholarships, tuition reimbursement, and co-op.

Federal Grants include Pell, Academic Competitiveness Grants, SEOG, LEAP, Byrd, Work Study, AmeriCorps, TEACH, various graduate programs and smaller programs.

Military includes the GI Bill, ROTC, military educational bonuses, and various benefits to dependents of veterans.

College Resources include scholarships and loans from the colleges' own resources. It does not include tuition remissions.

The States include state grant programs, state work-study programs and special loan programs that supplement Stafford. It does not include operating subsidies given to public universities.

*Figures are estimated for 2009/2010 based on FY2009 budget requests or data from prior years.

Looking to the Future

Paying for college isn't a one-shot deal. You must think in terms of this year's costs, next year's costs, and the following year's costs. If tuition strains you now, how desperate will you be by your Senior year? Lots will happen over the next few years. Here's a look at the biggest trends:

Trend A: College Costs Continue to Outpace Inflation

For several years, colleges across the country hiked their prices by as much as 10-20%. Shrinking endowments and state budget woes were largely to blame, however, increasing fixed costs—insurance premiums, health care, and energy bills—made a tight situation tighter.

Today, endowments are on the rise and state coffers are healthier, but annual tuition increases are likely to hover around 5-6%, continuing to outpace inflation. Why not a rate equal to inflation? There are many reasons why college costs can't be likened to the price of bread. For example:

Higher Education is Labor Intensive

For this reason, technological gain does not have as great an impact on "productivity" in the academic world as it does in the industrial world. College students cannot be turned out like Model Ts. Great teaching, as Socrates and Plato knew, comes from conversation between two inquiring minds. And 10:1 student-faculty ratios don't come cheap. Furthermore, in fields such as engineering and computer science, industry provides much higher salary scales than college departments. In consequence, graduate students are turning to industry rather than teaching, and professors keep moving from campus to corporate suites. To fight this trend, colleges must offer more attractive salary packages.

Fuel Costs and Deferred Maintenance

These are, proportionally, a far greater burden on colleges than on families. Old buildings, drafty halls, and students who overload the circuits with gadgets ranging from hair dryers to VCRs to multimedia computers keep the meters spinning. Also, colleges are plagued with leaky roofs, crumbling foundations, cracking asphalt and inaccessible pipes. Ivy won't hold up the walls forever. Our campuses need over $50 billion in repairs.

Fewer Students to Pick Up the Tab

Over the next 10 years, the U.S. Department of Education estimates that the number of undergraduates will level off, and decline, as the last of the baby-boom offspring hit college age. Furthermore, the composition of college campuses will continue to change, as a larger share of new enrollees will come from low-income immigrant and minority families, and be more likely to need financial aid. So not only will schools no longer be able to spread their fixed costs—physical plant, maintenance, staff and faculty salaries—among more "customers," many of the remaining "customers" won't be able to pay without help from student aid.

The squeeze will be most severe at public universities and community colleges; they are being asked to absorb most of these enrollment increases at the same time state appropriations to public colleges have levelled off. The (unpopular) solution? Program cuts combined with tuition increases. "We are heading toward reduced access and reduced quality" warns the American Council on Education.

Decreasing State Appropriations

Unlike a for-profit business, colleges sell their product (education) at a price substantially below cost. This is especially true at public universities, where tuition dollars cover only one-third of a school's operating costs, up from 21% in 1980. Why this increase? In tough economic times, funds for higher education are often the first to get the ax, since budget-cutters figure that colleges have alternate revenue sources—parental pocketbooks in the form of higher tuition charges. In the cash-strapped early years of this decade, most states increased their public university tuition rates by an average of 10%-15%.

While revenues have improved, many states are again trying to close massive budget gaps, and unlike the federal government, most states are required by law to balance their books. Furthermore, there is considerable competition for every tax dollar, especially from elementary and secondary schools, prison-spending and medicaid.

In it's own bureautcratic way, the Department of Education will soon start "encouraging"states to maintain certain spending levels. First, it will require states to meet "maintenance of effort" requirements to receive funding under a new "College Access Challenge Grant" program. Second, it will start posting five-year comparison charts on its web site, hoping to shame states into helping keep higher education affordable. The charts will show:

1. The change in spending by each state (per full-time student) at that state's public universities;
2. The change in tuition/fees charged by each state's public universities;
3. The change in need- and merit-based aid provided by the state to full-time students at public universities.

Laptops, Labs and Libraries

College after college is grabbing headlines by announcing their latest technological advances. At a minimum, every student will have access to a free Internet hookup, including high speed or wireless access with unlimited bandwidth. These now-essential computers must be linked by networks. They need maintenance and a training staff. The networks must be made secure. And since systems become obsolete faster than you can click a mouse, everything must be upgraded or replaced at a dizzying pace. Some schools now are even handing out new iPhones to incoming students. All of this costs money.

Furthermore, if colleges are to be on the leading edge of research and technology, they must have the latest in laboratories, research equipment, and machinery. Getting it (and maintaining it) will cost billions. In fact, schools spend at least $7 billion on technology each year. Even a school lucky enough to be "given" a new $40 million lab will need three times that much of its own money to maintain it—unless the wealthy benefactor whose name now adorns the new science center thought to include extra money for custodial services and test tubes.

Thanks to all these fancy new facilities stocked with higher-than-hi-tech toys, it now costs nearly three times as much to teach a science course as it does to teach English or philosophy. And, of course, most enrollment growth has been among students majoring in these expensive-to-teach fields.

Finally, no matter how extensive the Internet's reach, schools still need libraries to house centuries worth of scholarship. And, as anyone who's purchased textbooks and scholarly journals can tell you, the printed word does not come cheap.

Red Tape

The specially-formed Commission on the Cost of Higher Education compiled a list of federal regulations affecting higher education—it was three pages long, single-spaced and included everything from occupational safety to care of animals in research to gender equity to campus crime to historic preservation. The new Higher Education Opportunity Act adds dozens of new reporting requirement. In fact, up to 12.5% of every tuition dollar goes toward complying with myriad state and federal regulations.

Club (M)ed

The Wall Street Journal calls it the "amenities arms race." As students and parents become more sophisticated shoppers, they expect more for their money—state-of-the-art sports and rec facilities (with climbing walls and miniature golf courses), 24/7 campus security, comprehensive health care facilities (with psychologists, psychiatrists and drug/alcohol abuse counselors), and extensive career services. Dorm rooms (with bunk beds) are being replaced by dorm-suites, complete with in-room washer/driers, kitchenettes, cable TV (including HBO), high-speed Internet access, weekly maid service, and private bathrooms. And dining halls have been turned into food courts to accommodate a variety of dietary requirements.

Going for the "wow factor" costs alot of money. So the irony is, the very people who complain about rising college costs are in part responsible for urging tuitions upward.

Fees, Fees, and More Fees

Many schools are proudly holding steady on tuition, but charging students separate fees for communication and Internet costs, health services, library costs, student association activities, and athletic facilities. Colleges claim that linking fees to specific activities makes the college bill easier to understand. After all, students have come to expect these services (and more). Others argue that these items used to be covered by tuition, and it's just a way for schools to dramatically boost their revenues without being criticized for hefty tuition hikes. At some public schools fees now amount to fifty percent (or more) of tuition.

For many schools, the increasing reliance on fees to generate operating income might indeed be a backdoor way to increase tuition, but it's also about control—at most public schools, fees stay on campus, while tuition revenue must go back into state coffers. In any case, when looking at the true cost of college, be sure to include mandatory fees in your calculations.

Recruiting Costs

Visiting high schools. Providing toll-free phone numbers. Designing and maintaining ever-hipper web sites. Printing and mailing glossy viewbooks. Hosting campus visits for students as well as counselors. Recruiting costs at four-year private colleges average $2,075 per student enrolled; recruiting costs at four-year public schools average $455 per student enrolled.

The Robin Hood Syndrome

Financial aid budgets, with few exceptions, can no longer meet the needs of all students. The common solution is to raise tuition through the roof; those who can pay, in effect, subsidize those who cannot. Slowly, however, as families come to realize how few students actually pay "sticker price," colleges are feeling pressure to rethink their pricing strategies. Instead of discounting tuition for as many as 90% of their students, a few schools make headlines each year by actually lowering tuition for everyone!

Why don't more schools follow this lead? Simple, they claim "targeted assistance" is a fairer way to ensure educational access. In actuality, they'd lose their ability to use financial aid as a tool in influencing the composition of the student body. Unfortunately, they soon may not have a choice. An increasing number of wealthy students are opting for public universities, where they receive the same state subsidies as their less affluent classmates. This will hurt the ability of more expensive colleges to use "full pays" to subsidize other students' tuitions.

Graduate Student Subsidies

Along these same lines, undergraduate tuition often subsidizes the education of graduate students, especially in the social sciences and humanities where grant money is increasingly scarce.

College is Less Expensive Than People Think

Not all colleges cost $45,000 a year. According to the College Board, 35% of all students go to public two-year colleges, where annual tuition averages $2,600; another 40% attend state universities, where annual tuition averages $6,829. Of students attending four-year colleges, over 63% pay less than $9,000 per year for tuition and fees. Only 12% pay more than $27,000. (For the total cost picture, add another $7,000-$9,000 for room, board, transportation and miscellaneous expenses.)

While most parents worry about the cost of college, they are also widely misinformed about these costs. In a recent poll, 30% overestimated the annual price of public four-year colleges, some by as much as $10,000 or more, while 26% overestimated the price of private four-year colleges, some by as much as $5,000 or more.

Trend B: Tuition Price Controls

Some lawmakers feel that colleges could do more to control tuition, and wanted "price controls" to become part of the Higher Education Act (the legislation that spells out most federal student aid programs).

Higher education groups weren't crazy about this proposal, pointing out the many ways that market economics don't apply to college pricing (especially the fact that tuition increases quite often reflect lost revenues from sources the schools do not control, like state appropriations). Furthermore, *published* tuition is often much higher than the price students actually pay, thanks to large increases in institutional financial aid. Over the past ten years, for example, private colleges have kept net tuition increases (tuition less scholarship and grant aid) slightly UNDER the rate of inflation.

While price-control initiatives did not make it into the final version of the new Higher Education Act, Congress did impose some reporting requirements that will (hopefully) bring greater transparency to college pricing. For example, the Act requires colleges with the greatest cost increases to submit detailed reports to the Secretary of Education explaining why their costs have risen, and what steps they are taking to hold costs down.

In addition, the government is beefing up its *College Navigator* web site (nces.ed.gov/collegenavigator) to create a "Wall of Shame"—a public listing of colleges that have the highest tuitions, the highest net prices, and the highest tuition increases. It will also showcase colleges that have the lowest tuitions, and the lowest net prices.

Finally, Congress is encouraging colleges to use more innovative methods to keep costs down, and perhaps borrow from corporate America (or is it Dilbert?) for help in improving their operations. Business buzzwords like downsizing, rightsizing, repositioning, benchmarking, outsourcing, and reengineering have become campus mantras as schools find ways to live within their means. With personnel costs making up nearly 70% of some collegiate budgets, what this really means is lots of layoffs, buyouts and early retirements. (Or, as they say in the business world, the "release of resources" and an increase in "career-change opportunities.")

Trend C: Fascination with Excellence

Major studies have focussed on the decline of excellence in elementary and secondary schools. Nearly every proposed solution requires tons of money. Lengthen the school day. Lengthen the school year. Pay some teachers more than others. Pay all teachers more. Make everyone wear uniforms. Build single sex schools. Plug a computer into every socket. Put a computer in every home. All these solutions cost money, and while a nation of literate, math whizzes sounds wonderful, in a finite economy, that money must come from somewhere. Most likely, it will come from money that otherwise might have gone to supporting higher education.

But again, there is an upside. The enshrining of excellence legitimizes the states' and colleges' use of academic scholarships to attract high-performance students. Expect continued growth in such awards.

Trend D: Colleges Want You

For all but about 250 schools, selectivity is out the window. Today, 89% of all students attend one of their top two college choices. This widens your opportunity to shop wisely and well. And the more marketable you are— good grades, leadership, musical talent, athletic ability—the more financial aid opportunities you will find. Most tuition discounts go to high achievers (regardless of their financial need). The average discount at private colleges is nearly 40%, with 83.5% of freshmen receiving an institutional grant.

Let's Make a Deal

Do you enjoy the car buying process? Do you feel confident that you've beaten the salesperson at his or her own game? Or do you feel like every one else gets a better price? Some of us will do just about anything to avoid haggling over a price, and feel very badly that some financial aid administrators have been put in a position where even the wealthiest parents and students feel as though it's their right to negotiate for more aid. Unfortunately, as more and more schools use tuition discounts (or "merit scholarships") to meet recruiting goals, the process of awarding financial aid based entirely on "need" is now an ideal rather than an actuality. Even schools that say "no deals" are usually willing to consider "additional information" about "special circumstances." As The *Washington Post* editorialized, those who are more sophisticated or better advised will haggle while the less connected or less confident will not. This cleavage between the "information haves" and "information have-nots" is doubly dangerous when located at the very gateway to education-based upward mobility.

Discounting Toward Disaster

Most schools discount tuition for certain (desired) students in an effort to raise their academic profiles (and national rankings) and make it easier to recruit new students in the future. At the same time, tuition discounting has long frustrated educators who see strategic packaging as nothing more than an unneeded bonus for students from middle- and upper-income families. They are especially troubled when it comes at the expense of aid to students from low-income families. So will tuition discounting soon come to an end? Not in the immediate future. For better or worse, these discounts do seem to have a positive influence on enrollment and retention and the ability to help schools shape the incoming class. But if these discounts continue to increase in size, without accompanying increases in class size, then overall tuition revenue will start to decline, forcing colleges to find some other way to attract and retain desirable students.

Trend E: .Com and Get It

More and more college information is but a mouse click away; especially admission and financial aid advice. Thousands of colleges maintain home pages containing everything from virtual campus tours to virtual course catalogues to virtual alumni news. You may also find links to student home pages and blogs, letting you "meet" potential classmates. And you can usually follow a school's athletic teams, read its student newspaper, visit the campus art museum, and submit your admission application.

Throughout this book we've included Web addresses where appropriate, but like snail mail addresses, they change frequently (and unlike snail mail, they are not reachable if so much as a "~" or a "/" is out of place).

Trend F: Your Fickle Uncle Sam

Uncle Sam is the main dispenser of student aid. But Uncle changes his programs every year. Money that is authorized may never be appropriated. Money that is appropriated can be rescinded. Eligibility formulas are as variable as the dollars. In Year One you may be in. In Year Two you are out. In Year Three you are in again—but for a different amount of aid. Uncle needs close watching. To watch him intelligently, you must develop a working acquaintance with "authorizations," "appropriations," "budget reconciliations," and "rescissions." Better still, read the new edition of this book which comes out every fall. We'll do the Uncle-watching for you.

Impact of Tax Reform

To complicate matters, Uncle uses the tax code to encourage "desirable" behavior, like getting students to go to college. Education tax relief measures amount to an $11 billion annual windfall for the college-bound, provided they're willing to cope with both IRS and Department of Education regulations as they make their college plans. In addition, new rules for "Qualified

Tuition Plans," Education Savings Accounts, dividends and capital gains mean many families will have to re-evaluate their investment strategies if they want to take advantage of new tax breaks. Of course, understanding all the new tax provisions may require families to spend more in consultant and accountant fees than any resulting tax break is worth.

Trend G: Cash Flow Problems— Cash Flow Help

When tuitions rise faster than available student aid, families must make up the difference. But this is not a "vive la difference" to be cheered. It's a nasty cash flow problem which, in case you don't understand, is when you have money, but it's not "liquid." It is tied up in assets like your house, and you certainly don't want to sell your house just to pay the college bills.

But take heart. Problems create solutions. Financial innovators have developed plans to ease your cash flow without requiring you to place a "For Sale" sign in front of the family castle. A lot is going on. And, we'll cover it just about the time you throw up your hands and say, "We can't do it. No way." Research shows this happens around Chapter 7.

Trend H: Hire Education

Children from wealthier families are more likely to go to college. Those with a college education earn more money. Their children are even more likely to go to college. Their children will earn even more money. And so it goes. A college education indeed prepares you for a fulfilling life—through broader cultural awareness, deeper knowledge, greater self-confidence, keener citizenship and vastly expanded resources for personal happiness.

But if philosophical reasons aren't enough, a college education will also help you earn more money. Here are some recent Census Bureau averages (www.census.gov) showing the average income of full-time workers:

Educ. Level	Men	Women
< High School	$28,415	$20,508
High School	$40,112	$28,657
Some College	$48,369	$34,291
Associates	$51,894	$37,556
College	$75,130	$49,326
Masters	$95,794	$59,569
Doctorate	$116,657	$83,141
Professional	$153,234	$98,989

CHAPTER 3

■■■■■■■■■■■■■■■■■■■

COMMON MYTHS & MISCONCEPTIONS

Most parents (naturally) think their kids are scholarship material, and equate the search for financial aid with a haphazard search for this elusive pot of gold. Unfortunately, that's not the way the system works, and by the time families realize this, it's often too late for them to find alternate (low-cost) ways to ease the unexpected tuition burden. Instead, they might force unpleasant confrontations with the college's financial aid administrator in a last-ditch effort for "free money" that seldom serves any productive purpose.

To avoid finding yourself in this frustrating situation, become a smart college consumer. The following steps can be worth thousands of dollars. Any other approach will be a waste of time and money.

1. Understand how your financial situation affects eligibility for aid.
2. Apply early, accurately and honestly for all the major assistance programs for which you are eligible (federal, state and collegiate).
3. Select colleges most likely to present you with a good aid package.
4. Discuss (if appropriate) the possibility of an improved aid package with the financial aid administrator.
5. Become knowledgeable about favorable options—commercial or otherwise—for financing expenses not covered by aid awards.
6. Finally, search for portable scholarships.

Now read this chapter on the myths that envelop the financial aid field. And remember: You don't profit from these beliefs; only the people who sustain them do.

Won't a Scholarship Replace My Money?

Most people believe scholarships put money in their pocket. Example: You have been assessed a $5,000 per year contribution to High-Priced U. One lucky day, you win a $1,000 scholarship. You now say your contribution will be $4,000. Right? Wrong. Your contribution is still $5,000. Most colleges take the $1,000, add it to your available resources, and take away $1,000 of the loan or grant or work-study opportunity it had planned to give you. In other words, scholarships help pay your college bill, but they do not necessarily reduce your share of the bill.

Question: If that's so, why do clubs and organizations work so hard to raise scholarship money?

Answer: They are not familiar with financial aid packaging. If they were, all the money raised through car washes and candy bar sales might go to a different purpose.

Question: Why do colleges urge students to find scholarships?

Answer: Your scholarship frees up money the school can now use to help another student. In other words, Student A's scholarship actually benefits Student B. This may not have been the donor's intent, but it is a generous act and should not go unthanked. *Remember*: Only the money goes to the other student. You retain the honor of having won the scholarship.

Question: Is it ever worthwhile to look for scholarships?

Answer. Yes. If the school will use the money to replace a loan component of your aid package, that's money you won't have to repay. Also, if you are left with "unmet need" (see Chapter 5) or if you aren't eligible for need-based aid, then the scholarship helps pay your share.

Is There a Special Scholarship for Me?

Every day we get letters from people who tell us their life stories and then ask "is there a special scholarship for me?" These letters sadden us, because we know the writers haven't followed the smart route for getting financial aid. Most financial aid comes from Uncle Sam, your state, or your college and is based on academic merit, or financial need. Your age, sex, race and career ambitions have nothing to do with it.

And even if you do find a "special scholarship," there's a big difference between being eligible and winning. For example, your odds of winning a 4-H award (250 awards, 500,000 seniors as 4-H members), are 2000:1. To increase your chances, you could purchase a one-week old piglet, feed it 20 times a day until it weighs 1700 pounds. Then rent a forklift and a truck, take it to the state fair, and hope it wins a blue ribbon in the heavy hog competition. This might improve your odds to 20 or 30 to 1. But what about the costs of raising a 1700 pound porker?

Think we're kidding? Coca-Cola gets 137,000 applications for its 250 awards; odds of winning, 548:1. US Bank had 14,000 applications for its 25 awards; odds of winning, 560:1. The American Dairy Farmers received 9,000 applications for its 25 "Got Milk" awards; odds of winning 360:1.

Our advice: Go the traditional route first. Then, if you have submitted all your admission materials, and still feel the need to write more essays, get more recommendations, and complete more applications, then start looking for a "special scholarship." You may even find one.

What About Unclaimed Scholarships?

Every year you hear reports of millions (or billions) in unclaimed scholarships. These reports usually come from computerized scholarship search companies who hope you will send them money to find those millions, or at least register your personal data on their ad-filled web sites. We're sure a few scholarships do go unused every year, but for once, we'd like to see companies citing these vast untapped resources provide some concrete examples.

According to financial aid professionals, most of the money you hear about represents unused employee tuition benefits.

Money From Foundations & Corporations

Private foundations and corporations give colleges over $13.5 billion each year, but it's not money you apply for directly. Foundation money mainly goes directly to universities where it's used for faculty research, or to help students at the doctoral or post-doctoral level. There is some foundation money for undergraduates, but that money usually has narrow local restrictions, e.g., for students in Teenytiny County. Such grants are well publicized in the local paper.

Corporate money usually goes to employees or children of employees, either in the form of tuition reimbursement or company scholarships. Some corporations do give money to students whose parents aren't on the payroll, but this is usually done via grants to colleges; the colleges in turn select the recipients—you can't apply for them directly.

Computerized Scholarship Searches

Most experts agree, computerized search services seldom help you find private aid. At their very best they provide you with a few leads, but it's up to you to turn those leads into actual dollars.

Fee-Based Scholarship Matching Searches

If you need information on federal, state or collegiate aid, don't pay a computer service. Uncle Sam, your home state, and your chosen college offer free information (online and in print) detailing all their programs.

If you need information on scholarships offered by your employer or church, don't pay a computer service. Ask your boss or minister.

If you need information on local scholarships, don't pay a computer service. Check the HS bulletin board.

We've heard too many horror stories of families being duped out of $50 - $250 fees to recommend this route to anyone.

Free Web-Based Scholarship Searches

Are there any exceptions? Yes, you can do free Internet searches thanks to several online databases. Most make their money via site advertising and peddling your name to other companies, which means you have to register before you can use the service and divulge a great deal of personal information—is that an OK price to pay for loads of useful leads? Your choice.

- College Board (www.collegeboard.com/student/pay)
- FastWeb! (www.fastweb.com)
- MACH25 from CollegeNET (www.collegenet.com/mach25/app)
- Sallie Mae's College Answer (www.collegeanswer.com)
- Scholarships.com (www.scholarships.com)

Before you get carried away, however, re-read the paragraphs explaining how scholarships don't necessarily replace your money, then take another look at the pie chart in Chapter Two. *Tracking down private scholarships should not be your first priority in your financial aid search.*

Besides, even if you find a possible "match," you still have to complete the scholarship applications, write the scholarship essays, and gather the scholarship recommendations—all this on top of your regular admission applications and financial aid forms.

If you're doing all of this just for a chance at winning a $500 (non-renewable) award, maybe you should think about simply working a few extra hours at a paying job instead.

"Free" Financial Aid Seminars

With the proliferation of free, online scholarship searches, some companies (formerly in the scholarship-search business) have expanded their focus to include "free financial aid seminars." Unfortunately, these seminars can turn out to be little more than sales pitches for $700-$1,000 boilerplate consulting services.

Of course there's nothing illegal about selling college planning services, just be certain it's a service you need. And be sure to get references—it can be very hard to separate legitimate companies providing worthwhile, personalized service from those offering a cursory scholarship search and one-size-fits-all advice.

Here's what we advise: Don't sign any contracts while you're at a seminar and under pressure. Take the information home with you, show it to your high school counselor, check the ScholarScam web site below, ask for references, read the rest of this book, and if you still want to pay a fee for financial advice, go ahead. But do so as an educated consumer. It is up to you to decide whether the service is worth the money.

Project ScholarScam

The Federal Trade Commission shuts down shady dealers every year, but anxious parents desperately searching for financial aid make an easy target, so a new crop simply springs to life.

Project ScholarScam (www.ftc.gov/bcp/conline/edcams/scholarship) lists companies that the FTC has targeted in the past, and offers families useful suggestions on avoiding scams. For example, in "Six Signs That Your Scholarship is Sunk," the FTC warns against unsolicited sales pitches like, "The scholarship is guaranteed or your money back," or "We'll do all the work," or "You're a finalist." No one can guarantee you a scholarship. No one can apply for scholarships on your behalf. And no one can make you a winner in a contest you've never entered.

We Earn Too Much to Receive Financial Aid

Hogwash. All too many families don't bother to apply for aid because they assume they won't qualify. At the very least, you'll be eligible for a low-interest federal loan. And you may receive a great deal more, depending on the price of the college, and the resources it has to dispense. But you'll never know if you don't apply. Remember, there are no income cut-offs in determining eligibility for financial aid.

Income Shifting Seldom Pays

Many people can't accept the fact they are in a higher tax bracket than their children. They shift assets from themselves to their offspring through the Uniform Gift to Minors Act (UGMA), often times losing control of the assets, thinking the income from these assets will then be taxed at a much lower rate. Sometimes they even construct elaborate trusts with the help of lawyers and accountants whose fees can run upwards of $2,000.

But all this maneuvering is usually for naught. Investment income in excess of $1,800 for students under age 24 (assuming their own income provides less than half their support) is soon to be taxed at the parents' rate. Tax rates for trusts can be higher than tax rates for most families. And student assets are assessed at a higher rate than parent assets in determining your contribution to college costs, wiping out any small tax savings you may have realized.

A few years ago, tax-free Coverdell Savings Accounts and "Section 529" Plans made UGMAs yesterday's news. Then, tumbling stock prices and lower tax rates on dividends and capital gains caused some families to rethink the wisdom of this investment device, as well.

The Lesson? Make sensible, sound plans. And worry less about "beating the system." You'll understand better after you read Chapters 7 and 8.

Know Your Sources

Everybody knows Consumer Reports' *Income Tax Guide* takes a different slant to its subject than publications from the IRS—Consumer Reports' wants to help you save on taxes while the IRS seeks to extract the last drop of blood. You may value the IRS guide for its mechanical instructions, but not for its substantive advice on holding on to more of your money.

So it is with paying-for-college guides. Before you use one, make sure you know its origin. Is it (like this one) written from the viewpoint of those who pay the money (parents and students)? Or does it come from those who give and receive the money (Uncle Sam, colleges and the states)? The two guides may address the same subject, but their treatment could be many dollars (your dollars) apart.

"Reading" Online References

While some of the best Web resources are education-oriented, remember, there is no virtual editor checking facts and biases, so if at all possible, identify the information source and heed the warnings above. What often passes for "information" is really more of an advertisement—bankers trying to lure you into borrowing more than you really need, stockbrokers trying to scare you into investing more than you can afford, and publishers trying to tease you into buying their books and magazines (Guilty. You'll find us at www.ThinkTuition.com). Also, on a recent browse, many of the sites which boasted helpful names turned out to be scholarship search firms. Avoid them (except the free ones listed earlier).

Finally, most site sponsors play to our dwindling attention spans, and fill their pages with attractive graphics and superficial program summaries. In the time you spend clicking from site to site to site, reading the same thing, over and over and over, you can learn far more by curling up with a good book, for example, *Don't Miss Out*.

Reading Old References

When it comes to student aid, rules change every year and if you use an older reference, you will be badly misled with regard to loan subsidies, interest rates, eligibility, grants size, tax laws, saving techniques, government regulations and college costs. Even web sites frequently display dated material. Check the tag line showing when the page was last updated.

CHAPTER 4

■■■■■■■■■■■■■■■■■■■■

DEFINITIONS & PLAYERS

Short Definitions

Grants and Scholarships are aid awards you do not have to repay. They are gifts, however some require you to perform a service. The recipient of a band scholarship, for instance, may have to dress up in a costume complete with spats, march around a football field, and blow into a tuba whenever the college so directs.

Loans are sums of money you must repay. To qualify as financial aid, loans must carry a lower interest charge than prevailing commercial rates. They must also offer favorable repayment provisions. For example, in the Stafford Loan program, borrowers do not start paying interest on the loan nor do they have to retire any of the principal until after completing their studies.

Work-Study counts as financial aid when the financial aid office arranges your employment. Your earnings are excluded from the expected family contribution calculation (see Appendix). Work you find yourself is not considered financial aid. These earnings are included in the expected family contribution calculation.

Accreditation is a process that ensures the school's programs meet at least a minimum level of quality. Make sure your school has been accredited by a nationally-recognized association. You don't want to waste your tuition dollars getting a worthless education, and if you attend a nonaccredited school, you will not qualify for federal or state student aid.

Eligible Program is one that leads to a degree or certificate and meets other "integrity" rules established by Uncle Sam. To get federal aid, you must be enrolled in an "eligible program" at an "eligible institution." Students working toward associate, bachelor, professional or graduate degrees need not worry about what constitutes an "eligible program" or "eligible institution." Students looking at proprietary schools (for a two-month study, for example, of computer repair) should take heed. Most student aid fraud takes place in vocational programs of less than one year, and Uncle Sam is trying his best to separate the wheat from the shaft.

The 1st Player—The Student

Financial aid programs define students by dependency status. They are either dependent students or independent students.

A dependent student is one who is at least partially dependent on his or her parents for support. The income and assets of both student and parent are used to calculate the family's contribution to college costs.

An independent student is not dependent on parental support. Only the student's financial resources (and those of any spouse) are evaluated to determine contribution to college costs. To be considered independent, under federal regulations, you must meet one of the following conditions:

1. Be 24 years of age by December 31 of the award year (December 31, 2009 for the 2009/2010 award year).
2. Be a graduate or professional student.
3. Be married (or separated, but not yet divorced).
4. Have children who receive more than half of their support from you.
5. Have legal dependents (other than children or a spouse who live with you and receive more than half of their support from you.
6. Be an orphan, ward of the court, or in foster care (at any time after turning 13 years of age.)
7. Be a veteran of the U.S. Armed Forces; or be serving on active duty in the U.S. Armed Forces (for purposes other than training).
8. Be an emancipated minor, or in legal guardianship (as determined by a court); or an unaccompanied youth who is homeless, or at risk for homelessnes.
9. Be judged independent by the financial aid administrator based on documented unusual circumstances.

Establishing independence can give you an advantage: By not having to include parental income and assets on your financial aid application, your college contribution will most likely be lower and that will result in more student aid. To preserve scarce funds, however, some states and colleges go beyond the federal test to impose additional restrictions on your declaration of independence. These include written proof that your parents (or even grandparents) cannot provide any support whatsoever. This is especially true for students who are "independent" according to the federal definition, but who have moved back home with mom and dad to save some money.

If you have a nontraditional family situation, or you're a single undergraduate under the age of 24 who truly is "independent," see Chapter 9 for advice on appealing your dependency status.

The 2nd Player—The Parents

Parents may be loving, caring, supportive role models. The financial aid process doesn't care. Its main interest: Are they married, separated, divorced? Is there a stepparent who can foot the bill? Here is the impact of marital status on financial aid:

Both Parents Are Alive and Married to Each Other. The income and assets of both parents are fair game for the financial aid computer.

Parents Are Divorced or Separated. The federal financial aid form is only interested in the income and assets of the parent with whom the student lived for the majority of the twelve months preceding the date of the application—it does not matter who claims the student as an exemption for tax purposes. If the student did not live with either parent, or divides time equally between the two, then use the income and assets of the parent from whom the student receives the most financial support.

A Parent Remarries. If the parent whose data goes on the aid application remarries, the stepparent's income and assets are evaluated just as though he or she were a natural parent. No exceptions, even for prenuptial agreements.

Legal Guardians. Students need not report information about legal guardians. If a student lives with a legal guardian, but has biological parents, the student must report the parent(s)' income. If the student's parents are deceased, he or she files as an independent student.

These rules apply to federal aid and, generally, to state aid. Colleges, when deciding how to dispense their own money, are not bound by these rules. They can probe deeply into the resources of the divorced or absent parent who got off scot-free under federal regs. Many colleges use a College Board-created form to collect information from these non-custodial parents.

The 3rd Player—The Colleges

Colleges are classified as either private or public.

Private colleges can be more innovative in developing attractive aid packages and tuition assistance programs. They are not as circumscribed by red tape as tax-supported schools. Private colleges also have more latitude in how to spend their money. Again, it's their money, not the taxpayer's (this also means they're apt to pry more deeply into your family's finances to decide if you are deserving of their limited funds).

Public colleges, being tax-supported, are usually less expensive. As a general rule, students seldom pay more than 30% of the actual cost of education. The state pays the balance. Also, public colleges have two sets of fee structures: a lower one for state residents and a higher one for out-of-staters. At one time, it was easy to establish state residency to qualify for the lower rate. Today, it's more difficult. Most states have created elaborate bureaucracies, the efficiency of which appears to be judged in direct proportion to the number of residency denials issued.

One more thing. Private and public colleges have no great love for each other. The lack of affection is rooted in money. The privates resent the subsidies that permit public schools to offer lower tuitions. They would love to end this "unfair competition" by qualifying for subsidies of their own. Moreover, they see their own turf invaded when public schools, not fully sated by subsidies, seek funds from corporations and philanthropies. In fact, endowment funds at state flagship universities are now greater than those at most private universities. The public schools, for their part, resent the infusion of state money into private college coffers, especially when states are strapped for cash, and cutting their commitment to public schools. Also, they would like to be able to set their own tuition rates, and do a little more "enrollment management" and "tuition discounting" of their own.

Most of this hostility ends when the two must present a united front to fend off repeated efforts to slash the federal education budget.

The 4th Player—Need Analysis Processors

Before a college can consider you for aid, it must know how much you can pay. Families that can pay $10,000 won't be eligible for as much as families that can spare only $1,000. Determining how much you can pay without becoming a burden to your neighbors is called *Need Analysis*. Public and private schools now use what amounts to two varying systems.

Federal Methodology

The process for determining eligibility for federal aid begins with the Free Application for Federal Student Aid (FAFSA). You may complete the FAFSA online or use a paper-based form. Uncle Sam then compiles your data and calculates your Expected Family Contribution (EFC) to college costs. More will be said about FAFSAs in Chapters 6, 7 and 10.

Because the formula used to calculate EFC is set by Congress, it is called the Federal Methodology. And since all EFCs are calculated using this same formula, you gain nothing—except time—by submitting your FAFSA one way or the other.

Institutional Methodologies

The process of determining eligibility for collegiate aid is another story. Why? There is no uniformity. Many colleges (especially wealthy, expensive, private colleges) insist on additional knowledge about your family's finances to determine eligibility for their own programs. They will ask you to fill out an institutional aid application, or, they will contract with The College Board to collect (and evaluate) this information for them using Financial Aid PROFILE. You'll learn more about PROFILE in Chapter 6.

Because the formula is used only to award institutional aid, and it can be modified to comply with individual institutional needs, it is known as an Institutional Methodology. The results can vary from school to school.

The 5th Player—Financial Aid Administrators

For college students, the financial aid administrator can be the most important person on campus. The FAA can take the family contribution and—ouch—increase it or—hooray—reduce it. The FAA can draw from money under the college's direct control or certify the student's eligibility for federal and state funds. The FAA can decide on the contents of the student's aid package. Is it to be grants the student will not have to repay? Or will it all be loans? In short, the FAA is the final arbiter of how much the family must contribute to college costs and how much outside help, and of what kind, the family will receive.

Unfortunately, FAAs are working under increasingly stressful conditions. They usually have no say in setting tuition rates, developing operating budgets, or establishing enrollment goals (in terms of numbers or diversity), yet their offices are under constant pressure to make sure enough of the "right" students can afford tuition so the school meets its enrollment goals and balances its budget. The admission office wants to know why musical Johnny didn't enroll (would an extra $2,000 have done the trick?) while the budget director wants to know why needy Dee Dee got $4,000 when splitting that money might have lured no-need Joey and low-need Marky thus bringing in twice the tuition. To add to this stress, FAAs must keep their aid decisions ethical and consistent and make sure their schools don't run afoul of one of the 7,000 sections of Uncle Sam's Higher Education Act.

So why do people become financial aid administrators? A quick look at some top ten lists on the FinAid Web site revealed the following:

Ten... No salary cap like in the NBA and NFL.

Nine... Get to develop lots of forms, then cut them up for scratch paper.

Eight... More nifty acronyms than the military.

Seven... Love meeting irate people.

Six... Can order all the FAFSAs I want.

Five... Get all the respect of a Little League umpire.

Four... Enjoy watching students cry.

Three... Staff meetings. Staff meetings. Staff meetings.

Two... Get to answer every question with, "It depends."

AND THE NUMBER ONE REASON GIVEN

FOR BECOMING A FINANCIAL AID ADMINISTRATOR . . ,

I Need Analysis!

Seriously, get to know your school's financial aid administrator. He or she can make the difference between winning and losing (and besides, is truly one of the nicest, most helpful people you'll meet on campus).

CHAPTER 5

■■■■■■■■■■■■■■■■■■

THE CONCEPT OF "NEED"

Ubi Est Mea? (Old Latin Proverb. Translation: Where is Mine?)

Many high school students believe they cannot receive financial aid for an expensive private school if their parents can afford to send them to a state school. Others think almost all financial aid is set aside for minority students. Of course, neither of these assumptions is true.

The Official Definition of Need

Most financial aid is based on the concept of "need." Need is a number—nothing more, nothing less. It should never be confused with "needy." This is how financial aid administrators determine the need number:

Visualize three bars, Bar A, Bar B and Bar C.

BAR A is the cost of attendance at the college of your choice.

BAR B represents your family's expected contribution to college costs, as determined by need analysis (see previous chapter).

And **BAR C** is the amount of "outside" student aid you receive (for example, private scholarships and veteran's benefits).

Bar A—the cost of attendance—is a variable. It varies from college to college. It can even vary within one school, depending on your student status, the courses you take, how far away you live, etc. Bar B and Bar C are constant (unless there is a drastic change in your family's situation). It doesn't matter where you plan to buy your education. The amount you must contribute from your own resources should be the same.

If Bar A is larger than Bar B and Bar C combined, you have need.

Bar A— Cost of Attendance		
Bar B— Family Contribution	**Bar C— Outside Aid**	**Need**

The Student Definition of Need

While schools define need as "cost of college minus expected family contribution," students seem to define it as "cost of college minus financial aid." This kind of thinking won't get you far!

A Numerical Example

Let's illustrate "need" for a family judged capable of contributing $10,000 per year to each of three colleges: College X which costs $35,000; College Y which costs $20,000; and College Z which costs $12,000. Assuming the student finds a $2,000 scholarship, that family's need is:

$23,000 at College X (Calculation: $35,000 - $10,000 - $2,000 = $23,000);

$8,000 at College Y (Calculation: $20,000 - $10,000 - $2,000 = $8,000); and

$0 at College Z (Calculation: $12,000 - $10,000 - $2,000 = $0).

Unmet Need

The reality, unfortunately, is that about half of all families will find themselves with "unmet need"—the gap between their calculated "need," and the amount of financial aid offered them by the school.

According to a recent survey from the National Center for Education Statistics, for students with unmet need, the average amount of that unmet need is $5,300, ranging from an average of $3,800 at public two-year schools to $7,600 at private, four-year schools. Students must close this gap with part-time jobs, extra help from their families, outside scholarships, federal PLUS loans, or private loans.

A Whole New Can of Worms

Colleges that rely primarily on federal and state resources to make up financial aid packages seem satisfied with the FAFSA system.

Unfortunately, colleges with lots of institutional aid to distribute feel the FAFSA does not gather enough information to judge a family's true ability to pay. Accordingly, many no longer use the word "need" to describe FAFSA results. Instead, they refer to the results as a "family's eligibility for federal student aid." These schools then use an application of their own (or the College Board's PROFILE) to gather additional information and determine a student's "need" for institutional funds.

Chapter 6 explores how this affects aid packages. For now, just be warned that at most schools, awarding aid based entirely on "need" (as determined by a uniform method of analysis) is an ideal rather than a practice.

Finally...

Neither "family contribution" nor "cost of college" is carved in stone. They can be stretched and squeezed to increase your eligibility for need-based financial aid. In Chapter 7 you will find a plethora of ideas for stretching and squeezing.

CHAPTER 6

■ ■ ■ ■ ■ ■ ■ ■ ■ ■ ■ ■ ■ ■ ■ ■ ■ ■ ■ ■

THE MECHANICS
OF APPLICATION

Taking Charge of the Financial Aid Process

At most schools, you can't start the financial aid process until after January first (so computers can be fed data on how much your family earned the previous year). Then you are kept in the dark for several months before you learn (1) how much you will have to contribute, (2) whether you have need, (3) whether you qualify for need-based aid and (4) what your actual financial aid package will look like.

If you want to assume your family contribution will not cause you a cash-flow problem, and that your need will be met at whatever college you attend, then you can trust the system and submit all your applications in the dark. But if you assume, realistically, that (1) your family contribution will impose a cash-flow burden, (2) your full need will not be met, or (3) your need will be met in a financially-burdensome manner, then you have to take charge of the process.

What is Meant by Taking Charge?

You won't have to enroll in a muscle-building course or graduate from Officer Candidate School. All you have to do is read this chapter and act on its advice. The take-charge process has three elements:

1. **Learn the Money Numbers Ahead of Time.** Before you complete your aid applications, learn the costs of your selected colleges, the size of your family contribution, and your resulting need at each school. If you don't, you'll be surprised by the results and have little time to raise the necessary funds.

2. **Execute the Application Process With Speed and Precision.** You want to be first in line for aid, before the "Sold Out" signs light up.

3. **Know About Influence Points.** College selection, preparing for need analysis, the speed and accuracy with which you apply, the evaluation of aid offers—these are all influence points. How you handle yourself as you approach these points will impact on your family contribution, aid eligibility, and size and composition of your aid award.

■■■■■■■■■■■■■■■■■■■■■■■

STEP ONE: LEARN THE MONEY NUMBERS AHEAD OF TIME

Once you answer the following three questions—even if it's just an approximation—you can begin some sensible financial planning:

1. How much will my chosen college(s) cost? This is a variable.
2. How much will our family be expected to contribute to college costs? For federal aid, this will be a constant. For institutional aid, it may vary.
3. What's our need going to be at each college of my choice?

Question One: How Much Will College Cost?

College costs and tuition are not synonymous. College costs, also known as "Cost of Attendance," "Cost of Education" or "Student Expense Budget"—are an aggregate of many elements.

1. *Tuition* is usually based on credit hour costs and is generally the same for all students taking the same courseload.
2. *Mandatory fees* can vary. Some schools assess flat fees to cover communications and Internet costs, health services, library costs, student association activities, and athletic facilities. But they can also charge extra fees for "expensive" courses, like lab sciences and studio art.
3. *Book and supply expenditures* depend on the number and type of courses you select. Students taking a heavier-than normal course load may receive a larger allowance, so might film and art students.
4. *Housing charges* may vary depending upon where you choose to live; in a dorm, off-campus in an apartment, or off-campus at home, in your old room.
5. *Meal charges* can also vary. There is one figure if you purchase a school meal plan. There is another if you plan to cook for yourself (translation: pasta, pizza, popcorn, and fast food). And there is still a third figure if you're enjoying home-cooked meals—it makes no difference how much this arrangement might add to your parents' costs.
6. *Miscellaneous expenses* represent all the money you spend at places other than the college—keeping up with fashion trends, music trends and food trends. The personal expense category can be very flexible. If you are handicapped, for example, or have child care bills to shoulder, this item can be set very high. Co-op students may receive an allowance to cover employment costs. And, if you qualify for a student loan, the guarantee fee and insurance premium will be added to your budget.
7. *Transportation*, too, is flexible. It may cover several round trip flights between campus and home, or it may represent commuting expenses.

8. *Computer Expenses.* With most university services moving online, it's no longer smart to go to college without an up-to-date computer. Accordingly, colleges may now include "reasonable" rental or purchase expenses (usually no more than $3,000) as part of your student budget. Some schools simply give laptops (with wireless capabilities) to each of their incoming freshmen.

Financial aid administrators establish expense budgets for each category of student who attends their college. There may be separate budgets for dependent students living in a dorm, in an apartment, or at home, and subcategories for single and married independent students. Here are some points to ponder about expense budgets:

- The "cost of attendance" figure includes at least $11,000 for non-tuition expenses. By being frugal, these expenses may be lower than the college allots. For example, room and board, if you live at home, may not represent a special outlay for your family.
- If the "cost of attendance" does not appear to accurately reflect some of your college-related expenses, let the aid administrator know. Any increase in the expense budget increases your eligibility for aid.

College web sites, as well as college guides, give good cost estimates—augment this information by asking colleges for their most current catalogue. Also remember, if you're using information for the 2008/2009 year, and you aren't starting college until 2009/2010, you should add 5-6% to the total cost figure to get a better idea of the rate you'll be paying. Note that your last year could cost thousands more than your first.

To give you a quick idea of the cost of college, we've used College Board data for last year (from *Trends in College Pricing*) to project the average cost-of-attendance out to 2013. Last year's increases averaged 5.9% at both private and public schools, but we are always optimistic, so we have assumed 5% increases for both.

To keep things in perspective, since most students pay considerably less than "sticker price," we've also used College Board data (from *Trends in College Pricing)* to project out "net price"—the total cost-of-attendance less the average grant and education tax credit per student.

In general, schools are more expensive in New England and the Middle States (e.g., New York and Pennsylvania) and less expensive in the South and Southwest, for example:

- You'll pay an average of $1,550 *more* per year for 4-year public schools in the Middle States; an average of $7,635 *more* for 4-year private schools in New England.
- You'll pay an average of $1,910 *less* per year for 4-year public schools in the South; an average of $5,200 *less* for 4-year private schools in the Southwest.

- You'll pay an average of $10,450 *more* per year to attend public school outside your home state (ranging from $7,700 more at public schools in the Southwest to $11,920 more in New England).

	4-Yr Private	4-Yr Public	2-Yr Public
2009/2010			
Sticker Price	$39,000	$19,110	$14,470
Net Price	$28,750	$15,145	$12,220
2010/2011			
Sticker Price	$40,950	$20,070	$15,200
Net Price	$30,180	$15,900	$12,830
2011/2012			
Sticker Price	$43,000	$21,070	$15,950
Net Price	$31,700	$16,700	$13,475
2012/2013			
Sticker Price	$45.150	$22,125	$16,750
Net Price	$33,280	$17,530	$14,150

Question Two: How Much Must We Pay?

OK. You know about how much college will cost. Now you need to estimate how much each of these colleges will expect you to pay. For dependent students, family contribution is made up of four elements:

- Parents' Contribution from Income
- Parents' Contribution from Assets
- Student's Contribution from Income
- Student's Contribution from Assets

For independent students, family contribution is based on only their own income and assets (as well as those of their spouse, if they are married).

Family contribution for the purposes of determining eligibility for federal aid is calculated by Uncle Sam. Family contribution for the purposes of determining eligibility for institutional aid might be calculated in a slightly different fashion, either by the College Board or by the institution itself. Both systems of need analysis operate on the same principle: They preserve some of your income and assets for taxes, living expenses and retirement— then they want whatever's left.

You should know that the income protection allowance—the money left to you for shelter, food, clothing, car operations, insurance and basic medical care—is very close to the poverty thresholds established by the Department of Health and Human Services. If you have been living close to the poverty line, the need analysis formula will fit you like a glove. But if you have become locked into a higher standard of living, with mortgage payments, fat utility bills, two cars, summer vacations, and an occasional trip to the theater, the small allowance won't cover your expenses. And your assessed family contribution will appear impossibly large.

Question. Why should I calculate family contribution myself? Lots of Internet sites will do it for me; so will the guidance office computer.

Answer. By making the calculation yourself, you will develop an appreciation of the formula, its components, and the weights assigned to each component. This knowledge will serve you well if (later) you should have to discuss your award with a financial aid administrator.

The Federal Methodology

The Federal Methodology (FM) determines your eligibility for all need-based federal student aid programs, and most need-based state, private and collegiate programs. It has the biggest impact on your eligibility for student aid. To calculate Expected Family Contribution (EFC) under the Federal Methodology, go to Appendix 1, 2 or 3, depending on your student status. Your calculations won't match the need-analysis computer to the penny, but the result will be close.

Here are some things to know before you fill in figures:

Dependent Students

- All income and tax data comes from the previous calendar year. If you start college in September 2009, the previous calendar year is 2008.
- All asset data is as of the date you submit the need analysis form.
- If your parents are divorced or separated, use the income and asset figures of the parent with whom you will live for the greater part of the twelve months prior to the date of the application.
- If your parent has remarried, you must include your stepparent's income and asset information.

Independent Students

- All income and tax data comes from the previous calendar year. If you start college in September 2009, the previous calendar year is 2008.
- All asset data is as of the date you submit the need analysis form.

The Simplified Need Test

This simplified version of the Federal Methodology excludes all family assets from the need calculation. It applies to families in which (1) the parents (or independent students) are eligible to file a 1040EZ, a 1040A, or who do not file a tax return at all; and (2) total parental adjusted gross incomes (or, in the case of independent students, the student and spouse's total AGIs) are under $50,000. It doesn't matter what type of tax form the dependent student files.

Auto-Zero EFC

Parents (of dependent students) and independent students (with dependents) who have incomes under $30,000 and are eligible to file a 1040EZ, a 1040A, or who do not file a tax return at all, automatically receive an EFC equal to $0. Independent students without dependents (other than a spouse) are not eligible for the auto-zero EFC.

Recent Formula Changes

The Higher Education Reconciliation Act of 2005 made several substantive changes to the Federal Methodology. For example, it eliminated family-owned small business assets from consideration, it standardized treatment of qualified education benefits (like 529 savings plans), and it decreased the asset assessment rate applied to student assets.

The Higher Education Opportunity Act of 2008 (and other education-related legislation passed within the last two years) made a couple of additional (minor) changes. For example, it expanded the categories of "Independent Student" to include groups like emancipated minors and youth who are at risk for homelessness. It also excluded certain veterans education benefits from need analysis and declared that all Coverdell and "529 Plans" held by the student would be considered assets of the parent.

The Institutional Methodology

The Institutional Methodology (IM) is used by some states, some private donor programs, and about 16% of all colleges, mostly higher-priced private colleges, to determine eligibility for state or private or collegiate resources. The IM has initiated over a dozen formula changes, so it bears little resemblance to the Federal Methodology. For example:

In the income area, it adds business, farm and capital losses back into AGI. It gives families an annual savings allowance for each of their pre-college age children. It restructures income assessment rates and increases parental contribution when more than one family member is enrolled. It provides an allowance for unreimbursed medical expenses. And it institutes a minimum expected contribution level from student income.

In the asset area, the IM counts home equity. It eliminates the standard asset protection allowance and institutes an emergency reserve allowance based on family size. It includes siblings assets with parental assets. It implements an educational savings allowance for other children in the family and it increases the assessment rate on student assets from 20% to 25%. In addition, the IM has no simplified needs tests—no matter what the family's income, their assets are always a factor in measuring their ability to pay.

Depending on your family situation, you could come out better or worse. To see what IM colleges might expect you to contribute, go to the College Board web site (www.collegeboard.com) and use its online estimator.

Every College is Different

Many schools further tweak the IM based on their own policies, or use a methodology of their own. For example:

1. If your concurrently-enrolled sibling's cost of education is less than their share of the parental contribution figure, your school could take a little extra. For example, if parental contribution equals $20,000, and your sibling is enrolled half-time at a community college with costs of only $5,000; your school might want three-quarters ($15,000) of the contribution.

2. If your parents are divorced, you may be asked for financial data of the parent not listed on the FAFSA. If the divorce was recent, a school may expect a larger contribution than if the divorce was 16 years ago.

3. If your parents are divorced, and you were asked to report the income and assets of both of your natural parents AND your stepparent, the school might examine the situation and only factor in the income and assets of two parents, rather than three (or four).

4. If you live in a pricey urban area like New York or Washington or San Francisco, the school may account for your higher cost of living.

5. If you have assets in a tax-advantaged college savings plan, these might be assessed at a higher rate than other assets.

6. If the value of your assets is disproportionate to your reported interest and dividend income, the school may simply boost their value, assuming you must have "hidden" them in some way.

7. If you want to prepare for the absolute worst, add in other assets, like the value of your retirement accounts and luxury vehicles (cars as well as yachts). Often, these questions are to assess your borrowing ability.

8. If the ratio between your mortgage payments and income is outside the 37% debt-to-income ratio favored by financial experts, the school may start probing for (suspected) additional money streams.

9. If you come from a middle income family, the school may cap your home equity at two or three times your family income.

10. If a school really wants you to enroll, it can ignore all need analysis results, and fill your family's coffers with institutional aid. (Dream on.)

Reconciling the Differences

In most cases, EFC as calculated by the Federal Methodology (FM) will be lower than EFC as calculated by an Institutional Methodology (IM). In these instances, schools award federal and state aid using FM results, then re-evaluate your finances using IM results before awarding institutional aid.

If IM results are lower, schools must tread carefully, since (by law) they can't award federal aid in excess of need, as determined by the FM:

- Most schools ignore IM results and package all aid to FM need.
- Some schools adjust FM results to account for special circumstances, thereby lowering a family's EFC so it matches IM results.

- Some schools eliminate need-based federal aid from the package, and award only institutional aid, including an institutional loan.
- About a quarter of all schools do a combination of the above.

In Summary

Again, the Federal Methodology determines eligibility for federal aid (and most state aid). It's a strict formula with little room for negotiation. The Institutional Methodology is used by many colleges to award need-based collegiate aid. The formula is not legislated so individual discretion can be wide and the room for negotiation sometimes great (depending on the policies of the school, and the desirability of the student).

Completely confused? You should be. As each school develops its own methodology for awarding aid, the financial aid process is quickly becoming as mysterious and arbitrary to families as the admission process.

Question Three: What's My Need?

Now you have all the materials you need to answer the third question: How much need will I have at each college of my choice? You do that by comparing your Family Contribution from Appendix 1, 2, or 3, with the Cost of Attendance at each school that interests you. Remember, if you're applying to one of the wealthier private schools you should perform this comparison twice: once using the federal methodology to determine your eligibility for federal aid, and again using the institutional methodology to estimate your eligibility for institutional aid.

■ ■

STEP TWO: EXECUTE THE APPLICATION PROCESS WITH SPEED AND PRECISION

The second step of the "Take Charge" plan is to execute the application process with speed and precision. To do this, you must submit your aid application as soon after the first of the year as possible. We say "as soon after" because many programs operate on a first-come, first-served basis.

Which Form Should We File?

That's up to the colleges and your home state. Be sure to find out before New Year's Day. Here are some general guidelines:

- Everyone must file the Free Application for Federal Student Aid (FAFSA) to be considered for federal and state student assistance.
- Some families will have to use the College Scholarship Service's Financial Aid PROFILE and/or a supplemental form from their home state to be considered for collegiate or state resources.
- Finally, some families will have to complete an institutional aid form and send it directly to the college they hope to attend.

In other words, you may have to file one, two, three or four forms depending on the wishes of your home state and the schools to which you apply.

Why So Many Forms?

Simple. College is expensive and there's not enough financial aid to cover everyone's tuition bills, so schools have to figure out who needs money the most and they haven't figured out a way to do this without asking a lot of questions! Here's what they do:

1. Use FAFSA results to award federal and state aid to all who qualify;
2. Use PROFILE or institutional aid application results to find out more about a family's finances;
3. Adjust the family contribution accordingly;
4. Award collegiate resources to the still needy; and
5. Suggest politely that everyone else borrow more money.

Students applying to in-state public schools must usually file just the FAFSA. Students applying to more expensive schools where federal and state aid doesn't cover tuition (e.g., private schools and out-of-state public schools) must usually complete multiple forms, as described above.

Where Do We Get Forms and What Do We Do with Them?

Paper FAFSAs

In the fall, students may call the Dept. of Education (800/4-FED-AID) and request up to three paper copies of the FAFSA. (Forms will no longer be supplied to high school guidance offices.) You fill it out as soon after January 1 as possible and snail mail it to the address listed on the form. You pay no fee. The 2009/2010 FAFSA will be green and purple, and include several new questions to gather information about the student's dependency status, eligibility for the Simplified Needs Test, and interest in becoming a teacher. The layout is also a little different from prior years—the worksheets have been incorporated into the form itself.

FAFSA on the Web (www.fafsa.ed.gov)

You may also file electronically using FAFSA on the Web. Uncle continues to enhance his online application and reports that most forms are now filed electronically. FAFSA on the Web includes worksheets, online help, detailed instructions and an EFC Estimator, however, families won't see their estimated EFC until *AFTER* they submit their form. FAFSA on the Web also includes internal edits that help prevent errors and reduce rejections. Finally, parents with multiple students in college can transfer their parental data to additional FAFSA applications with the click of a mouse.

At the FAFSA web site, families can print a pre-application worksheet to collect data and make it easier (and faster) to complete their FAFSA online.

Paper FAFSAs take 3-4 weeks to process; electronic FAFSAs take only one. *If possible, save time and file electronically.* You'll get a jump on your equally-needy, but technophobic classmates. Save often (in case you get bumped off-line), but in your eagerness, don't click "SEND" until you've checked your answers carefully!

State Aid Applications

If your state requires a separate aid application, you may get one from your state's higher education agency (see Chapter 11) or your guidance office. Again, you fill it out (usually after January 1) and send it to the address listed on the form. You pay no fee.

PROFILE

If you're applying to one of the 250+ PROFILE schools, you must register and complete the form online (profileonline.collegeboard.com)—it will be customized with each of your school's questions.

The basic PROFILE requires the same sort of data as the FAFSA, with a few extra questions about income, assets, expenses, and resources. But the College Board has accumulated nearly 200 additional questions that schools may ask. These questions pry into everything from the student's career

Table of Agencies, Forms and Programs

Form	Sponsor	Program	
		First-Come, First-Served	Not Time Sensitive
Free Application for Federal Student Aid (FAFSA)	Uncle Sam	Federal Campus-Based Programs	Pell Grant
		Most State Programs	Federal Family Education Loans (Stafford and PLUS)
Renewal FAFSA	Uncle Sam	Some College Programs	
			Federal Direct Loans (Stafford and PLUS)
FAFSA on the Web	Uncle Sam	Some Private Programs	
State Application	Your Home State	Some State Programs	Some State Programs
Financial Aid PROFILE	The College Board	Some College, Some State and Some Private Programs	Some College, Some State and Some Private Programs
Your College's Aid Application	Your College	Some College Programs	Some College Programs

objective, to whether the student has applied for outside scholarships, to whether the family has recently sold any income generating assets (and the purpose for which they were sold), to the year, make and model of all the family's motor vehicles. PROFILE can also include a business/farm supplement and collect information on the noncustodial parent.

You pay a fee for all this fun; $25 to register (which includes one school report) then $16 for each additional school that is to receive your information. Students from low income families may receive a fee waiver

You'll find extensive online help at profileonline.collegeboard.com.

You may register for PROFILE beginning October 1 (vs. January 1 for the FAFSA), which helps colleges get a head start on estimating aid packages.

Renewal FAFSAs

You must re-apply for aid every year. If you filed a FAFSA in 2008/2009, you will receive a Renewal Reminder Notice in early January that provides instructions about how to reapply for aid using Renewal FAFSA on the Web. (Renewal FAFSAs must all be filed online.) Some of the fields will be "pre-populated" with data you provided last year, so unless there's a change in information, you can skip some of the questions.

The renewal reminder notice will be sent to the e-mail address you listed on your 2008/2009 FAFSA. If you did not include a valid e-mail address, or the e-mail is undeliverable, you will receive a paper reminder.

Tips for Filing a Mistake-Free Form

Millions of students must file correction FAFSAs, listing new information or fixing errors. By filing a mistake-free form, you'll be ahead of all those people in the chow line. If a question or two seems confusing, call the federal student aid hotline (800/4-FED-AID) or ask a guidance counselor.

Here are some tips to help smooth the process.

Use the Right Forms

Some students must now file a FAFSA, PROFILE and a separate state or institutional aid application. Read each school's aid literature closely to make sure you know which forms to file.

Apply Now for Your PIN (www.pin.ed.gov)

If you want to file your FAFSA online, apply now for a "Personal Identification Number" (PIN) which will act as your electronic signature. Otherwise, you have to print and snail mail the FAFSA signature page, thus losing out on some benefits of electronic filing. Not only does your PIN verify your identity when completing a FAFSA, you can use it later to check on the status of your application, or to make online corrections. You request PINs directly from the Department of Education (www.pin.ed.gov).

If your parents must sign the FAFSA, they need their own (separate) PIN.

The Early Bird Gets the Worm

The absolute last day to file your FAFSA for the 2009/2010 award year is June 30, 2010. But don't be fooled by this late date. You should apply for aid as early as possible. Not only can schools run out of money for late applicants, but you help your admission chances as well: In filling the last few spots of the incoming class, more and more schools consider a student's "ability-to-pay"—especially after the financial aid well runs dry.

If each of your colleges has a different deadline, submit your forms in time to meet the earliest deadline.

A Good Use of the Winter Holiday

To make sure you're one of the early birds, start collecting the necessary financial records over the winter holidays. You'll need your family's annual income (including untaxed income) and the net worth of all your assets. You'll also need your income tax information close at hand. Certain items on your aid application must agree with items on your federal income tax form, most importantly, adjusted gross income, the amount of federal income taxes paid and the number of exemptions. Print a copy of the FAFSA on the Web worksheet to help you gather the correct information (but please don't submit the worksheet in lieu of a FAFSA—it's not an official document).

Use Fafsa4Caster (www.fafsa4caster.ed.gov)

Another way to get a head start is to use Fafsa4Caster. Prior to January 1, families can use this tool to receive an early estimate of their eligibility for federal student aid. Even better, when you start work on your FAFSA, much of the data you entered using Fafsa4Caster can be copied to the real form.

FAFSAs vs. 1040s

The FAFSA asks whether you've already *completed* your tax return, not whether you've already *filed* your tax return. The two are not synonymous. You may complete the return on January 1, and still wait until April 15 to file. Don't, however, delay filing your FAFSA because you've procrastinated on your taxes. You can get pretty good income and asset information using year-end pay stubs and bank statements. If you note, later on, that your estimates were incorrect, you'll have to provide corrections. Estimators are also the most likely candidates for verification (see below).

The FAFSA also asks whether you are *eligible* to file a 1040A or 1040EZ, even if you filed a regular 1040. If you and your parents can answer "yes," your family's assets may be excluded from the primary EFC calculation.

Comparison Between Need Analysis and IRS Forms

Aid administrators must verify data on up to 30% of all FAFSAs. That's when you get to produce copies of tax returns and other documents for comparison—FAAs can delve quite deeply into your finances during this process. Most FAFSAs are selected based on "preestablished criteria," which is bureaucratese for "something smells fishy." Lesson: Be accurate and honest in submitting your data. If your income and tax numbers are outside a $400 tolerance range, the college will make corrections.

Note: Many families opt to underreport income on their FAFSAs, some by as much as $100,000. Some schools ask all families for copies of their W-2s and tax returns—as a matter of policy. And if your school doesn't catch you, Uncle will. The Department of Education is authorized to do a FAFSA-IRS match. The bugs are still being worked out, but soon, the system will be able to automatically compare income information as stated on the FAFSA with income information as reported to the IRS .

Be Consistent

The FAFSA processor crosschecks data and flags questionable applications for verification. *Example One*: A student claims a one-parent family but records income for two parents. *Example Two*: A family's federal income taxes exceed 40% of its Adjusted Gross Income. There should be some correlation between your earnings and the taxes you pay. Otherwise, lights will flash, bells will sound, and investment advice will come pouring in (or, you'll be asked to share investment secrets). In either case, you're a candidate for verification.

Students who filed a FAFSA last year must be doubly careful. Uncle has developed a "Multi-Year Applicant Database" so it can cross-check your current data against previous years and detect possible inconsistencies and significant changes, for example, in the number of reported family members, total income, and taxes paid.

Name, Rank and Serial Number

You must have a social security number to apply for financial aid—Uncle verifies every applicant's name, social security number and date of birth with the Social Security Administration. He also does a "Date of Death" match to make sure you're a live person.

To minimize problems, use the name on your social security card (and avoid nicknames). The computer doesn't know whether "Bill Reese" and "William Reese, Jr." are the same person. Married or divorced students must be especially careful as their last names may have changed, while their social security numbers have not.

Also, be sure the street (and the e-mail) address you record on the form is one where you can be reached for the next year. Otherwise, you won't receive your eligibility report or requests for additional information (or your FAFSA renewal notice for next year).

Register for Selective Service

Males (18 to 25) are not eligible for federal aid unless they do. You may register using a check-off box on the FAFSA or online at www.sss.gov.

Answer the Question Regarding Past Drug Use

Question #23 on the paper FAFSA asks whether you (the student) have ever been convicted of selling or possessing illegal drugs during a period of enrollment in which you were receiving federal student aid. If you are not sure how to answer the question, use the worksheet at www.fafsa.ed.gov. If you file the FAFSA online, you can complete the worksheet online, as well.

You must answer the question, otherwise your application will be rejected.

Are You a Teacher-to-Be?

Question 32 on the paper FAFSA asks whether you are planning to complete the coursework needed to become a teacher. Answering "yes" is the first step to linking up with a new $4,000 per year federal grant for teachers-to-be (see TEACH Grants in Chapter 10).

Identify Your College Completely

You can use federal student aid at over 7,500 schools. It's your responsibility to list your schools correctly—this means getting the correct codes from your counselor, looking them up yourself (www.fafsa.ed.gov), or at least recording the full name and address of every school that is to receive your data. Remember "U. of M." could mean Maryland or Michigan. "University of California" could mean the campus at Davis or Irvine.

If you are applying to more than four schools, use the FAFSA for your top choices (or, those with the earliest application deadlines), then, when you receive your Student Aid Report (SAR), go online to www.fafsa.ed.gov and look for the link that allows you to add additional schools. You can also call 800/4FED-AID to have your data sent to your remaining institutions—you'll need to know your Data Release Number (which appears on your SAR).

Record Data Accurately

The FAFSA wants to know the *net worth* of your assets, in other words, their current market value minus any debt against them. Also, the FAFSA asks for federal income tax paid, not just the amount withheld on a W-2.

Don't Make Careless Mistakes

Mistakes cause the form to bounce. By the time you correct and resubmit it, you'll be at the end of the money line. *Common mistakes:* Recording an incorrect social security number; leaving questions blank when you mean zero (write "0"); recording the current date instead of your birth date; giving monthly instead of yearly amounts; entering decimal points, cents or commas; leaving off numbers ($5000 vs. $50000); failing to use black ink; writing illegibly (print clearly using ALL CAPITAL LETTERS); entering student income and asset information in the parental sections (or vice-versa) and checking the ovals (rather than filling them in completely).

You're far less likely to make mistakes if you complete your FAFSA online.

Unusual Circumstances

In general, if you don't feel the FAFSA adequately captures your true financial situation, contact the school's financial aid office to explain your situation. Here are a couple of common problems:

1. You don't meet the statutory requirements for being considered an independent student, yet you truly don't have access to any parental resources. In this case, complete your FAFSA as best you can (for example, without including any parental data) and let your colleges know what you've done. Many students today come from non-traditional families and schools are becoming experts at wading through prickly situations to be as fair as possible.

2. You have recently lost your job, or received a lay-off notice. In this case, you might qualify as a "dislocated worker" and be eligible for the Simplified Needs Test (which excludes assets) or an Auto-Zero EFC. The FAFSA now captures these situations if they occur before you file (Question 85 on the paper FAFSA).

3. Your status changes *after* you submit your FAFSA, due, for example, to a family death, disability, prolonged unemployment, divorce or separation. In this case, notify your colleges immediately. Aid administrators can recalculate your EFC to reflect your new situation.

Don't Forget to Sign the Form

The FAFSA includes a statement in which you promise to use your student aid for XYZ College only and certify that you aren't in default on any federal loans. Whether you file a paper FAFSA or an electronic version, you must acknowledge this statement before Uncle authorizes any funds.

If you're filing online, you can use an "electronic signature" which now has the same legal status as a written signature (see below).

Don't Falsify Anything

The FAFSA clearly states, "If you purposely give false or misleading information (on this form), you may be fined $20,000, sent to prison or both." And don't expect the financial planner you hired to bail you out.

Make Copies

Make copies of all financial aid forms and your responses to any information requests from Uncle Sam, the need analysis processor or the colleges. Make sure to send the original, however, and keep the copy for yourself.

What Happens Now?

Processing the FAFSA

1. You send your completed FAFSA to a processor; the address will be on the FAFSA, as well as the envelope that comes with your FAFSA.

2. The processor matches your information against several national databases to verify your eligibility for aid—it checks your Selective Service status, your Social Security number, and your citizenship status.

3. The processor evaluates your finances, checks data for inconsistencies and calculates your "Expected Family Contribution" (EFC).

4. The processor sends you a multipart eligibility document called a Student Aid Report (SAR) which incorporates your EFC. Students who include their e-mail address (on their FAFSA) are sent a secure e-link so they can review their eligibility report online.

5. Review your SAR carefully to make certain it was calculated using accurate information. If there are any mistakes (for instance, if a $500 has become $5000) send the correction back to the processor immediately. If your EFC has an asterisk next to it, the processor has found a potential problem and marked you as a candidate for verification. If your EFC has a "C" next to it, you're a big winner—you have an eligibility problem which must be resolved before you can receive any student aid.

6. The processor sends a detailed (electronic) analysis to all the colleges named on your FAFSA as well as your state's education agency, and the state education agencies for each college named on your FAFSA.

If you use FAFSA on the Web, the processor performs all the checks and matches described above, then sends you a link to your electronic SAR; you can make your corrections online.

Processing PROFILE

You must file PROFILE online. Within a week of processing your form, the College Board/CSS sends you an acknowledgment. The Data Confirmation section of this acknowledgment shows what information was entered from your application. As with the SAR, review the data carefully. If you see a mistake, make your corrections on a printed, paper copy of the Confirmation Report, and send these corrections directly to your colleges. The College Board also sends your schools a Report adjusting the Institutional Methodology calculation to meet each school's individual requests.

Building the Financial Aid Package

Before they start building aid packages, the financial aid staff establishes a packaging philosophy—guidelines to ensure consistency and equity in their treatment of all aid applicants. Unfortunately (and ironically), each school has its own ideas about consistency and equity which means your need will probably be met differently at each school to which you apply. Some schools award every student the maximum Stafford possible. Others award grant aid first, then self-help money (loans and work). Some have rules prescribing the ratio of grants to loans, a ratio that can vary with the income of the aid applicant (lower income students receiving more grants than loans, upper income students receiving mostly loans).

Now the financial aid administrator (FAA) goes to work.

First, the FAA determines your cost of attendance.

Second, the FAA reviews your EFC, compares it to your cost of attendance, and establishes your need (and eligibility) for most state and federal programs.

Third, the FAA takes another look at your EFC to determine your eligibility for collegiate awards—about 35% of all FAAs adjust the contribution based on policies of their office.

And finally, the FAA builds your Financial Aid Package.

In general, when awarding money from programs they administer but do not fund (i.e., federal programs), colleges give priority to the neediest of the able. When awarding money from their own funds, colleges give priority to the ablest of the needy.

Layer One—Federal and State Grants

The Federal Pell Grant is the foundation of every aid package (see Chapter 10). Only students with EFCs under about $4,500 are eligible for Pells. The school also checks to see if you are eligible for an Academic Competitiveness Grant (up to $750 for first-year Pell recipients and $1,300 for second-year Pell recipients) or SMART grant (up to $4,000 for third- and fourth-year Pell recipients).

State grants make up the other part of Layer One. Most states require students to attend an in-state college to qualify for a state award.

Layer Two—Outside Scholarships

Next, the FAA gleefully incorporates any outside scholarships you may have found—the $500 awarded you by your church or temple, as well as the $5,000 from your parent's boss. This is money the school need not worry about providing you.

Layer Three—Other Federal Programs

Third, if you still have need, the FAA draws on four other federal programs: Stafford Loans, Perkins Loans, Supplemental Educational Opportunity Grants and Work-Study (see Chapter 10).

The way FAAs use these programs varies from school to school according to their packaging philosophy and the size of their student aid budget. Most award Stafford loans (which are limitless) first, preserving (scarcer) federal resources for students who then still have need.

Layer Four—Collegiate Resources

If the cost of college is still greater than your resources (your EFC plus money from the aid programs above), the FAA can do one of three things:

1. Give you a huge award from the college's own resources. These resources include low interest loans and collegiate scholarships. The richer the college, the more resources it will have for this layer.

2. Use an IM (based on information you provided via PROFILE or the school's own aid application) to adjust your family contribution, and if you still have need, give you funds from the college's own resources. About 43% of private colleges, and 12% of public colleges, use multiple methodologies to determine eligibility for institutional aid.

3. Apologize for not being able to meet your financial need fully and suggest your parents borrow money under Uncle Sam's PLUS program (or use a commercial loan source) to help ease any cash flow problems.

Layer Five—PLUS Loans and Unsubsidized Staffords

Finally, the aid administrator will approve you for a PLUS loan. The size of your loan is limited to the school's total cost less financial aid—if school costs $20,000 and you receive $8,000 in financial aid, you may receive a $12,000 PLUS loan. The size of your family contribution does not matter. As an alternative, the school might certify you for an unsubsidized Stafford.

PLUS and Unsubsidized Staffords may be used to replace your EFC. For more information, see Chapter 10.

Families Without Financial Need

If the family has no need and the school really wants the student, the school may offer the student a no-need award such as an academic scholarship. Nearly every college, public and private, offers these awards. In fact, 45% of all institutional grant dollars are distributed based on merit or other criteria, for example, athletics or artistic ability. (Note: Much of this money goes to students who happen to have financial need, however, demonstrated need is not a criteria for receiving the money.)

The Award Letter

The FAA will present your aid package in the form of an award letter. These letters vary in format, but most contain the following items:

1. A statement of the expense budget developed for you. Again, this varies based on factors like whether you plan to live on- or off-campus.

2. Your expected family contribution, as calculated under the federal methodology and (if used) an institutional methodology.

3. The amount of your need.

4. A description of how all or part of that need is to be met, listing each aid source and dollar amount.

5. A suspense date by when you must return the award letter.

6. Information on "appealing" any information in the award letter .

If there is something you don't understand about the offer, or if you notice your EFC is different than what was sent to you by the processor on your Student Aid Report, ask the school for clarification.

Comparing Your Award Letters

While it's seldom wise to make the agonizing, final decision concerning which college to attend based on money issues alone, it's no longer realistic to exclude money as a factor. That said, it's important to make sure you're not just looking at the schools' sticker prices (that would be like comparing apples and oranges). Instead, you have to evaluate how much each school is going to cost your family in out-of-pocket money. And to make certain you're not comparing Granny Smiths to Red Delicious, be sure to factor in the amount of loan money you'll eventually have to repay.

You might find it helpful to create a spreadsheet with a side-by-side comparison of each school's package, or link to the College Board's "Compare Aid Awards" online tool at **www.collegeboard.com/student/pay**. If you'd like to review some sample letters, including a financial aid letter decoder, take a peek at **www.FinancialAidLetter.com**.

Don't delay responding to a letter, however, because you're still waiting to hear from other colleges. If you don't reply by the required date, the school can cancel your award and give the money to some other deserving student. Responding to the award letter does not commit you to attendance. It just safeguards your award, should you elect to go to that college.

In responding, your have four choices: You can accept the award in its entirety; accept some components of the award and reject others; reject the award entirely; or request a revised award (more grants, less loans).

Appealing Your Award

Few people still ask us if they can challenge admission decisions. Now, everyone wants to know if they can get schools to re-evaluate their aid package. Our answer? An unqualified "Maybe." But before you bully your way into a financial aid office demanding a recount, learn what actions will help (or hurt) your cause. Your success depends on several factors:

1. *The availability of discretionary funds.* Private colleges usually put more money toward scholarships than public universities. They also have more flexibility in how they distribute their money. In any case, make your request as early as possible, because money runs out fast even at our wealthiest schools!

2. *The skill (and tact) with which you present your case.* If your family has had a recent change in situation, document the change carefully and contact the FAA. He or she can adjust the EFC calculation to allow for special conditions—mostly unpleasant things like job loss, death, disability, divorce, or unexpected or unusually high medical expenses. In these cases, the FAA will probably lower the family's income figure and

recalculate. You might ask the FAA to reduce the value of reportable assets as well. For example, you can easily argue a recent job loss will not only affect a family's earnings, but also eat into its savings.

3. *The caliber of the student.* If the school really wants you to enroll, the FAA can sometimes be of more help, usually by adjusting the composition of your aid package. Remember: Grants are infinitely more desirable than loans. Here's also where the line between "financial aid" and "enrollment management" can begin to blur: Informal studies show it takes about $10,000 (spread out over four years) to nab a student who might otherwise not consider a particular school. Are you the kind of student on the college's shopping list?

Will This Route Satisfy My Need?

Maybe. Maybe not. It could be a dream package. Or it could leave you a thousand dollars short or mired deeply in debt. Remember: Few colleges have enough resources to help all applicants. Also, different colleges assess need differently. If you apply to three schools, each of which costs $8,000 more than your family's EFC, you may be offered three very different packages, ranging from the very attractive to the completely unacceptable.

■■■■■■■■■■■■■■■■■■■■

STEP THREE: KNOW ABOUT INFLUENCE POINTS

Now that you've mastered the mechanics of need analysis, it's time for the last step of the take-charge process: Know about influence points.

Influence Point: Wise College Selection
What You Can Gain: Improved aid package; no-need scholarships.
More Information: Chapter 9.

Influence Point: Careful Preparation for Need-Analysis
What You Can Gain: A lowered EFC and increased eligibility for aid; Longer planning time for help with cash-flow requirements.
More Information: This chapter, Chapter 7, Appendices 1, 2 and 3.

Influence Point: Speed and Accuracy in Applying
What You Can Gain: Increased chance of tapping into limited aid sources; Improved financial aid package.
More Information: This chapter.

Influence Point: Working with Aid Administrators
What You Can Gain: Improved financial aid package.
More Information: This chapter, Chapter 7, Chapter 9.

CHAPTER 7

■■■■■■■■■■■■■■■■■■■

There are six strategies for tilting the aid process in your favor. Only two are mutually exclusive—the Napoleon of aid seekers would investigate all six:

- Strategy One—Reduce Your Expected Family Contribution
- Strategy Two—Increase the Cost of Attendance
- Strategy Three—Obtain an Improved Aid Package
- Strategy Four—Replace Your Money with OPM, Other People's Money
- Strategy Five—Lower the Cost of College
- Strategy Six—Improve Your Cash Flow

Strategy One—
Reduce Your Expected Family Contribution

Objective: Reduce your expected family contribution so your need becomes larger and you become eligible for more student assistance. Of course, there's a fine line between getting your fair share and abusing financial aid rules at the expense of needier students. Besides, if you're caught cheating (and you would be), you'll pay the price in fines and lost aid. Most financial aid, remember, is "need-based" not "want-based"—family contribution is calculated independently of a family's lifestyle choices. Here are some ideas to ponder:

Thoroughly Understand Need Analysis

We assume that while reading Chapter 6 you took time to complete the worksheets in Appendix 1, 2, or 3 and noted the various percentages and weights assigned to your data. These items should have caught your eye.

1. **Parent Assets vs. Student Assets.** Dependent students do not rate an asset protection allowance. Their assets are taxed at 20% of their value. (Previously, they were assessed at 35% of their value.) Parents do rate an asset protection allowance. Money held by parents, as you trace it through the formula, is taxed no more than 5.6%. That's quite a difference! $40,000 in junior's bank account becomes an $8,000 contribution to college costs. The same $40,000 in the parental account becomes a mere $2,240 contribution. *Lesson*: Accumulate money for college, yes. But don't be so quick to accumulate in the child's name.

2. **Business Property.** Family-owned and controlled small business assets (including family farms) are excluded from net worth in the need analysis process. Other business assets rate an adjustment factor (e.g., 40% of net worth up to $115,000). Think hard. Do you have any assets that you can move into a small business or limited partnership?

3. **The True Value of a Student Aid Dollar.** If you are in a 25% tax bracket and don't get student aid, you must earn $1.33 to have one dollar available for tuition bills. Let's turn this around. If you are successful in getting one dollar of student aid, that one dollar is really worth $1.33 to you. Lesson: The higher your tax bracket, the greater the value of any student aid dollar received.

4. **Tax Dollars Are Not Created Equal.** For each dollar you pay in federal income taxes, you increase eligibility for financial aid by up to 47 cents. Local taxes, including property and sales taxes, bring no such windfall.

5. **The Previous-Year Rule.** Your 2008 earnings determine your aid eligibility for the 2009/2010 academic year. Your 2009 earnings impact the 2010/2011 year. If your income fluctuates, and you have control over the fluctuations, you might defer income from the base year to the next. That would enhance your eligibility in the coming academic year. What about the next year? Life is filled with soap opera twists. Take it one year at a time.

6. **No Credit for Consumer Debt.** Under need analysis, you get no write-off for consumer debt. If you have $10,000 in credit card debt, or you owe the bank $20,000 in car payments, that's your problem. But let's say you own stocks and have a brokerage account that lets you borrow against your portfolio. If you draw $20,000 to finish paying for the car, you reduce the value of your reportable assets by that amount. You pay less for college and have a new car in which to drive Junior off to school!

7. **High Income Assessment Rates.** After a certain threshold, each additional dollar of student income is assessed at 50%; each additional dollar of parent income is assessed at 47%. In other words, high income (rather than assets) is what sinks most families hopes for eligibility.

"What If" Calculations

If you have spreadsheet software, you can program our appendices and simplify the following kinds of "what-if" scenarios. Another option is to use an online calculator, or our Federal Methodology (FM) software (see last page). The results can surprise you. Whenever possible, we've noted strategies that aren't viable under the Institutional Methodology (IM).

Reduce Your Reportable Income

1. *Take less pay.* Can you defer income or year-end bonuses? Remember, need analysis looks at previous year income—2008 for the 2009/2010 award year. With constantly changing rules, if you can increase eligibility even for a year, do it!

2. *Accelerate income.* If your student won't start college until 2010, try to lower your 2009 income. For example, accelerate bonuses into 2008, ask your ex-spouse for an early alimony (or child support) check, and make sure you don't receive 2008 state or local tax refunds in 2009.

3. *Accelerate or postpone gains.* If you plan to sell stocks or property (for a gain), do it two years before college, or wait until graduation year. Capital gains count as income which is heavily "taxed" during need analysis.

4. *Watch out for year-end dividends.* If the mutual fund you're eyeing is about to pay a dividend, wait until after the payout before you buy.

5. *Do you have any losing investments?* Sell them off and take the loss. It's a two-fer—if your capital losses exceed your gains, you may use up to $3,000 in losses to lower your other taxable income. This, in turn, lowers the income you report for need analysis.

6. *Do you have all your assets in income-bearing accounts?* Move money you won't need for college into "growth" funds which aim to increase the value of your investment rather than provide high current income. Need analysis assesses assets much less heavily than income.

7. *Are you paying alimony or child-support for another child?* If so, can you accelerate payments?

8. *Can you contribute to an employer-sponsored flexible-spending account for childcare or medical expenses?* These contributions are not added back into income on the FAFSA.

9. *Is it time for a career change?* Should Mom or Dad take some time off work to rethink options? Sadly, as much as 85% of each extra dollar your parents earn go to state taxes, federal taxes or the college bursar.

Reduce Your Reportable Assets

Not all assets are created equal.

1. *Home equity is not a reportable asset under the Federal Methodology.* So what happens if you use savings to pay down your home mortgage? You'll probably be in a better position to qualify for a low-interest federal loan. Remember, however, aid administrators are free to ask questions about home equity, and may reserve the school's own funds for renters (and expect families with pricey homes and no mortgage to borrow against this great asset). The IM assesses home equity.

2. *Do you need to make a large purchase before you sign and date your FAFSA?* A new car to replace the one Junior wants to take to college? How about a new refrigerator or washer-dryer? Is your heat pump about to give out? Pay cash, or borrow against a stock portfolio. That will reduce your reportable assets—and provide you with a smooth ride, cold drinks, clean clothes and a comfortable home climate.

3. *If you've been saving in your child's name,* prior to filing your FAFSA, get his permission to use that money for pre-college expenses, like SAT Prep, or to buy the now-essential computer (or maybe even a used car). Or, if Junior is a good athlete, send her to a summer camp in her sport. This can have an extra benefit if she catches the eye of a recruiter, and can parlay her skills into an athletic scholarship. Talented musicians (and other artists) can benefit similarly from summer camps. Otherwise, use Juniors assets to pay your entire EFC for the first year of college. This will improve your chances for aid during years two, three, and four. Warning: This won't work at all schools. Some expect 20% of a student's assets in Year One, 20% of the remaining balance in Year Two, etc. Tricky, tricky, tricky! Also, don't just throw the money away—it's not worth wasting $1 just to gain an additional twenty cents in aid.

4. *Do you have a favorite charity?* Make your annual contribution before you file your FAFSA and see how that gift impacts on your family contribution (and your taxes).

5. *Can you use reportable assets to pay down your credit card debt?* Or pay off an automobile loan? Getting rid of consumer debt can be good financial planning, as well as good college planning.

6. *Do you have any bills to pay?* Deplete your checking account balance before you file by paying all your bills, and maybe next month's, too.

7. *Do grandparents need some extra money?* You can each give each of your student's grandparents a gift of up to $12,000, which would reduce your assets by up to $96,000.

Declare Yourself Independent

Independent students do not include parental income and assets in their need analysis calculation; only their own, (generally) more limited resources so their contribution will usually be smaller, and their need larger. Should you declare yourself independent to gain access to more aid? Certainly, if you are really independent. Absolutely not, if it is a ploy. Note: Single, undergraduates under the age of 24 who are not in the military are "dependent" in all cases, except at the discretion of the financial aid administrator.

Start a Family Business

Can you move some assets into a business venture? It doesn't have to be complex, but it must show a profit in at least 3 out of 5 years, otherwise the IRS calls it a hobby. For example, the Bakers started Babycakes to sell muffins every Saturday at their local farmer's market. Rose loves going to yard sales on weekends, so, she started a second-hand furniture business with the objects she finds.

Uncle rewards private enterprise with a reduced contribution to college costs. First, small business assets are excluded from need analysis; and second, any money you pay your children becomes a business expense, and under the FM, students receive an income protection allowance of $3,750. (They receive no such allowance under the IM, and freshmen are expected to contribute at least $1,550 from earnings.)

Save for Retirement

Need analysis wants to know how much you contribute to a retirement fund the year before college (it considers this a discretionary contribution and adds it back in to your income). It does not, however, ask how much you've already saved. In other words, you can accumulate retirement funds tax-free (or tax-deferred) at the same time you reduce your assets for need analysis. For example, currently you can put $15,500 each year into a 401(k). Of course, you shouldn't put all your assets in funds that penalize you for early withdrawal (e.g., before age 59 1/2). You may need some money sooner.

The IM also excludes retirement assets, however some colleges ask about their value to determine your family's overall financial well-being. These colleges may either expect you to borrow more money, or use your hefty retirement account "against" you if try to "upgrade" your aid package.

Use a More Favorable Need Analysis Method

Can you lower your AGI to under $50,000? If so, and you're *eligible* to file a 1040A or 1040EZ (even if you file a regular 1040), parent and student assets are excluded from need analysis. *Lesson.* If you can keep your AGI under $50,000 (even for one year), do it! The IM makes no such distinction.

Increase the Number of Family Members in College

Your parental contribution figure is divided by the number of students you have in school at any one time. If you have two children, one year apart, with one starting college and one starting the senior year in high school, would it be advantageous for the older child to "stop out" for one year and wait for son or daughter #2 to catch up? The IM is less generous; 60% of the parental contribution is assessed for each of two children.

Neither formula includes parents in the "number of family members enrolled" figure, however, if Dad truly needs to complete his degree at the same time one or more children are in college, let the school know. Aid administrators may decide to include him. Or (more likely), they may treat his tuition payments as another exclusion from the family's AGI.

Explain Your Extraordinary Expenses or Unusual Situations

The FM leaves consideration of special conditions to the discretion of aid administrators. Colleges have even more wiggle room in deciding how to allocate their own resources. Don't try to explain away high vacation expenses, four Jags in the driveway, or a newly-remodeled kitchen. But do note legitimate "involuntary" expenses or unusual situations that might convince an aid administrator to re-evaluate your contribution.

In deciding whether or not a family has "unusual expenses," the Department of Education suggests that schools allocate 30% of the income protection allowance (Table A in the Appendix) to food; 22% to housing; 9% to transportation; 16% to clothing/personal care; 11% to medical care; and 12% to other family needs. How do your expenses compare?

FYI. Schools aren't allowed to change the Federal Methodology formula, or adjust your "bottom line" EFC directly, but they can modify the data elements used in the calculation, for example, lower the value of your assets, or use expected year income, rather than prior year. Of course, they may wait until Spring semester to adjust your award, so they can examine your 2009 tax return. Here are some questions to ask yourself:

- Does your family have enormous medical or dental expenses?
- Does your family pay secondary school tuitions for younger siblings? Or graduate school expenses for older siblings?
- Are your parents repaying their own students loans, or those of an older sibling?
- Are your parents paying nursing home costs for their own parents?
- Will you be attending camp (for example, in dance or tennis) or serving the community in lieu of taking a paying summer job?
- Is your contribution from student income inflated because you took a year off to work?
- Is your contribution from student assets inflated because the family saved its money in the student's name? Did the parent put it there? Or did it come from some other source, like grandparents, aunts or uncles?
- Is your contribution from parental income artificially high due to an unexpected bonus or capital gain? Is that money being double-counted as an asset, as well?
- Do you have consumer debt resulting from past unemployment?
- Do you have high child care costs?
- Did you pay more in state and local taxes than the need analysis formula allowed?
- Do you have siblings attending pricey private colleges (who received less-than-generous aid packages)?
- Did the school exclude consideration of your Hope or Lifetime Learning tax credits?
- Is a parent about to retire? Do you have a skimpy retirement fund?
- Has your College Fund declined in value since you filed your aid application?
- Is your new business eating up assets, rather than generating income?
- Did either of your parents lose a job after you filed your application?

- Are you an independent student who was required to report parental income and assets on the aid application?
- Was your home affected by earthquakes? Floods?
- Did your parents divorce or separate after you filed your application?
- Do you live somewhere with a higher-than-average cost of living, for example, urban areas like San Francisco or New York?

Before they start adjusting the EFC calculation to account for special circumstances, some aid administrators will take a quick snapshot of your situation—20% of your income and 5-6% of your assets (excluding home equity)—and use that as a rough guide to your ability to pay.

If you make an appointment to discuss your situation, bring all of your supporting documentation with you—and be ready to make your case in one session. Frequent repeat visits (and demands) before you enroll can make the college suspicious that you're using their potential generosity to leverage a better deal elsewhere.

Go Complex, Consult an Expert

College is one of life's biggest investments, yet many families fail to treat it that way! Financial planners who really understand financial aid can help you in important ways. They'll help you (1) understand the long- and short-term financial impact of different cost-saving strategies; (2) gain insight into how schools might view your case; (3) draft a Letter of Special Circumstance to explain any unique situation; and (4) manage your cash flow so you can educate your children *and* have enough for retirement.

But don't expect a free college education. As Bonnie Hepburn writes, "Financial planners can save you money but they can't work miracles. They are best at helping you reduce your cost of college, if possible, and then figuring out how to pay for what remains over the number of years you'll have kids in college."

Ms. Hepburn is with MONEYSENSE Financial Planning, a fee-only practice with college funding expertise (240 Massachusetts Ave., Boxborough, MA 01719, 978/264-4088, www.win.net/~moneysense).

If you ask for a re-evaluation of your aid package don't let the hired gun speak on your behalf. Schools respect your financial privacy and won't talk about your income and asset situation with a third party.

Strategy Two—
Increase the Cost of Attendance

Objective: Increase the cost of attendance so your need becomes larger. This will improve your chances for a Stafford Loan or collegiate aid.

Don't Rule Out More Expensive Schools

Your EFC is $15,000 and you plan to attend a $17,000 school. The maximum (subsidized) Stafford for which you qualify is $2,000. If you now select a $25,000 school, you could get a $3,500 loan, $1,500 in work-study and $5,000 from the school's own funds. Your family contribution is the same.

Remember, more expensive schools often have more aid to hand out. You never know until you apply.

Does Your Student Budget Reflect All Your Expenses?

Does the aid administrator have a true picture of your transportation costs, special medical expenses, disability needs, child care costs, loan fees, or other legitimate expenses the school may have overlooked? For example:

- If you're a fine arts majors, you might need to buy costly art supplies.
- If you're planning to study abroad, you might need extra money for transportation expenses and supplemental medical insurance.
- If you're a music major, you might need to take private piano lessons.
- If you're a film student, you might have to pay your own film production costs.
- If you're a co-op education student, you might need extra money for employment costs. You probably won't get enough to cover a new Armani wardrobe, but you may get an extra $500 for bus fare.
- If you're changing climates, you might even get a boost for "miscellaneous" expenses—so you can afford to trade your 99-cent Florida flip-flops for 99-dollar Minnesota snow boots.

The school may also include computer expenses in your cost of attendance. If it doesn't, and you need a new laptop, be sure to let the school know. Finally, many colleges charge separate fees for a variety of campus essentials; for example, "technology fees" to counter the exploding costs of maintaining up-to-date computer labs. While these fees may only amount to a few hundred dollars, make sure they are all included in your budget.

Strategy Three— Obtain an Improved Aid Package

Objective: Change the composition of your package to emphasize aid you won't have to repay. Grants and work-study are much better than loans.

Careful College Application

Apply to colleges as early as possible, before the money runs out.

Also, pick colleges where your academic qualifications place you in the top 25% of the applicant pool. The most desirable applicants get the most agreeable aid packages. That's as true at the Ivies as it is at Horned Toad

State. Two-thirds of all private colleges, and one-quarter of all public colleges, target their aid packages to increase their enrollment yields.

Avoid Early Decision

If financial aid is important, think twice about applying early decision. Here's why: If you are accepted early for admission, the college knows you will be attending and does not need to sweeten an aid package to help influence your decision. You could lose some of your leverage.

Dialing for Dollars

Call (or write) the school and request a review of your aid offer, especially the share that comes from the college's own funds. Will you get more money? That depends on whether the college really wants you, and has resources to spare. What gives you bargaining strength? Good grades and SAT scores, athletic ability, artistic talent, alumni ties, ethnic background, geographic origin, even a substantial aid package from one of the school's "competitors." Colleges like to brag about their diversity and they might be missing a pole vaulter from Idaho or a soprano from Rhode Island.

You might even ask a department head (if you are a genius) or a coach (if you are a jock) to be your advocate in such negotiations. Why do colleges care about this? Long term survival! First of all, a diverse student body makes for a more rewarding academic experience for all enrolled students, but also, having enthusiastic, diverse alumni spread over the entire country is a good way for a college to ensure a continued stream of applicants in future years.

Strategy Four—
Replace Your Money With OPM

Objective: Getting Other People's Money (OPM) to pay for your family contribution is the most desirable but also the most difficult strategy. You could beg for cash via your own Web site (www.sendannatocollege.com) or auction yourself off on eBay. Or you could follow the lead of an enterprising, financially strapped economics student who (according to the *Wall Street Journal*) staged a one-person bike-a-thon to benefit himself. Unfortunately, pledges to his scholarship fund ($725) barely covered his expenses ($510), and after biking nearly 200 miles, alone and in the dark, he offered these words of wisdom, "stupid idea, stupid idea, stupid idea."

Here are some better ones.

Money from Grandma

Direct payments to the school for tuition are not subject to gift tax limits, so grandparents who want to help their smart grandchildren can help pay the college bill, without having that generosity affect the financial aid calculation or anyone's tax return. No fuss. No muss. On the off-chance the payment impacts future aid packages, make sure to let the school know that the cash infusion from grandma was a one-time gift.

Money from Your Boss

Many employers will reimburse you for part of your tuition expenses; the first $5,250 is tax-free. See Chapter 12 for more information.

No-Need Awards

No-need awards are given without regard to financial need. If you win a $5,000, no-need scholarship, you are $5,000 ahead. The recipient of a no-need scholarship can fall into one of two categories: They either have need or they don't. Let's examine each situation in more detail:

Situation 1—You have need and receive a no-need award

The award is included as part of your expected family resources, effectively increasing your EFC by the amount of your award. This increase may eliminate (1) part of your need; (2) your entire need; or (3) your entire need and part of your family contribution. Actual numbers will determine which of these it will be. Assume the cost of college is $20,000 and your family contribution is $15,000. This makes your need $5,000.

Example 1—Your no-need award is $1,000. Offered aid package: The school increases your expected family resources from $15,000 to $16,000 which reduces your need from $5,000 to $4,000.

Example 2—Your no-need award is $5,000. Offered aid package: The school increases your expected family resources from $15,000 to $20,000 which eliminates your need.

Example 3—Your no-need award is $6,000. Offered aid package: The school increases your expected family resources from $15,000 to $21,000, however, the cost of college is only $20,000, so you can use the extra $1,000 to reduce your out-of-pocket contribution from $15,000 to $14,000.

This packaging may seem unfair, but federal regulations prevent schools from using no-need money to replace your EFC (if the school plans to distribute need-based federal student aid funds). In Examples 1 and 2 above, you still benefit from the no-need award since the money is likely replacing a loan element of your aid package.

Situation 2—You have no need and the award is a no-need award

In this case, the money goes directly to you. You write a smaller check when you pay the college bill. Let's assign numbers to this. Your family contribution is $20,000, the cost of college is $20,000 and your no-need award is $3,000. Your family contribution now shrinks to $17,000.

Where can I find no-need awards?

No-need awards tend to congregate in the following three areas.

1. *Uncle Sam.* Most of Uncle's no-need awards have a military connection and carry a service obligation, e.g., service academies and ROTC.

2. *States.* Merit money from the states is the fastest growing source of aid. Two programs: (1) Honors scholarships for use at in-state schools, to keep top students close to home; (2) Tuition equalization grants for students attending in-state private colleges rather than public universities. See Chapter 11 for the address of your home state's higher education agency.

3. *The Colleges.* Colleges are the main source of no-need awards. Over 1200 offer academic scholarships to entice bright students to enroll. See *The A's and B's of Academic Scholarships* ($15, www.octameron.com).

Strategy Five—
Lower the Cost of College

Objective: Lower costs so you reduce or eliminate your need and spare yourself the hassle of applying for aid or saddling yourself with debt.

Pick a Lower-Priced School

Choose schools that receive church subsidies (Brigham Young, St. Olaf, or any Catholic college) or where the cost of living is low (Texas, Michigan). Or consider these options:

1. **Investigate your own State U.** Not just the flagship school, but all the others, as well. Even the wealthiest of families receive what amounts to a $12,000 - $18,000 tuition subsidy, courtesy of their state government.

2. **Investigate the State U. in other states.** Even with the non-resident "surcharge," the average cost is $6,000 - $10,000 less than at a private school.

3. **Consider community colleges.** Go for two years, then transfer to a four-year school to finish your degree. You pick up the "halo" of the prestige college's sheepskin, but at a fraction of the cost. Some community colleges even have Honors Programs to better prepare top students for the eventual transfer. If you opt for this route, make sure you take academic core courses so your credits will transfer. Also, don't let yourself get derailed—it's all too easy to pick up "real world" responsibilities, and never finish your degree.

4. **Look for "Best Buys."** *U.S. News* and *Kiplinger's* each publish "Best Value" rankings. In general, schools that score highest do so because they charge less than schools of similar quality, or they offer greater amounts of non-need-based aid. You'll find both magazines on your real or virtual newsstand (www.usnews.com or www.kiplingers.com).

5. **Study in Canada.** Winters are long, and class sizes can be large (especially for first-year students), but Canadian schools are excellent. Furthermore, Canadian taxpayers subsidize tuition, making room and board quite affordable. In fact, Canadian prices rival public tuition in the U.S. For example, well-known McGill charges international students just $15,420 for tuition which currently equals $14,730 in U.S. dollars. If you choose a Canadian school, you won't be eligible for need-based federal grants, however, you can receive subsidized federal loans and qualify for tuition tax credits. For more information, contact the Association of Universities and Colleges of Canada (www.aucc.ca) or Canadian Academic Study Abroad (www.studyincanada.com).

6. **Study Abroad.** Tuition costs can be lower in many other countries as well, especially if you look at schools outside of Western Europe (Prague and Buenos Aires are current hot spots). If you're only going for a year, or a semester, make sure the credits you'll be earning will be accepted by your U.S. university. Also find out whether you'll be paying tuition to your host program or your home university. Because the dollar is still weak against the Euro, the difference can be huge. For program information, visit the Council on International Education, www.ciee.org, or StudyAbroad.com, www.studyabroad.com.

Take Off-Hour Courses

More and more schools are lowering tuition costs for classes taught at less popular times, for example, evenings and weekends or summertime. You save money for each credit hour taken during these off-peak times.

Take Extension Courses

Many universities, public and private, offer extension programs at satellite facilities. These extension programs were originally designed to serve working adults looking to take a course or two, usually to advance their careers. For this reason, courses are usually taught on weekends or in the evenings. But economic considerations are making extension schools a much more popular option with traditional-age undergraduates. Not only do extension schools make it easier to work and attend college at the same time, they are generally less costly than their parent universities; for example, a course at Harvard costs over $4,000; a course at Harvard University Extension might cost only $550. Furthermore, extension schools often feature open admissions and their credits can be fully transferable.

Extension schools are nothing new. In fact, UCLA extension is celebrating its 90th anniversary.

Pay Less For Textbooks

Textbook costs can average up to $1,000 per year. But there are several ways to cut this cost in half. For example:

- Five of the largest textbook publishers, including Pearson, Wiley and McGraw Hill, have joined together to create CourseSmart, a collection of nearly 5,000 online textbooks. These eTextbooks cost about half the price of the print versions. You may highlight text and take notes electronically. You may even do some printing. But at the end of a year, your digital code expires, along with access to the textbook, www.coursesmart.com.

- If you don't want to keep your textbooks, you might also consider book rental programs and book buy-back programs. If your campus bookstore doesn't offer these options, get your books online using BigWords, www.bigwords.com or BookRenter, www.bookrenter.com.

- Students studying the classics should check Project Gutenberg, which has over 25,000 out-of-copyright works available as free downloads, www.gutenberg.org.

- Compare book prices at www.bestbookbuys.com—used books cost less than new ones, softcover costs less than hardcover.

Examine Other Elements of the "Cost of Attendance"

You can influence most of them. For example:

- Cut your travel costs—many airlines offer low student fares.
- Save on housing by living off-campus with roommates.
- Choose a meal plan that fits your lifestyle—don't pay for breakfast at the dining hall if you never wake up before noon.
- It's never-too-soon to start clipping coupons. Your Sunday paper is a gold mine; so is www.hotcoupons.com. *Remember, never pay full price for pizza!*

Look for Other Savings

Miscellaneous expenses can run from $3,500 to $7,000 per year, depending on your chosen lifestyle. For example, when it comes to phone calls, you might skip the land line, but be careful not to go over your minutes. Compare cell phone plans at www.MyRatePlan.com. Also, learn to make your own coffee—a daily trip to Starbucks can cost more than $100 a month.

To see how much money you can save by drinking water instead of soft drinks, or skipping the oversized muffin at breakfast and fast-food sand- wiches at lunch (to say nothing of the possible health benefits), try the fun calculators at www.hughchou.org/calc.

Leave the Car at Home

Gas, insurance, maintenance, parking (and parking tickets) really add up— car-related expenes could cost over $200 per month. Furthermore, parents may qualify for lower car insurance when their risky teenage driver heads to college and leaves the car behind. Use some of your savings to buy a bike.

Be Careful With Your Credit Cards

One of the best ways to control your college costs is to stay away from credit cards. It's easy to run up large debts trying to maintain a standard of living you can't afford—credit card shopping sprees are usually not for school-related essentials. It's never too soon to learn one of life's little lessons: The only way to stay out of debt is to spend less money than you have! You'll learn more than you want to know about debt when your student loans come due; don't add high-interest credit card debt to the mix.

If you absolutely must own a credit card, be wary of on-campus promotions and those daily solicitations that arrive in your mailbox; instead, use CardWeb's Card Locator (www.cardweb.com) to find the best rates.

Don't Spend (or Gamble) Money you Don't Have

Even more dangerous is the lure of online day trading. Eager to make a quick buck, some students schedule classes around Wall Street's opening bell, using their college loan money as "start-up" capital. You may hear classmates brag about their latest financial gains—the stock that doubled its price in just a few days. But in all likelihood, these daredevil investors have no clue as to what they're doing and will also pick some stocks that collapse, and lose their tuition money in the process. You *won't* hear them bragging about that!

Watch Your Pre-College Costs

Campus visits, test prep courses, testing fees, application fees and private counselors can cost thousands. Be judicious.

Accelerate College

The best way to cut the cost of college, is to cut the time you spend there. Here are some ways to shorten your college career:

1. **Take college courses while in high school.** Many states fund "dual enrollment" or "early college" programs that let you take real college courses while also earning credit toward high school. Philanthropic groups (like the Gates Foundation, www.earlycolleges.org) are also pouring money into these programs. All in all, it's a great way to beat "senioritis"—the tendency to slack off once the admission applications are in the mail—and get an early taste of the rigors of college life. The credits should be easily transferable, but it never hurts to check.

2. **Earn credit for advanced placement exams**. Last year, students took nearly 2.3 million tests in 37 different areas. About 1,200 schools give credit for good AP scores; hundreds (including Harvard) grant incoming students sophomore standing. Each course for which you receive credit can be worth up to $2,000-$4,000 (depending on the college's tuition costs). A test costs only $83. To counter criticism that scoring well on an AP exam is not as tough as passing a college course, many schools are

boosting their minimum accepted score from 3 to 4 (or 5). And some delay giving credit until students pass the next course in the sequence. In other words, you won't receive credit for that "4" on your Calculus exam, unless you pass a higher level math course after you enroll. In following this strategy, be careful not to skip too many introductory-level classes; many students are adequately prepared to start out in more advanced classes, but others struggle with all of the adjustments.

- If your school doesn't offer AP courses, you can take them online through APEX learning, www.apexlearning.com.

- If you do start college as a sophomore, the IRS says your family can still qualify for two years of the Hope credit, even though eligibility is generally limited to students in their first two years of college.

3. **Look for three-year degrees.** High profile figures from Stanford and Oberlin have praised the idea. Others feel most students need the full four years to grow, intellectually, emotionally, and occupationally. They're afraid the liberal-arts will get short-changed as students won't have enough time to take the necessary spectrum of courses.

4. **Combine your degrees.** If you're planning to go on to graduate school, look for combined-degree programs, for example, a BA-MBA combo that takes five years, instead of the usual six.

5. **Get credit for life experience.** Every school has its own rules on what counts for what credit. The American Council on Education publishes guidelines in *The National Guide to Educational Credit for Training Programs*. Another option is to take the College Board's College-Level Examination Program (CLEP) Test or the ACT's Proficiency Examination Program (PEP). Both are ideal for students who have college-level mastery of a subject because of their backgrounds or job experience. For test descriptions, registration information, and a list of schools that give CLEP credit, click www.collegeboard.com and search for "CLEP."

6. **If you're a full-time student, don't take more than four years to gradu-ate!** A tight job market makes it tempting to hang out in college for an extra year, a move that could cost you $15,000-$50,000 (or more) in college bills, plus another $25,000-$50,000 in lost wages. (We're sure you would've found a job!) As an alternative, finish your degree, join AmeriCorps, and use your education-award to repay some of your student loans.

Become a Cyberstudent

Do you have a travel-intensive job? Or maybe young children at home? Are you short on cash? Time? Thanks to computers and phone lines, you can now get a quality education in the CyberLeague without ever setting foot in a classroom. Costs range from $60 to $400 per credit hour.

Currently, students have their pick of thousands of credit and non-credit classes. Even our most selective schools are trying to incorporate new learning technologies into their curriculums (without, of course, diminishing the value and prestige of their degrees). How do they work? Students use e-mail to attend classroom "discussions," get reading assignments, submit papers, and communicate with faculty and classmates.

Some colleges have found that online teaching leads to increased demands on faculty time, making it more expensive than old-fashioned face-to-face learning. In other words, you won't always save tuition money by taking this route. The best way to learn about all these new options is to investigate them online. The following links will get you started.

Degree.Net! (www.degree.net). Links to useful resources as well as a searchable database of distance-learning schools.

Globewide Network Academy (www.gnacademy.org). A thorough list of nearly 32,000 distance learning courses and 6,250 programs.

World Wide Learn (www.worldwidelearn.com). A large directory of online courses, as well as advice on choosing the right program.

World Lecture Hall (web.austin.utexas.edu/wlh). Links to online course material in every field of study; created by faculty worldwide.

Graduate from http://www.almamater.edu

If you want a more traditional college experience (instead of taking a hodge-podge of courses from computers around the world), you can pay tuition to a single virtual school. You won't get to cheer at football games, or toss water balloons out your dorm window, but you will get to enjoy pictures of smiling students and a graphically-pleasing college campus every time you click on your college's home page. Sometimes you can even hang out with your new cyberfriends in a virtual student union or join an alumni association and attend virtual college reunions.

Before you enroll, find out if you can take all your courses online or whether there is a residency requirement. Visit a virtual classroom to make sure your computer can handle all the graphics. And find out how many enrolled students have actually graduated (in fairness, many of these programs are still new, so they don't have any graduates yet).

Capella University (www.capellauniversity.edu). One of the oldest distance-learning schools in the country.

Jones International University (www.jonesinternational.edu). This fully-accredited online university awards business- and education-oriented degrees on the undergraduate and graduate level.

New School Online (www.online.newschool.edu). The New School has a reputation for excellence. Its cyber-campus offerings are top-notch.

Servicemembers Opportunity Colleges (www.soc.aascu.org). A consortium of over 1,800 colleges that provide educational opportunities for servicemembers and their families—either on-campus or on-line.

Southern Regional Electronic Campus (www.electroniccampus.org). Online campus with degree programs from colleges across the South.

University of Phoenix (www.phoenix.edu). With both real and virtual classrooms, this for-profit university caters to working students.

Western Governors University (www.wgu.edu). A collaborative effort among several Western states to serve the needs of nontraditional students, not replace the traditional college experience.

A Note on Accreditation:

If your program is not accredited, you can't receive federal student aid. It's that simple. Unfortunately, officials are still trying to figure out how to evaluate cyberschools, which leaves thousands (millions?) of students in the lurch. The problem is two-fold: how to guard against fraud and how to ensure a quality education. Most worrisome is the possibility of virtual universities with virtual students who receive real Pell Grants.

The most recent higher education legislation makes it easier to receive federal student aid while attending online schools, but you'd still be wise to choose courses carefully; for example, look at those attached to already-accredited "bricks and mortar" campuses. *For more information, contact the Distance Education and Training Council (www.detc.org) or the Council for Higher Education Accreditation (www.chea.org).*

Consolidate Your Credits

Excelsior College offers associate and baccalaureate degrees. Students may enroll at any time and move through the program at their own pace. Excelsior offers classes of its own, and lets students consolidate credits they've earned from other sources including distance instruction, campus-based courses at other colleges and special assessment. Students work with an advisor by mail, phone, fax and e-mail to plan their course of study. Excelsior College, 7 Columbia Circle, Albany, NY, 12203, www.excelsior.edu.

Strategy Six—
Improve Your Cash Flow

Objective: To pay your family contribution without liquidating assets, hocking the family jewels, or playing Uncle Sam's paper games.

Your family contribution must be paid each semester. For most families, it represents a rather sizable sum that usually comes with a friendly note "unless this bill is paid by such and such a date your student will not be allowed to register for classes... ."

How can you pay this bill without selling the family home, jeopardizing your after-retirement financial security or taking out a high-cost commercial loan? You could turn to federal (PLUS) loan programs, but they can be subject to the whims of the political process. Here are some other options.

Choose Colleges with Innovative Payment Plans

Many colleges offer favorable loan programs, using money from their endowment funds or from money raised by tax-exempt bond issues. Other schools let you pay the family contribution in installments. See Chapter 9.

Participate in Commercial Tuition Payment Plans

These plans let you pay all or part of your education expenses on a monthly basis, and keep you from borrowing more money than you really need. For example, if your family contribution is $8,000, you pay the commercial organization $800 per month for ten months and the commercial organization forwards your payments to the school. You pay no interest, but must start making payments well before your tuition is due, usually in June or July. Frequently, plans charge a flat $40-$50 fee and have a life insurance feature to cover bills in the event of your death. Plan sponsors include:

- **TuitionPay Monthly Plan,** 800/635-0120, www.tuitionpay.com.
- **Tuition Management Systems,** 800/722-4867, www.afford.com.

Choose the College You Can Most Easily Afford

Apply to colleges of varying costs—there are good schools for you in every price category. Then, look over the offered aid packages and choose the school you can most easily afford. Be sure to weigh your out-of-pocket costs as well as the loans you must eventually repay.

Tap Your Home Equity

With the fall of housing prices, some families (for example, those with larger mortgages) might find that home equity loans are no longer an option as nervous lenders have become reluctant lenders.

If you are able to open a home equity account, you can often do so at no cost, and borrow whatever you need, whenever you need it, without having to reapply. To use the funds, simply write a check or use a credit card. Interest rates float about one percentage point above the prime. And here's an added bonus. Any items you charge—like college tuition—become part of your home mortgage, so your interest payments on loans up to $100,000 become tax-deductible. For families who earn too much to deduct interest payments on education loans, borrowing against home equity may be the better option (especially since interest rates on federal PLUS loans have increased to 8.5%).

There are two ways to access home equity: via an equity line of credit or an equity loan. A line of credit turns your home into a checking account.

Interest accrues only when (and if) you use the money. Home equity loans turn your home into a pot of cash. You start repaying principal and interest whether you use the money or not. *Which is the better deal?* Unless you plan to write a single check for four years worth of tuition, stick with the line of credit. The reason? First of all, the interest rate is usually slightly lower. Second, you won't need all the money at once. In fact, in between tuition bills you should pay down as much of your debt as possible, so you never use up more of your equity than necessary.

Home equity is an extremely easy and flexible way to obtain cash flow assistance on favorable terms. In fact, it allows many families to live way beyond their means, so take care that ease of access to all this money does not result in deep financial problems and cause you to lose your home. The total monthly payments on all of your loans should not exceed 35% of your pre-tax monthly income.

When shopping for the best deal, beware of teaser rates which are usually good for only the first six months or a year. Also ask: If the interest rate is variable, how often can it change? On what index is it based? Does it carry a cap? Is there an annual fee? An application fee? An origination fee? Are any points charged? What about closing costs? Can terms change without my approval? Can the bank ever require repayment of the outstanding credit? Is there a penalty for paying off the credit line within a short period of time?

Borrow from a Commercial Loan Source

College costs are rising faster than the combination of family income and grant resources leaving many families little choice but to borrow more money to pay their tuition bills. Unfortunately, the nationwide turbulence in the credit market now extends beyond mortgages, and is affecting the availablity of commercial education loans. Dozens of lenders have left the market, and those that remain have tightened their standards and raised their rates—frequently excluding families with credit scores below 650, as well as families looking at schools with poor graduation rates (citing a correlation between poor graduation rates and high loan default rates).

If you are unable to find a lender, ask your school for its recommendations, and compare plans carefully. They will likely have varying interest rates, capitalization schedules, borrowing limits, disbursement schedules, incentives, and repayment options. Ask lenders for sample repayment schedules, and read the fine print. Compare Annual Percentage Rates (APRs). Make sure they were calculated using current interest rates. (Most lenders have web sites that include these repayments schedules.) As you evaluate options, remember that your interest payments might be tax deductible.

If your school doesn't have any recommendations, here are some of the largest commercial sources still offering education loans. In general, you can borrow up to the cost of college (less any financial aid received) with 12 to 20 years to repay. The interest rate will be based on either the Prime or the three-month LIBOR (London Interbank Offering Rate). And, the better your credit rating, the lower your interest rate, and the less you'll pay in origination fees. Finally, you can often apply online and learn your eligibility within minutes.

- **Access Group**, 800/282-1550, www.accessgroup.org
- **CitiBank CitiAssist**, 800/967-2400, www.studentloan.com
- **Discover Student Loans**, www.discoverstudentloans.com
- **Key Alternative Loan**, 800/KEY-LEND, www.key.com/educate
- **NELLIE MAE EXCEL**, 800/FOR-TUITION, www.nelliemae.com
- **NextStudent**, 800/299-4639, www.nextstudent.com
- **SALLIE MAE Tuition Answer Loan**, 800/749-9100, www.TuitionAnswerLoan.com
- **TERI**, 800/255-TERI, www.teri.org

Tip: If you (the borrower) don't yet have a credit history, get a co-signer with a good credit score. Your interest rate will be several points lower.

Comparing Your Student Loans

Several web sites will help you evaluate student loan options, but some of the biggest lenders (including several of the ones mentioned above) might not participate in these services, so if you rely exclusively on these sites you may still miss out on the best rates.

And to truly find the best deal, remember to compare the commercial loan rates to those of a home equity loan or Uncle's PLUS loan.

- **SimpleTuition** (www.simpletuition.com) asks you a few questions about your home state and future college, and then sorts through a hundred different loan options from top lenders and displays the best ones for you. There is no charge to use the service. Instead, SimpleTuition receives a referral fee if you select a loan product from one of its lender-partners. This is the "Lending Tree" of student loans.
- **eStudent Loan** (www.estudentloan.com) offers side-by-side comparisons of top loan options to help you find the best deal.

You might also try Loan Analyzer at www.finaid.org/calculators.

My Rich Uncle

MyRichUncle (www.myrichuncle.com, 888/697-4248) will lend you the funds you need. Your interest rate and repayment terms will be based on your achievements, grades and goals rather than your prior credit history. For example, good grades can lower your interest rate by as much as .75%.

The "Friends and Family" Plan

Several new commercial sites link student borrowers with individual investors who are willing to take a chance on them, and (perhaps) make a small profit at the same time. You pay the company a small fee to formalize the agreement (so it's legal, like a bank loan), but otherwise a peer-to-peer loan (between strangers, friends, or family members) can be a cheaper, easier option than a commercial education loan—lower interest rates, more flexible repayment plans, and greater discretion when it comes to deferment and forgiveness options. Some of these companies are brand new, so think carefully before you decide to share your personal data.

- VirginMoney (part of Richard Branson's vast Virgin empire), www.virginmoney.com
- Fynanz, www.fynanz.com
- GreenNote, www.greennote.com
- Prosper, www.prosper.com

Hold a Yard Sale

Now that Junior is heading off to school, maybe it's time to start unloading his or her "stuff." Even a modest yard sale can net $1,000.

Borrow Against Your 401(k)...

If you participate in a pension plan like a 401(k), you may be able to borrow against it—usually half the vested amount up to $50,000, less your highest loan balance during the preceding twelve months. The interest rate hovers around the prime, you pay no fees or points, and the cash is available very quickly. To avoid tax and penalties you must repay your account within five years (longer if you use the money to buy a home). You usually make payments via payroll deductions. If you must use this option, borrow enough to cover a full year's tuition, not just a semester, since employers may limit you to one loan per year.

Is borrowing against your 401(k) a good idea? Maybe. Maybe not. Even though you're paying interest to yourself, you're still stunting the growth of your retirement fund. For nuts and bolts information on everything related to 401(k)s, visit www.401khelpcenter.com.

Deplete Your IRA...But Try Not To

Traditional IRA: No matter what your age, you can withdraw money penalty-free (but not tax-free) to pay for higher education expenses.

Roth IRA: No matter what your age, you can withdraw the value of your original contributions penalty-free and tax-free to pay for higher education expenses. If you're under 59 1/2, you can withdraw your earnings penalty-free (but not tax-free) to pay for higher education. If you're over 59 1/2 and your account has been open at least 5 years, you can withdraw money (for any reason) tax and penalty-free.

Rules regarding IRA distributions rival *Ulysses* in their complexity. If at all possible, consider borrowing from other sources—raids on IRAs (like raids on 401(k)s) cause funds to grow much more slowly, and most parents really do need this money for retirement. Also, you must report the distribution (even if it's tax free) as income on your FAFSA thus hurting your eligibility for student aid—thanks to the 47% parental income assessment rate.

Are You Credit-Worthy?

Many cash flow helpers are available only to credit-worthy families. Others reserve their lowest interest rates for prompt payers. *Tip*: If you plan to take out a commercial loan, don't wait until the last minute to apply. Lenders have learned that procrastinators can be bad risks. You should review your credit report once a year to make certain all the information is correct. If it isn't, let the bureau know—it must follow-up. You can get one free report per year from each of the three main credit bureaus (via www.annualcreditreport.com), or you can contact each bureau separately:

* Equifax, 800/685-1111, www.equifax.com
* TransUnion, 877/322-8228, www.transunion.com
* Experian, 888/397-3742, www.experian.com

Credit-Scoring

Credit scoring is a mathematical evaluation of your credit report; it reduces your general repayment patterns to a single 3-digit number—the higher the number, the more likely you are to repay. If you are denied a loan (or offered poor terms) because of your credit score, don't panic. Several lenders offer a one-time reconsideration of your loan request. First, request a copy of your credit report and check it for accuracy. (The report is free if you've been turned down for credit.) Second, appeal the lender's decision in writing, addressing the reasons you were denied a loan. Finally, consider a co-signer.

Fair Isaac & Co (FICO, www.fairisaac.com)

Fair, Isaac & Co. is the creator and gatekeeper of credit scores which range from 300 to 850. The best rates generally go to those with scores above 760; the median score in the United States is 723.

FICO assigns weights as follows:

1. *Payment history*, 35%, including the frequency of any delinquencies.
2. *Outstanding debts*, 30%, including the number of debts, the average balances, and how close the balances are to the credit limits.
3. *Credit history*, and the age of the credit lines, 15%; the older the better.
4. *New account openings*, including the number of accounts opened over the past year, 10%; frequent balance shifting is considered a bad sign.
5. *Types of credit* in use, including bank cards, department store cards and installment loans, 10%; don't open accounts you don't plan to use.

VantageScore (www.vantagescore.com)

The three main credit bureaus (Equifax, TransUnion and Experian) have teamed up to create a competing system called "VantageScore" with scores ranging from 501 to 990. Furthermore, they have assigned letter grades to each range of scores to help consumers understand what the score means, 901 - 990 gets you an "A"; 501-600 warrants an "F."

Stock Market Woes

Did a bearish market leave you with unexpected cash flow woes? What *should* you do if all your college money is tied up in (formerly) high-growth mutual funds? And the market tanks before the tuition bill comes due? If you've been following smart planning strategies, you have shifted some of your college savings into safer vehicles. But if not, all is not lost.

First, don't pull all your tuition money out of the market when stocks are at a low. Instead, consider using a home equity loan or a federal PLUS loan to pay the first year's tab; you'll be paying tuition bills for at least four years, and that's plenty of time for a market rebound.

Second, talk to the school's financial aid officer. If you *didn't* apply for aid (because you thought you had the tuition bill covered), the school may offer to extend the aid application deadline. If you *did* apply for aid, and reported a net worth considerably higher than your current bank statements show, the school may decide to consider this in packaging your aid award.

What People Won't Try

Students Buy Campus Property

Linda Wallace, a University of Wisconsin student, purchased a condo near the campus for $90,000. When she graduated, she sold it for a $30,000 profit—enough to pay off her college loans. Becky and Louis James bought a three-bedroom house and collected rent from house-mates. The James' are tickled pink with their investment. The rent covers mortgage payments. And, by owning property, they established state residency, saving each more than $7,000 a year in out-of-state tuition. Of course, Linda and the James' also saved on room and board charges.

Mom and Dad Buy Campus Rental Property

Not only do you get the benefits of deducting mortgage interest, operating expenses and depreciation, but your college student can receive a nice salary while in school; a salary you may deduct as a business expense. How? By having your student live in one of the units and draw pay as property manager. At the same time, he or she saves on room and board. In addition, your campus visits can be written off, because, as far as the tax collector is concerned, the purpose of the trip is to inspect your property.

And, if your real estate appreciates, you can sell the property and pocket the after-tax share of the capital gain. There is still one more advantage. If you purchase the property with personal assets, and the property becomes part of a formally-recognized small business, you have moved assets into the business category which eliminates them from need analysis.

To benefit from this, be sure your property qualifies as rental (not personal) property. In other words, Mom or Dad cannot use it for more than 14 days or 10% of the total days they rent it out. Here's why: The IRS limits deductible losses from personal property to the amount of rental income received. The IRS places no such limit on losses from rental property—families with AGIs under $100,000 who actively manage their property, may use up to $25,000 of real estate losses to shelter "nonpassive " (salary) income.

Get on Mom or Dad's Payroll

Can either of your parents give you a job in the family business? If so, it's a great way to shift some income! Your earnings become a tax-deductible business expense. If you're under 18, you don't have to pay social security tax on your wages. And, if you limit your annual earnings to under $5,450 ($10,450 if you contribute to an IRA), you will owe no federal income tax. Assuming you start this when you enter high school and your parents pay about 40% in federal, state and local taxes, they will receive $16,720 in deductions. Of course, under the federal methodology, schools will grab $7,710 of the $41,800 you've earned. Calculation: 20% of non-retirement assets (c. $21,800) plus 50% of prior year income ($10,450) over $3,750, but isn't that what the money was for anyway? Meanwhile, you're beginning to save for retirement. Even without additional contributions, your $20,000 IRA (at 7%) will grow to over $480,000 by the time you're 65. (It will grow to nearly $745,000 at 8%!)

Start a Company Scholarship Program

The program must meet an IRS test to qualify as a business expense. The test usually involves a set of standards. For example, beneficiaries must have a B average; their mother or father must have worked for the company at least five years. A second part of the test deals with eligibility. All employees' children must be eligible. If too many scholarships go to the children of corporate officers and directors, the company will flunk the test.

CHAPTER 8

■ ■

LONG-RANGE PLANNING:
COLLEGE IS YEARS AWAY

The current credit crisis extends beyond the mortgage market, and has resulted in a dwindling number of private educational loan opportunities. If you are reading this Chapter, you probably have a few years before the tuition bill comes due (as well as four years to save while the student is in college), so be proactive, and start investing. The College Savings Foundation estimates that every dollar invested in a "529 College Savings Plan" saves families four dollars in future debt costs.

How Much You Need to Save

You've seen them. Calculators that tell you to save $800 a month from now until your newborn turns 18 if you want to afford college in the year 2026 (to say nothing of the savings requirements for families with two or three children). You are best advised to ignore these and any other "scare-the-pants-off-you" marketing strategy employed by organizations who, of course, will be pleased to help you save (and invest) that $800 per month. Instead, save as much money as you can afford, do it systematically, but be realistic, and remember, when your student enters college, you can supplement your savings with a contribution from earnings and a small loan.

If you absolutely must try a "How Much You Need to Save" calculation, a better goal might be to cover half the cost of college. And remember, you don't need the entire amount the day your student first enrolls. He or she will be there for at least four years, so make certain the calculator reflects this expanded time frame. Besides, it's not unreasonable to expect your kids to pay for some of their education, for example 10 - 15% of the tab, through summer earnings and a part-time job during the academic year.

One good calculator is "The Savings Plan Designer" from the FinAid page, www.finaid.org/calculators.

Another option is to calculate your Expected Family Contribution today, project that amount into the future, set that as your savings goal, and hope student aid picks up the balance. Example: Your EFC today would be $5,000. Five years from now, assuming 8% increases in your income and asset situation, your first year EFC would be $7,346 (calculation: $5,000 x 1.08 x 1.08 x 1.08 x 1.08 x 1.08). Over four years, that projects to around $33,100. Now, how does that amount compare to what you have on hand?

How Your Savings Grow

Heed the advice above, then go to the Savings Growth Projector at FinAid (www.finaid.org/calculators) to see how your savings grow. If you aren't near a computer, the following chart shows how your fund grows if you save $100 per month. In the short run, the return rate makes little difference. Over 20 years, however, the difference between 5% and 12% comes to $58,635.

Lesson: The sooner you start saving, the better. Early on, take a chance on riskier investments; let compound interest work for you. Later, switch to safer investments as college bills loom near.

	5%	7%	10%	12%
Year 1	$1,235	$1,245	$1,267	$1,281
Year 2	2,525	2,580	2,670	2,725
Year 5	6,825	7,200	7,810	8,250
Year 7	10,075	10,860	12,195	13,200
Year 10	15,600	17,410	20,655	23,235
Year 12	19,760	22,600	27,875	32,225
Year 15	26,840	31,880	41,790	50,460
Year 20	41,275	52,400	76,570	99,910

Rule of 72

The Rule of 72 is a quick way to see how fast your money will grow. If you divide 72 by your expected rate of return, the resulting answer is the length of time it will take for your money to double. For example, if your $10,000 investment is earning 6%, it will be worth $20,000 in 12 years (72/6). If it's earning 8%, it will be worth $20,000 in just 9 years (72/8).

Dollar-Cost Averaging

The best way to accumulate money is to use an investment strategy called Dollar-Cost-Averaging. The premise is simple. You have a fixed amount withheld from your paycheck each month and invest that money in some-thing like a mutual fund; you don't have to worry whether the market is up or down, and you're pretty certain to be safe from financial disaster. In fact, you'll probably do better than most professional fund managers.

Why does this work? Let's say you have $200 withheld from your paycheck and wired into a brokerage account each month where it buys shares of your favorite mutual fund. When the market is up, your $200 buys relatively fewer shares than when the market is low, so the average cost of your shares is lower than the average price during the period.

Your average cost per share is $24.66 ($1,200/48.66) while the average market price per share is $25 ($150/6). You win! Here's another way to look at your smart investment: Had you simply purchased eight shares each month, you would have only 48 shares for your $1,200. Now you have 48.66. You win again! This method of systematic savings allows you to accumulate funds fast, especially if you start when your children are young!

	Monthly Investment	Price per Share	Shares Purchased
	$200	$25	8.00
	$200	$25	8.00
	$200	$30	6.66
	$200	$25	8.00
	$200	$20	10.00
	$200	$25	8.00
Totals	**$1,200**	**$150**	**48.66**

Similarly, if you plan to invest a lump sum in the market, you might consider protecting yourself against daily fluctuations by dividing the money into twelve equal portions and investing one portion each month.

It's not easy to force yourself to continue to invest while the market continues to decline, however "true believers" will tell you, that's when your commitment is most important! Buy low. Sell high. (This assumes, of course, that you don't have an immediate need for the funds.)

Savings Strategies For the Less Disciplined

Are you doomed if you aren't this disciplined? Of course not. What's important is that you save. An alternative approach is to put all your "surprise" money into a college savings account, for example, tax refunds, year-end bonuses or gifts from grandma. Or, make a small sacrifice or two, and invest the proceeds. For example, skipping the family vacation one year might save you $2,000-$3,000; keeping an older car for an extra two years might save you $300 per month (for 24 months) in new car payments.

If your budget is really tight, you might try something as simple as emptying your pockets each night, and putting your change into a piggy bank, to be deposited once a month into a college fund. Or, you might try entering a contest like BrainQuest's (www.brainquest.com) "Win Your College Tuition Sweepstakes" for parents with children aged 2-13.

Finally, encourage your kids to save for college—using birthday money or babysitting money—and offer to match all their savings.

Getting Good Financial Advice

During most of the 1990s, investing was pretty easy—you just had to put your money in a mutual fund, any mutual fund, and watch your dollars grow. Unfortunately, the bull market has grown more grizzly of late, and an increasing number of shell-shocked investors are turning to certified financial planners for advice on maximizing savings, both for college and retirement. Most of these planners are bright, resourceful professionals who can be of genuine help. Unfortunately, some of them are more interested in their own lucrative retirement than they are in yours. Before you enlist in any services, learn something about investing, write down your objectives, and ask questions.

1. *Are they fee-only planners or do they work on commission? About how much are you going to pay for their services?* Fee-only planners charge by the hour. Comprehensive financial plans can cost you from $2,000 to $6,000. While this may be more expensive in the short-run, fee-only planners point out that their counterparts don't always have real incentives to provide you with totally unbiased service (i.e., some planners will give you nothing but a glossy sales pitch for whatever products bring the largest commission). If possible, find out how much of the planner's income comes from each of four sources: commissions, fees you pay for advice, fees you pay for them to manage your funds, and fees they receive from companies that pay them to sell their products. And don't confuse fee-only planners with fee-based planners who charge both fees AND commissions.

2. *What is their area of expertise? Their investment strategies? Are they selling you boilerplate from a parent company or is truly a personalized plan?* Traditional advice on retirement planning and estate planning is not necessarily compatible with sound college planning. Your advisor should be able to explain these possible conflicts and help you maximize your resources (while minimizing your tax consequences). If you're confused about any piece of advice, keep asking questions until you're clear. Find out how often you're likely to hear from them, and how much time they spend monitoring your individual portfolio. Finally, your planner should be a good listener, incorporating your tolerance for risk into your financial plan.

3. *What is their prior work experience?* Did they start out in law? Accounting? Insurance? Stock market? A college financial aid office? Charm school? How long have they been in business? Are their typical clients at all like you? How many clients do they have? How many new clients per year? Unless the firm specializes in short-term college planning, heavy turnover is a bad sign!

4. *Is the planner providing you with a service you can't get from your accountant, your stockbroker or your lawyer?* There is no sense in paying for the same service twice.

Finally, ask for references. Reputable planners will be happy to oblige. Most will be registered as investment advisors with their home state or the Securities and Exchange Commission. Ask for a copy of your planner's state or SEC disclosure form (Form ADV). It will tell you all about his or her academic, professional and work history. To view it online, or check for complaints filed against a planner, go to www.adviserinfo.sec.gov. To verify your planner's CFP designation, call 888/CFP-MARK, www.cfp.net/search.

For more information, or to find a planner in your area:

- *Financial Planning Association,* www.fpanet.org, 800/322-4237. A membership organization of 28,500 Certified Financial Planners (CFPs). The Planner Search helps find local CFPs and shows their certification.

- *National Association of Personal Financial Advisors*, www.napfa.org, 800/366-2732. Trade group of more than 1,000 fee-only planners.

- *Society of Financial Service Professionals*, www.financialpro.org, 610/526-2500. Planners with an insurance orientation.

- *American Institute of Certified Public Accountants,* www.aicpa.org, 888/777-7077. Personal Financial Specialists (PFS) who are CPAs and have demonstrated expertise in a wide range of financial matters.

- *Garrett Planning Network,* www.garrettplanningnetwork.com, 866/260-8400. A network of fee-only planners (with many middle-income clients) who specialize in "advice for everyday life."

You can also get terrific advice from consumer-oriented finance magazines like *Kiplinger's, Money,* and *Smart Money. Kiplinger's* even offers a free "How to Pay for College" hotline for two weeks at the end of August.

Seeing the Sites

Professional money managers no longer have the same information advantage they used to. Personal finance sites litter cyberspace, and with a few mouse clicks you can find everything from introductory investor education to full research reports to financial news headlines to mutual fund prospectuses to ten-minute stock tickers.

1. *For a general start place*, Investor Guide (www.investorguide.com) includes daily news, company research and an online, personal-finance university, as well as links to stock sites, bond sites, mutual fund sites and thousands of other finance-related sites. Also worth a look is Investors Insight (www.investorsinsight.com) which includes useful commentary like "Forecasts and Trends" and "Outside the Box." And Yahoo Finance (finance.yahoo.com) could be the best site of all— it's easy to navigate and full of useful investment tools, stock re-search, financial news, a mutual fund screener and much, much more.

2. *If you're interested in mutual funds*, try Mutual Funds Interactive (www.fundsinteractive.com/newbie.html) or FundAlarm (fundalarm.com). The latter site is the PageSix of the mutual fund industry—learn who's in, who's out, who's making the grade, and who's not.

3. *To learn more about bonds*, including bond basics, news and real-time price information, try Investing in Bonds (InvestingInBonds.com).

4. *If socially-responsible investing appeals to you,* explore the Social Investment Forum (www.socialinvest.org) and Sentinel Investments (www.sentinelinvestments.com/sustainable_investing.php). You'll be steered away from polluters and companies that produce weapons, nuclear power and tobacco, and toward companies that are "clean and green." *Of course, if you prefer stocks* from the gaming, tobacco, alcohol and defense industries, try the Vice Fund (www.vicefund.com). As the prospectus says, "It is our philosophy that although often considered politically incorrect, these industries...will continue to experience significant capital appreciation during good and bad markets. We consider these industries to be nearly 'recession-proof.'"

5. *If you want a more cooperative experience,* and a wider range of "expert" opinions, join Motley Fool's (www.fool.com) rapidly growing club. Investment advice comes from former stockbrokers, as well as thousands of monthly site visitors with unknown credentials.

6. *If you're serious about investing,* several sites will help you measure total returns and estimate portfolio risk with the best of them. First do research on The Street (www.thestreet.com). Dozens of market analysts will keep you up-to-date with breaking news and sophisticated discussions. Also, go to Zacks Investment Research and "Profit from the Pros" (www.zacks.com/pfp)—it's the background data used by many institutional investors and portfolio managers.

7. *If you want to keep a closer eye on your portfolio,* try Zack's free portfolio tracker (www.zacks.com/portfolios) and get daily e-updates on major events affecting your stocks. Also let Morningstar's very cool tool, "Instant XRay," analyze your current portfolio for balance and diversity. Search for it under "tools" at portfolio.morningstar.com.

8. *If you need an online broker, SmartMoney* and *Kiplinger's* give high marks to Muriel Siebert & Co. (www.siebertnet.com). Also, try OptionsXpress.com, eTrade.com, TDAmeritrade.com, or www.BuyandHold.com.

The following sites (belonging to more traditional players) also have little treats for you. Of course, what they really want is for you to subscribe to their publications or give them all your money to invest, but that's no reason to forsake their largess. Just be a savvy surfer.

- *Investment houses:* www.jpmorgan.com, www.lehman.com
- *Brokerage firms:* www.ml.com, www.morganstanley.com, www.schwab.com, www.smithbarney.com
- *Personal finance magazines:* www.kiplinger.com, money.cnn.com, www.smartmoney.com
- *Mutual fund companies:* www.dreyfus.com, www.fidelity.com, www.franklintempleton.com, www.janus.com, www.morningstar.com, www.troweprice.com, www.vanguard.com

Choosing An Investment Account

Before you choose your specific investments, you must decide what type of account is best for your situation: A custodial account? trust? Coverdell Education Savings Account? "529" Plan? Or a no-frills, hassle-free, segregated college fund? Each offers advantages and disadvantages in terms of flexibility, control, tax liability, and financial aid eligibility. Of course, constantly changing tax laws and financial aid regulations mean no one can predict with certainty what rules will be in effect when your tuition bills come due—5, 10, 15 or 20 years from now.

So what should you do? Read the following pages, including the advantages and disadvantages of each type of savings vehicle, then decide for yourself what is right for your individual situation. Your main concern should be with your tolerance for risk and the time you have left to invest, and not the tax consequences or financial aid implications. And remember, there is no perfect choice.

Tip: Most need-based aid takes the form of low-interest loans rather than grants. Families with healthy college funds are usually ahead of the game.

Tax Planning vs. College Aid

In previous years, plans to minimize tax liability ran counter to plans to maximize financial aid eligibility—making investment decisions even more complex. For example, families could save money in their child's name and the unearned income (e.g., interest or dividend income) of children over the age of 14 would be taxed at their own lower rate. For financial aid purposes, however, parental assets were assessed at no more than 5.6% while student assets were assessed at a flat 20% thus eliminating any savings for families who qualified for need-based aid.

Beginning in 2008, income-shifting strategies no longer make sense as a way to save substantial amounts of money for college. Here's why: For children under the age of 19 (or age 24 for full-time students whose own earned income provides less than half their support), the first $900 of investment income is tax-free, the next $900 is taxed at the child's rate, and any investment income in excess of $1,800 is taxed at the parents' rate. In other words, there is no longer much of a tax advantage, furthermore, student savings are still "penalized" in the financial aid formulas.

So what should you do with money from Grandma? If it's a small amount, you might still establish savings accounts for your children. And encourage them to contribute as well—it's never to early to start learning good savings habits. But if it's a larger gift, use the money to fund a Coverdell Education Savings Account or a "Section 529" College Savings Plan.

Coverdell Education Savings Accounts

Formerly called Education IRAs, these accounts were renamed in tribute to Paul Coverdell, the Georgia Senator who pushed for their enactment. They let you sock away up to $2,000 per year per student-to-be under 18 years of age. Contributions are not deductible, but earnings accumulate tax-free, and remain tax free upon withdrawal assuming the proceeds are used for tuition, fees, books, room and board. You can also use the money for pre-college education expenses, for example, private secondary school, extended-day programs, tutoring programs, school uniforms, computer equipment, even monthly Internet access.

These accounts are more flexible than 529s (see below). You can invest the funds however you choose—in stocks, bonds, mutual funds or whatever your comfort index permits—but the money must all be used by the time the "child" turns 30, or rolled into a younger family member's account; family members include first cousins. This benefit will be phased out for single filers with incomes between $95,000 and $110,000 and joint filers with incomes between $190,000 and $220,000.

"Section 529" College Savings Plans

To encourage early college planning, every state now sponsors at least one form of education savings plan, either a prepaid tuition plan or a simpler college savings account. These plans have taken-off thanks to Section 529 of the tax code which clarifies that money in "Qualified Tuition Programs" may grow tax-deferred, with families paying no federal tax on the appreciation if the proceeds are used for "qualified" educational expenses—college tuition, fees, books, room and board—otherwise plan participants are assessed a 10% penalty, and face immediate taxation. (The penalty is waived for students who receive full scholarships.) The money can, however, be used by another family member, including first cousins.

Everyone may benefit from 529s, regardless of income, and some states permit maximum (aggregate) contributions of over $350,000. To build funds fast, individuals can make lump sum contributions of up to $60,000 without incurring a gift tax by consolidating five years of their $12,000 gift-giving exclusion. And parents are certainly taking the bait—experts estimate that 10.5 million have already invested over $130 billion in these plans; 83% of this money is in savings plans, 17% percent is in prepaid plans.

Prepaid Tuition Plans

Eighteen states sponsor Prepaid Tuition Plans in which parents can guarantee four years of tuition at any of the state's public (or in some cases, private) colleges by making a lump sum investment or periodic payments.

No two plans are the same, but most operate under the same assumptions: The investment amount depends on the child's date of entry into college, the percentage of costs the family wants to cover, and the degree of flexibility parents desire in withdrawing funds. The state invests the money and pays the student's tuition when he or she enters college, and takes the risk of actually guaranteeing tuition. The annual prepayment amount will be taken into account when the student's aid is packaged.

In past years, smaller tuition increases eroded the value of prepaid plans so even less-sophisticated investors could earn greater returns on their own. Today, however, the shaky stock market, combined with soaring tuition rates, has convinced many families to give prepaid plans a second look. After all, most people aren't comfortable playing investment games. They want an easy way to guarantee they'll have enough money for their children's education, and, if necessary, will sacrifice a percentage point or two of interest to buy that security.

Unfortunately, the same conditions that make prepaid plans look like a good deal to investors can prove devastating to Plan sponsors. To stay in the black, most states will honor current contracts, but they may charge hefty premiums that dilute net returns; a few states have put the brakes on new contributions and contracts, until they can re-adjust pricing models.

Independent 529 Plan. States aren't the only ones permitted to offer prepaid plans. For example, a group of over 270 private colleges now offers a national plan that allows families to buy "tuition shares" for use at any member institution. This "Independent 529 Plan" includes many Ivies, as well as a variety of large private universities and liberal arts colleges. It is managed by TIAA-CREF but participating colleges pay the administrative costs, so parents pay no fees. The plan must be held for at least three years, so consider investing here during the middle school years—by then, families should be looking for more conservative options AND have a better idea what school the student might wish to attend, www.independent529plan.com.

The College Savings Bank sells CollegeSure CDs indexed to the average cost of 500 independent colleges with a minimum yield of 2%. CDs may be held within a 529 plan, so your earnings are tax free. Maturities range from one to 22 years so you can time them to mature during the college years. Call 800/888-2723, or click www.collegesavings.com.

Savings Plan Trusts

The real growth, however, continues to be in state-sponsored savings accounts. Nearly every state is operating at least one program to give families big incentives to save for college. These plans have several advantages over prepaid plans. First, they offer families greater flexibility. Families can generally use the full value of their investment at any college. Second, they offer potentially greater returns. State savings plans do not "guarantee" they will keep pace with tuition, however, they typically invest in stock- and bond-markets, which (over the long run) should earn a higher return than 6-7%—the average tuition increase over the past few years.

Of course if tuition soars while stocks sour, even the best-performing "529s" can lose money. A few years ago, the worst performing ones lost over 20%. Tax breaks aren't worth anything if you have no earnings.

Since few plans are restricted to state residents, shop around, comparing annual and lifetime contribution limits, age restrictions, investment options, management fees, cancellation penalties and special state-resident-only incentives—the most common are tax deductions and matching funds.

1. Currently, 33 states give residents a state-tax deduction for contributions to an in-state plan. For example, Arkansas, Connecticut, Michigan, Oklahoma, New York and North Dakota couples may deduct up to $10,000 against their state taxes. Illinois and Mississippi couples may deduct up to $20,000.

2. Thirteen states will match a portion of your contribution. For example, Minnesota provides a $400 match; Kansas will contribute up to $600. Sometimes these gifts are limited to students from low- and middle-income families.

While management "philosophies" vary between states, the portfolios are quite conservative. In general, when children are young, money is split between a bond fund and a stock growth fund with the majority going into the stock fund. Then, as the child grows up, the balance shifts so by age 18, 40% of the "portfolio" might be in a bond fund, 5% in a stock fund, and 55% in an ultra-safe, but low-yielding money market fund. The IRS allows states to offer multiple investment options, so usually you get a choice of portfolios with varying degrees of risk and reward. Most 529 Plans are managed by outside investment specialists. For example, nearly ten states invest with TIAA-CREF while a half dozen use Vanguard.

Unfortunately, in using a state-based savings plan, you relinquish control of your money. If you are not happy with your fund's performance, you have few options: You can (1) roll the account over to a different plan, but only once every 12 months; (2) stop adding to your investment; or (3) withdraw your money and pay a 10% penalty.

So Which "529" Is Best?

Each plan has so many variables it is very difficult to compare them on an "apples to apples" basis, however, personal finance magazines often review the plans and publish their evaluations in-print and on-line. For example, *Kiplinger's* recently favored "Iowa College Saving," "Michigan Education Savings Program," "Minnesota College Savings Plan," "and "Virginia's Education Savings Trust" for having lower management fees and a good variety of investment choices. *Morningstar's* top marks went to plans from Virginia, Illinois and Maryland.

Start Shopping

Several enterprising organizations have tried to make it easier for families to set up college savings plans simply by going shopping. For example:

UPromise. Shop online at JCrew or Old Navy, Speigel or The Sports Authority, and earn money for college. UPromise has signed up thousands of partners, including restaurants, grocery stores, credit card companies, and online merchants. Spend money with any of them, and the sponsoring company will put a percentage of your purchase (generally 2-10%), into an account which you may transfer into a Vanguard 529 Plan.

Your friends and family members can sign up, too, with the bonuses they earn going to your account. Now owned by Sallie Mae, 888/434-9111, www.upromise.com.

BabyMint also lets you shop online with participating retailers and earn money for a college savings plan of your choice. You may also use the money to make a payment on your student loan. In addition, each "BabyBuck" you earn is matched by a dollar off tuition at over 175 "Tuition Rewards" colleges across the country, www.babymint.com.

College Rewards American Express from Fidelity puts 1.5% of everything you spend into a Fidelity-managed 529 Plan to a maximum of $1,500 per year, 800/551-0839, www.fidelity.com.

FutureTrust MasterCard. You'll earn a 1% rebate on all your purchases and up to 10% by shopping with FutureTrust partners. The money can go into a 529 plan of your choice.

Little Grad is yet another program that lets you earn rebates while shopping with online retailers, and put those rebates into a 529 plan, www.littlegrad.com.

Impact on Financial Aid

For dependent students, Coverdell Accounts and Section 529 Plans are considered parental assets. It doesn't matter whether the student or the parent is the account owner; the value of the account is included with parental assets on the FAFSA, and less than 5.6% of its value will be assessed for college. Annual distributions are excluded from need analysis. (If someone else owns the account, like a grandparent, the assets might still be "overlooked.")

Beginning this year, treatment of educational savings plans during the aid process has been made more uniform, however, significant accumulations in these accounts can still hurt your chances for need-based aid. But with all these resources at your disposal, you won't require any aid, right?

Of course, by the time your student is ready for college, the methodology for determining aid eligibility may have changed so your savings will provide you with a nice cushion against all this future uncertainty.

Impact on Education Tax Credits

The IRS won't give multiple tax benefits on the same dollar, so you can't claim a Hope or Lifetime credit using money from a Coverdell Account, or a 529 Plan unless (1) you meet the lower income requirements, and (2) your tution payment is in excess of your Coverdell or 529 Plan earnings. See Chapter 10 for more detail.

So, Should I Sign Up?

Citing high management fees, limited investment choices and arcane financial aid rules, some investment advisors suggest that 529s have lost some of their appeal. They also point to lower divided and capital gains rates on assets held in taxable accounts as reasons to consider your college savings plans carefully. So, what should you do? We know it's confusing, but don't let paralysis set in. Answer the following questions, then start saving. Even a small college fund is better than no college fund.

- Do you want to be able to choose your own investments?
- Do you want to retain complete control of your own investments AND have the flexibility to use them however you please—to pay for tuition, or to bail you out of an unexpected financial jam?
- Is there a chance your children may opt not to go to college?
- Do you want your children to be responsible for their own tuition tab?

If the answer to any of these questions is "yes," then "529s" might not be the right investment vehicle for you. Instead, think about Coverdells to save some money, and using your retirement fund to build extra wealth, or just putting your savings into a simple segregated college-savings account.

Good News

Congress has eliminated the "sunset" provision on 529s, so plan benefits are now permanent—previously the tax benefits were set to expire after 2010. Coverdell benefits, however, *are* still set to expire, unless additional legislation is passed before 2010.

For More Information

1. *The Internet Guide to 529 Plans* (www.savingforcollege.com) offers a detailed summary of each state's offerings, as well as quick ratings based on plan flexibility, liquidity, special state benefits, and investment approach.

2. *College Savings Plan Network* (www.collegesavings.org) offers sound information from the states themselves, courtesy of The National Association of State Treasurers, PO Box 11910, Lexington, KY 40578.

Choosing Investments—Risk and Reward

Choosing the "best" investment is highly subjective. In fact, if you ask ten financial advisors to recommend the best type of college investment, you're likely to get ten very different answers. Why? Because it's very difficult for them to offer sound advice in a vacuum, i.e., without knowing your family's balance point between risk and reward—that precise place where you sleep easily at night, no matter what's happened to your stock or bond fund on Wall Street that day, and where you aren't kicking yourself for some missed financial opportunity.

As a general rule, the safer the investment option, the lower the reward. The riskier the option, the greater the reward (as well as the potential for a huge loss). The investments described in this remainder of chapter are safe, or as some would say, plain vanilla, and don't require professional fund managers to turn a profit. *Tip:* If you don't understand an investment—its liquidity, its true costs, or how it works—that's also a clue to stay away.

Capital Gains, Capital Pains

To further complicate your decisions, the top rate on dividends and long-term capital gains is now 15% (the top rate on long-term capital gains actually drops to 0% through 2010 for families in the 10% and 15% brackets). Of course, as soon as you figure out how to choose wise investments based on these new low rates, Congress will change the rules. In the meantime, here are some points to consider.:

- You must hold an asset for at least 12 months to benefit from lower capital gains rates. *Lesson:* Avoid frequent trading.

- All investment earnings in tax-deferred accounts (like annuities and 401(k)s) are taxed as ordinary income when withdrawn, even if the earnings come from capital gains. *Lesson:* Put stocks and stock mutual funds in taxable accounts and bonds in retirement accounts.

Sample Portfolios

If you decide to direct your own college savings account, the composition of your portfolio should change with the age of your children. When they are young, you can afford to take more risks than you can when tuition bills are just around the corner. Here's one example:

The Early Years (Under 6). Time is on your side. About 90% of your money should be in stock funds, split between aggressive growth (the most risky) and growth and income (less risky). The other 10% should be in something safer like a high-yield bond fund.

The Middle Years (6 to 13). Keep your stock funds, but as your college-bound student ages, direct new contributions into more conservative bond funds and growth and income funds.

The Pre-College Years (14 to 17). During each of these years, start getting out of equities, so that by the time your student turns 17, just 25% of your money is still in growth and income funds. The rest should be in bond funds, CDs, money market funds or US Treasury strips that mature during your student's first two years of college. By moving funds slowly, you protect your investment against daily market fluctuations.

If you think you're going to qualify for financial aid, time these moves so capital gains don't inflate the income figures you must submit for need analysis.

The College Years (18 to 21). Don't be tempted by dreams of double-digit market gains. Keep your money safe. Some planners recommend putting everything into CDs and money markets. Others recommend a combination of short-term bond funds and treasury strips that mature during your student's last two years of college. In any case, by now your college funds should be completely out of equities—otherwise you might be forced to sell during a market downturn. Past tumbles caught many families unprepared.

CDs and T-bills

Some of the safest and easiest ways to save money are through short- and long-term Certificates of Deposit, Treasury bills, Treasury notes, and U.S. Savings Bonds. With their minuscule returns, these should be a small piece of your college portfolio (unless your student is starting college within the next year). In August, 2008:

- six-month CDs were yielding 2%
- three-month Treasury bills were yielding 1.66%
- two-year Treasury notes were 2.5%
- five-year notes were 3.22%
- and ten-year notes were 3.95%

Treasuries are exempt from state and local taxes, so for most families, these yields are a bit higher.

U.S. Savings Bonds

Parents who purchase Series EE Savings Bonds and the inflation-indexed I Bond will not have to pay federal tax on the accrued interest, provided they use the proceeds for their children's education. To qualify, they must pay the money directly to an eligible institution, or to a state tuition savings plan. Full benefits are available to couples with modified adjusted gross incomes under $100,650 and to single parents with incomes under $67,100 when it's time to redeem their bonds. Benefits taper off for families with incomes above these limits, and disappear completely for couples with incomes above $130,650 and single parents with incomes above $82,100. Income limitations are indexed for inflation, so, by the time you redeem your bonds, the ceilings may be much higher.

One Catch: Your AGI for the year in which you redeem your bonds includes all the interest earned on bonds you redeem that year. This may push some families right past the income cut-offs and ironically eliminate their exclusion! Regardless of income, these bonds are exempt from state and local income taxes.

Bonds may be purchased at any time during the year, but to qualify for the tax exclusion, purchasers must be at least 24 years of age. In other words, families with incomes too high to benefit from the tax break may not have their children take advantage of the benefit by buying the bonds themselves. For the same reason, grandparents and couples who file separate tax returns are also ineligible to participate.

Both bonds are available in denominations ranging from $100-$1,000 through payroll deductions and $50-$10,000 through most banks.

To encourage long-term saving, investors who cash in either of these types of bonds within five years of purchase forfeit three months of interest. For rate information after November 1, call 800/4US BOND.

EE Bonds. These earn 90% of the average yield of five-year Treasury securities over the preceding six months. EE bonds earn fixed rates of interest announced semi-annually, May 1 and November 1. The interest rate currently stands at 1.40%.

Inflation Bonds. For people who worry about the impact of inflation on the value of their bonds, Uncle Sam offers inflation-indexed Bonds (I Bonds) with yields pegged to the inflation rate. Currently, they carry a fixed rate of 0% plus a semiannual inflation adjustment for an earnings rate of 4.84%.

To purchase these bonds online, or get more information, visit the **Savings Bond Home Page** (www.savingsbonds.gov).

Mutual Funds

The best way for small investors to play the market is via a mutual fund. By having your money pooled with money from lots of other investors, you gain the advantage of diversification and professional fund management.

You can either research and buy mutual funds yourself, or work with a broker. Currently, there are over 13,000 mutual funds, all categorized by investment goal. For example:

Growth Funds aim to increase the value of your investment rather than provide you with a large stream of dividends. Growth Funds generally invest in stocks and are best suited for people who plan to hold on to the fund for a longer period of time, for example, people who won't need to tap their college fund for many years.

Income Funds focus on providing investors with high current income (i.e., large dividends). Income funds generally invest in corporate and government bonds, or stocks with good dividend-paying records.

They bring higher yields than money market funds, but their share price can move up or down, making them a little riskier.

Money Market Funds are very safe, and accordingly, offer the lowest return. Money Market Funds generally invest in high quality securities with short maturities (e.g., bank CDs, US Treasury bills).

Other types of funds include hybrids of the above, for example, Aggressive Growth, Balanced Growth, and Growth and Income. Investors will also find specialty funds grouped by company type (for example, energy, environmental, health care, real estate, utilities, etc.).

There are also kid-friendly funds like "First Start" from USAA which invests in companies like Disney, Pepsi and McDonalds and design-your-own- funds courtesy of ShareBuilder (www.sharebuilder.com) and FOLIOfn (www.foliofn.com).

Sage Tuition Rewards

So how do you choose "the best" mutual fund from the thousands (and thousands) of options? Sage Scholars hopes its *Tuition Rewards* program will convince you to give its partners a closer look. Parents (or grandparents) who invest with select companies will earn an undergraduate tuition reduction equal to 5% of their average annual account balance to a maximum of one year's tuition per student, spread over four years (of course, they receive their investment gains as well). Students may use this reward at any of over 175 participating "Tuition Reward" colleges—although admission is not guaranteed. Example: A $20,000 balance held for five years would earn a tuition reduction reward of $5,000.

If your child decides not to attend one of the participating colleges, the money you've invested is still yours to use as you choose, and the reward amount may be transferred to another student. Sage Scholars, 21 S. 12th St., 8th floor, Philadelphia, PA 19107, 215/564-9930, www.sagescholars.com.

Is it a Trust? Or a Mutual Fund?

American Century Giftrust (www.americancentury.com) is an aggressive mutual fund (focussed on long-term growth) that doubles as an irrevocable trust. Shares must be given as a gift, and remain in the fund for at least 18 years. The current one-year return is over 8%, and 11.81% over the past 20 years. It has had a volatile history, however, which angered investors who wanted out during some of the longer (and larger) downturns. As a result, a Missouri Court ruled that Giftrust accounts *can* be closed before the 18-year investment period is over. Unhappy customers can download the forms at www.americancentury.com/trustlaw.

Life Cycle Funds

"Life-Cycle Funds" may be your smartest choice, especially if you are overwhelmed by all of your investment options. These are pre-fabbed allocation pies sold by mutual fund companies. Best of all, there's a pie for every investment goal, including college and retirement. No need to worry about diversification or rebalancing your portfolio (between stocks and bonds) to control your risk. That's all taken care of for you. Automatically.

Zero Coupon Bonds

These are bonds stripped of their interest coupons. Owners receive no income while holding the bonds. Instead, income compounds and reinvests semi-annually. At some future date, you receive a fixed sum that is much larger than your purchase price. For example, for a 6.5% zero maturing in 2018, you pay $5,274 today to get $10,000 ten years from now.

Many families like to use zeros to save for college because they can time maturity dates to coincide with tuition bills. Also, they know exactly how much money they will receive when those bills come due, a certainty that for some families is more important than taking chances with a riskier portfolio. Zeros have, however, several drawbacks which families should consider before deciding on this type of long-term investment.

- Corporate and municipal bonds may be called before maturity, and if you miss the call, you may be in for a nasty surprise: When a bond is called (e.g., because of declining interest rates) interest stops accumulating, and its value freezes. The $10,000 face value you thought you were getting could turn out to be little more than the bond's original cost. Treasury "STRIPS" are safer—they carry a no-call provision.

- No income is distributed, yet tax must be paid yearly on the accrued interest. The exception is for tax-free zero-coupon municipals.

- There is no way to know the value of the money when the bond matures. If interest rates rise, the bond value drops. If interest rates drop, the bond value rises.

Variable Annuities

Many people are completely (and justifiably) confused by the endless variety of life insurance options, however, variable annuities are frequently advertised as a good vehicle for long term saving needs, like college.

These annuities (sometimes described as a "mutual fund bundled in an insurance wrapper") let you stash unlimited amounts of money into a tax-deferred account which may escape the eye of need analysis. But high sales commissions and annual maintenance fees, plus the fact that annuity earnings are taxed as regular income (and don't benefit from lower capital gains rates) can make these investments considerably less valuable.

Don't decide to invest in life insurance while under pressure or because of financial aid rules that place the value of your insurance outside the need analysis formula.

We suggest that you stick with a real mutual fund instead.

CHAPTER 9

■■■■■■■■■■■■■■■■■■

THE COLLEGES

Rethinking Your Ideas About Admission

In choosing your future college, your first consideration should be quality of education and your fit with the school—where will *you* be happy and successful? After you weigh traditional factors such as size, location, academic emphasis, extracurricular activities and composition of the student body, then you should look at costs and financial aid offerings:

- Schools with innovative payment plans can help ease cash flow.
- Schools with innovative aid programs can funnel extra money toward "desirable" students.
- Schools with mountains of cash can handle families' financial need.
- Schools with a strong reputation in your selected field of study might have extra funds to support students in these departments.

Financial Aid in the Admission Process

If students can't afford the school (or are unwilling to pay the tab), they aren't going to enroll! This simple truth means the line between financial aid and admission continues to disappear. New experiments in "enrollment management" and the intense competition for quality students translate into "no-need" awards, "tuition discounts" and "preferential packaging." In other words, aid administrators sometimes mold aid packages for certain students to lure them onto the campus and help the school meet its enrollment goals—for example, a brighter, or larger, or more diverse student body. While student's can't simply "name their price" (yet), here are some things to consider as you plan your college selection strategy.

1. Apply early for financial aid. Most schools have limited resources so the first people in line are more likely to have their need met than the last.

2. Forget about "Early Decision" if you need financial aid. Your admission chances may be better, but since the school knows you're committed to attending, it doesn't need to sweeten your aid package.

3. Don't worry about "sticker price" when you're deciding where to apply. Thanks to their myriad aid policies, private colleges, with their generous aid packages (including merit-based awards), may cost you less than

your home-state Public U. Even our most prestigious (and priciest) schools are among those re-evaluating their packaging to create more generous awards for middle- and upper-middle income families.

4. Apply to colleges where your qualifications place you in the upper 25% of the applicant pool. That standing will have a strong impact on the composition of your aid package. Schools make no bones about that.

5. Pair your applications. Then, if you're admitted to schools of similar prestige, you can try to improve your award. Schools may not mind losing you to lesser- or higher-regarded colleges. But they might try to keep you away from direct competitors. Carnegie-Mellon responds within 24-hours (and adjusts about half of the cases it reviews). Even Harvard says, "We expect that some of our admitted students will have particularly attractive offers from institutions with new aid programs, and those students should not assume that we will not respond."

It Doesn't Hurt To Ask

For many families, financial aid packaging is now as mysterious as admission committee deliberations. So how can you get an honest estimate of your aid chances? You certainly can't rely on the financial aid sections of college catalogues. Pious generalities outnumber hard facts while the tone is reminiscent of sweepstakes notices. Why do schools do this?

First of all, vagueness about financial aid is important when you know Uncle Sam will release some enormous rule change two days after 500,000 copies of your school's materials come back from the printer.

Second, it's hard to be precise about what kinds of aid a student might expect when decisions vary from student to student depending on their income and asset situation and their admission qualifications.

And third, the "you may be a grand prize winner" attitude is essential for colleges trying to convince students not to worry about the $15,000 - $50,000 bill they'll face if they enroll! While aid packages at many schools look quite generous, frequently, that generosity takes the form of loans, which you must repay.

Since candor is seldom found, to get answers, you must ask specific questions. Don't be bashful. You have the right to ask colleges as many questions as they ask you. Find out about innovative payment plans of the type illustrated in the next two sections. And get answers to the following:

1. Do you guarantee to meet a student's need (or a certain percentage of need)? *Reason*: Most families are eligible for financial aid. Unfortunately, there's not enough money to help all these eligible families.

2. Do you guarantee to meet need (or a certain percentage of need) for all four years? *Reason*: Some colleges offer generous grant-filled packages to lure new students, then give them loans in post-freshman years. Even if the school promises you a fixed size grant for all four years, remember,

annual tuition increases mean a package that seemed generous in Year One, may seem stingy by Year Four.

3. Do you have a per-student-limit on the aid you provide? *Reason*: Some schools set ceilings, such as a $10,000 per student maximum.

4. Do I have to demonstrate a minimum amount of need to qualify for aid? *Reason*: Some schools won't consider students for aid unless they have at least $500 in need.

5. Do you have a standard "unmet need" figure for each aid recipient? *Reason*: Some schools will leave each person $500 short.

6. What is your expected "student earnings" figure? *Reason*: Regardless of need analysis, some colleges expect students to contribute a certain amount (which can be as high as $2,000 per year), whether it actually comes from the student's or the parents' resources.

7. What is the breakdown of a typical need-based aid package, grants vs. "self-help" (loans and work-study)? How do you determine those percentages? Is there an income cut-off? Reason: Some colleges advertise generous aid packages, but a closer look reveals a heavy reliance on low-interest loans. Also, at some schools, the make-up of aid packages varies with family income—students from lower-income families receive mostly grants; students from wealthier families receive mostly loans.

8. Is there an application cut-off date for meeting a student's need? *Reason*: Some colleges say they can meet all need for students whose applications are received prior to Date X. But no such guarantee extends to students who apply after that.

9. Do you maintain financial aid "waiting lists" or accept students on an "admit-deny" basis? *Reason*: These practices mean financially-needy students are welcome but they will not receive financial aid.

10. How do you package "outside scholarships?" *Reason*: Different colleges have different "aid philosophies." For example, many schools will use your outside scholarships to replace loan components of your aid package. Others, however, take only a fixed amount, say 50%, and use it to replace a loan. They use the rest to reduce your grant from that school. At other colleges, the outside scholarship merely replaces, on a dollar for dollar basis, collegiate grants, causing the poet Leider to ponder from her garret:

> *You found a nifty scholarship,*
> *To loosen the tuition grip.*
> *But does this change what you must pay?*
> *Or do they take your grant away?*

Don't expect outside, need-based scholarships to lower family contribution. But do search for a policy that uses the award to replace part of the package's self-help component (loans and work-study).

11. What percentage of alumni contribute to the school's annual fundraising campaign? *Reason*: If you are worried about the college's financial survival, you can't ask for a corporate balance sheet. But you can check on alumni support. At some schools, it's as high as 65% and when colleges have this kind of loyalty, they are not going to fold.

12. If I don't apply for aid in my freshman year, am I likely to get aid in subsequent years? *Reason*: You can't be prohibited from applying, however, you may get nothing because many colleges give priority to "continuing recipients."

13. Do you place any time limits on financial aid? *Reason*: With fewer and fewer students finishing their degrees in four years, campus crowding, and excessive student subsidies have become real thorny issues. To hurry you along, colleges may just take away your on-campus parking privileges, or, they may limit your award to a maximum of four years.

14. Will my request for aid have any impact on my admission chances? *Reason.* To meet 100% of financial need, some colleges base their last few admission decisions on the family's ability to pay the bill.

The Taxman Cometh

Uncle taxes the portion of a scholarship that exceeds tuition, fees, books and equipment as ordinary income. This means room and board scholarships may be taxed. If you've received a large grant, use it to pay the tax-free items first, and keep track of everything left over.

Twelve Innovative Payment Plans

Colleges can be flexible about how you pay your tuition bill; here are some of the most common options:

1. **Installment Plans.** Not many families can write a check for $5,000 or $15,000 at the beginning of each semester, so many colleges soften the blow by letting them spread out the payments. Furthermore, by using an installment plan, you may not need to borrow as much as you originally thought. If a college doesn't have its own plan, ask about (1) *Tuition Management Systems* (800/722-4867, www.afford.com), or (2) *TuitionPay* (800/635-0120, www.tuitionpay.com). TuitionPay has contracts with over 1,500 schools. Here are some variants you may encounter.
   - Interest: (1) No interest (2) Fixed interest (3) Interest on the remaining balance (4) No interest, but a one-time fee.
   - Down Payment: (1) No down payment (2) Down payment of 25%.
   - Payment Frequency: (1) Ten monthly installments (2) Two installments per semester (3) Four installments per semester.

2. **Prepayment Discount.** Pay a year all at once, and your tuition is discounted, sometimes by as much as 10%.

3. **Advance Payment Bonus.** Place money into your account before it's due and the college adds a bonus to your balance. It can be a set dollar amount (e.g., $100) or a percentage of the amount on deposit (e.g., 2%).

4. **Low-Interest Loans.** Many colleges have become low-interest lenders to offset Uncle Sam's yo-yo student aid policies and provide parents with financial planning stability. Others have negotiated good deals with private lenders, by agreeing to share financial risks (i.e., they're betting you'll be a successful graduate and repay your loan promptly).

5. **Guaranteed Tuition Plans.** Guarantee that tuition will hold for a set time or won't increase by more than a fixed percentage (e.g., 3%). Schools may use freezes to improve retention and limit them to upperclassmen. At some schools, you must maintain a set sum on deposit—anywhere from $500 to $3,000. At other schools, you must pay four years tuition in advance, at the rate which prevails your freshman year. Parents who can make an out-of-pocket prepayment must decide whether the tuition increases they will be spared are worth more than what their money could earn if it had not been used for prepayment.

6. **Stretched Payments.** Similar to a loan. Parents who do not qualify for aid defer a fixed amount of their tuition bill. They have two years to pay the deferred amount and are charged a slight interest rate.

7. **Barter.** You provide a usable service in exchange for tuition.

8. **Three-Year Option.** Some colleges offer a "time-shortened degree" that lets students graduate in three years, saving one year in tuition costs. This is especially true at schools that give unlimited course credit for high scores on AP Exams.

9. **Two Degrees in One.** Students can also save a year's tuition by finding schools that offer joint undergraduate-graduate degree programs. For example, students can receive their BA-MBA in five years instead of the usual six, or a BA-MA in four years instead of the usual five.

10. **Choice of Accommodations and Meal Plans.** Do you need a spacious room with a spectacular view, or are you happy contemplating the backside of a dumpster? Do you need 21 meals a week in the dining hall or would you rather fend for yourself when the menu reads "Chef's Surprise" or "Mystery Meat?" Colleges give you options. Housing contracts can vary up to $3,000 per year, depending on location and type of room. Meal plans can vary up to $1,000 per year, depending on how often you want to eat dining hall food. If a college is having trouble filling dorm rooms, you might even get a "buy two years, get two free" offer. This keeps upperclassmen from moving off-campus, makes college more affordable and doesn't cost the school much of anything.

11. **Use of Credit Cards for Bill Payment.** Provides credit card holders with some flexibility but can cost them dearly in finance charges. If you pay

by this option, use an "affinity" credit card that at least gives you a bonus, like frequent flier miles. Or, use the college's own card.

12. **Use of Electronic Bank Transfers.** A set amount is transferred directly from your account to the college each month.

Forty-Two Innovative Aid Programs

Colleges offer a variety of discounts designed to attract quality students. Most often, these take the form of scholarships and academic incentives, however, colleges sometimes offer discounts to student leaders or siblings who attend college together. Here are some of the most innovative programs:

1. **Academic Scholarships.** To recognize and reward academic achievement, nearly every college offers no-need scholarships to lure bright students. In fact, about 45% of all institutional aid is now merit- or talent-based; the awards range from $300 - $45,000. For a college-by-college listing, see *The A's & B's of Academic Scholarships* (www.octameron.com).

2. **Research Assistants.** Some (hoity-toity) colleges claim not to offer merit-based awards, saying "all their students would deserve one." Instead, they lure preferred applicants with financial incentives—for example, research jobs with choice faculty (complete with large stipends) or high-paying internships.

3. **Merit Scholarships.** Some schools automatically give money (usually around $2,500) to every student recognized as a "Finalist" by The National Merit Scholarship Corporation, www.nationalmerit.org. To compete for this money, you must have received a high score on the PSAT/NMSQT during the fall of your Junior year of high school .

4. **Honors Colleges.** Many public universities have created Honors Programs or Honors Colleges which offer students the benefits of elite, liberal-arts colleges—smaller classes, closer contact with top professors, etc.—but at low, in-state tuition prices. (In many instances, students who are accepted into Honors Programs or Honors Colleges also receive full- or partial-tuition scholarships.) States like these programs because they act as magnets to help keep bright students in-state. In fact, over 800 schools are now members of the National Collegiate Honors Council, www.nchchonors.org.

5. **Quickie Loans.** Many colleges offer short term loans to tide students over in times of temporary financial crisis. These loans usually run from $100 to $500, but sometimes students can get up to $5,000.

6. **Replacing Loans.** Many schools let you use outside scholarships to replace loan components of your aid package. Some schools limit this bonus to bright students, or convert your loan to a grant only if you maintain a certain GPA. Others make the switch only if you find the scholarship before your loan gets processed. You should also ask if the school has a limit (e.g., $2,000) on the total amount it will replace.

7. **Forgiving Loans.** Some schools repay your loans if you do worthwhile (low-paying) things after graduation. Most likely beneficiaries: Health workers who practice in low-income communities and attorneys who sign up with non-profits or public-interest firms (for a list of schools, www.equaljusticeworks.org).

8. **Graduate Debt-Free.** Over 50 colleges (like Princeton, Harvard, Amherst and Stanford, as well as the Universities of Michigan, Virginia and North Carolina) now subscribe to "no loan" financial aid policies for students from families that meet certain income criteria, for example, the family's income must be under $60,000. For a list of schools, go to the Project on Student Debt, projectonstudentdebt.org.

9. **Capping Student Loans.** A few less-wealthy colleges offer a modified version of the above plan and guarantee that no student will have to borrow more than a fixed amount per year, for example $3,000.

10. **Family Plans.** If you and a sibling attend the same college, you may receive an extra discount. This tuition break may extend to other family members as well.

11. **Faculty and Staff Discounts.** Do you or one of your parents work for a college? Is it your dream school? If not, dream again. Most schools allow faculty and staff members, and their children to attend classes at reduced tuition. Discounts range from 50% to 100%. Some schools offer "professional courtesy" by extending this discount to dependents of faculty and staff at other institutions. For example, over 580 colleges now participate in "The Tuition Exchange," awarding 5,095 full-tuition scholarships (to a maximum of $29,000), www.tuitionexchange.org.

12. **Alumni Children.** Tuition breaks for alumni kids are also common. Colleges like to establish multi-generation relationships with families. That's how chairs get endowed and buildings get built.

13. **Peace of Mind.** Some schools waive (or reduce) tuition if the person primarily responsible for your support dies or suffers total disability.

14. **Incentives for Academic Achievement.** Many colleges reward their top enrolled (continuing) students. Other schools reward any student who was in the top 10% of their high school class.

15. **Remissions for Student Leaders.** Many colleges provide discounts to campus leaders—class officers, school newspaper editors. You won't get this money your first year, but you might want to start planning your campaign for student body president.

16. **Matching Scholarships.** Some schools match church scholarships. Other schools match state awards, or Dollars for Scholars awards.

17. **Remissions for Work.** Most schools provide room and board for residence hall assistants. You may not qualify your first year, but you should know about the opportunity.

18. **Emphasis on Student Employment.** Many colleges have beefed up their placement offices to help students find on- and off-campus employment. They also use their formidable alumni networks to locate summer work opportunities. Co-operative education (where students alternate school and work) is especially lucrative—students can easily earn from $8,000 to $15,000 per year.

19. **Free for Some.** A handful of our nation's most expensive colleges (for example, Duke, Harvard, Stanford, and Brown) are pledging to pay full tuition, room and board for students from families with incomes below certain levels (for example $60,000). And they will pay tuition only for students from families earning slightly more than that (for example, less than $90,000). Why this newfound generosity? Our wealthiest colleges are facing public (and Congressional) scrutiny for being too stingy with their endowments, and not doing more to hold down the cost of college.

20. **Free for All.** Some schools are tuition-free for all their students. For example, Berea (KY) only admits students from low-income families and requires everyone to work 10-15 hours per week in exchange for covering their costs. College of the Ozarks, Webb Institute and Cooper Union also offer free tuition for all of their students.

21. **Off-Hour Rates.** Look for lower charges for off-hour courses—those on evenings, weekends and summers. The difference can be as high as $300 per course or a 50% room rate reduction (for summer school).

22. **Moral Obligation Scholarships.** Not a scholarship. Not a loan. The college loans you money and attaches a moral—not legal—obligation to repay it after graduation.

23. **Trial Attendance.** "Try us you'll like us." Schools may offer free classes to high school juniors and seniors, it may let some students try the school for one semester for a low fee (e.g., $25), or it may run a free summer program to give students a little taste.

24. **Bucking the Trend.** Some colleges seek to win the enrollment competition by freezing or even lowering tuition.

25. **Special Scholarship Drives.** Some schools have launched special fundraising drives aimed at increasing their in-house financial aid kitty. At Grinnell, for example, money raised by each year's 50th Reunion class is used to help pay down the debt of current graduating seniors.

26. **Helping Students Find Scholarships.** Hundreds of schools have special offices to help students find grants, scholarships, etc.

27. **Border Crossing.** Some public universities offer special rates to out-of-state students who live near the state border. For example, the University of Nebraska discounts tuition for students from nearby counties in Iowa; the University of Tennessee (Chattanooga) offers generous rates to students from Alabama and Georgia.

28. Older Student Remissions. If you are over 24, some schools will give you a discount on tuition, however, at most schools, "older" means 50 or 60. In fact, many public schools offer free tuition to senior citizens as long as they are state residents and attend on a space-available basis.

29. Persistence (or Retention) Awards. To recoup the money they spend recruiting students, schools must keep them enrolled (and paying some tuition) for four years. Accordingly, to keep you from transferring or dropping out, some colleges offer financial inducements such as senior class trips, loan cancellation or scholarships for returning students.

30. Travel Awards. Some schools will reimburse you for campus visits or, if you are enrolled, for commuting costs.

31. Adopt-a-Student. In some communities, local churches and businesses help students with scholarship money.

32. Students Helping Students. When students take on projects that help build their school's scholarship fund, it's a sign of good morale and a friendly campus. For example: scholarship phonathons, class gifts, and waiving the return of room-damage deposits.

33. Running Start. HS students can spend their senior year, or the summer before their senior year on a campus, taking regular college classes. Colleges look on such students as a farm club. Before you sign up, however, be sure the courses are for college credit, and ask if the credits are transferable. Sometimes they are good only at the sponsoring school.

34. Help for the Unemployed. Some schools offer free tuition to students from families whose major wage earner is unemployed.

35. Free Tuition for Farmers. Some schools offer a year of free tuition to farmers who have had to quit farming because of financial hardships.

36. A Birthday Gift. Colleges often celebrate major anniversaries with special gimmicks. For example, one school celebrated its 100th anniversary by allowing selected students to pay the school's original tuition rates, $100/year. Keep your eyes open for similar "celebrations."

37. Campus Contests. Some schools reward students for their creativity— new slogans, clever recruiting posters, or innovative web sites.

38. Guaranteed Degree. Graduates who are unhappy with their major (because, for example, they couldn't find a job) may return to the alma mater and major in another field, tuition-free.

39. Toll-Free Numbers. Most schools have toll-free numbers and financial counselors with whom to discuss your financing options.

40. Reward for Community Service. Many schools encourage students to participate in community service. Some give course credit.

41. Tuition Equalization (1). To compete more effectively with public schools for top students, some private colleges offer their own tuition equalization programs, for example, discounts to bright state residents.

42. Tuition Equalization (2). To compete more effectively with other states for top students, some public schools will waive higher non-resident fees for exceptional out-of-state students, e.g., those in the top 5%.

The Rich Schools

Money attracts money. Schools with large endowments can build fancier facilities, hire brainier faculty and attract the most-connected (and powerful) trustees. All of this makes it easier to raise yet more money.

Of course, there is no proven relationship between the size of a school's endowment and the pool of money it makes available for student aid, however, rich schools do spend some of their endowments to limit tuition increases and sweeten aid packages. At some, the *average* need-based grant ranges from $10,000 to $25,000! Furthermore, rich schools have greater flexibility in awarding financial aid. It's their money, so they are better able to take individual circumstances into account than schools that dispense, in the main, public funds. (Schools also use endowment money to expand research, shrink classroom sizes, add majors, and beef-up campus facilities.) Here are schools with mountains of money:

Over $10 billion: Harvard, Yale, Stanford, Princeton, and U. of Texas.

Over $2 billion: MIT, Columbia, U. of Michigan, U. of Pennsylvania, Texas A&M, Northwestern, U. of California, U. of Chicago, Notre Dame, Duke, Washington U. (MO), Emory, Cornell, Rice, Virginia, Dartmouth, U. of So. California, Vanderbilt, Minnesota, Johns Hopkins, Brown, Ohio State, U. of Pittsburgh, U. of Washington, North Carolina, New York U., and Rockefeller U.

Over $1 billion: Williams, CalTech, Case Western, Purdue, Pomona, U. of Rochester, Grinnell, Boston C., Amherst, Wellesley, U. of Richmond, Wisconsin, Penn State, Indiana U., Illinois, Tufts, Swarthmore, Yeshiva, Delaware, Smith, Southern Methodist, Georgia Tech, Baylor C. of Medicine, Nebraska, Wake Forest, Michigan State, Kansas, Florida, Texas Christian, Cincinnati, George Washington, Carnegie Mellon, Oklahoma, Princeton Theological Seminary, Berea, and Tulane.

While these numbers may seem huge, universities spend an average of just 4.6% of their assets each year, regardless of how the market is performing, hoping that bull and bear years average out. For example, last year's gains averaged 17.2%, the highest in nearly a decade. But this year, markets are dropping, and colleges are bracing for the beginning of a few lean years.

For several years now, Congress has been looking at escalating tuition costs, and lawmakers from both parties are now prodding colleges to use more of their endowment money for financial aid. They note that private foundations are required to spend at least 5% of their endowments each year to preserve the tax-exempt status of their investment earnings. They say colleges should think about doing the same.

Leadership in Selected Fields

Colleges that are acknowledged leaders in selected disciplines are usually heavily endowed by private sponsors in the areas of their special expertise. You are more likely to find an agriculture scholarship in Iowa than in New York City, or a petroleum engineering scholarship in Oklahoma than in the District of Columbia. For opinions on who is best in what:

1. Ask the guidance office to pick up a copy of *Rugg's Recommendations on the Colleges* ($28.95 postpaid, Rugg's Recommendations, Box 417, Fallbrook, CA 92088, www.ruggsrecommendations.com); or,

2. Ask for recommendations from people you respect in your intended academic/career field. **Tip:** Strong departments usually have funds they control themselves rather than the financial aid office so ask the department head about the possibility of departmental assistance.

Working With Financial Aid Administrators

The median salary of financial aid directors in 2007/2008 was $70,745. You might keep that sum in mind as you get ready to explain how your $150,000 income has been ravaged by the current economy to the point of making it impossible—absolutely impossible—to handle your family contribution. You might also remember that the purpose of financial aid is to make college affordable, not to give families a free ride.

Financial aid administrators primarily dispense public funds—tax money—and such expenditures are usually strictly regulated. They have more flexibility in awarding the colleges' own funds and in treating changed circumstances—unfortunate events such as death, disability, disaster, and divorce, as well as unusual (non-discretionary) expenses like medical bills, private secondary school tuitions, prior education loans, failing businesses, or upcoming retirements.

"Responding to New Information"

Few schools will adjust your aid package to meet your other institutional offers, especially merit-based offers, but most will "respond to new information," especially if that information explains a disparity in your need-based offers. That doesn't mean schools will haggle over price, but they will listen if your situation prevents you from writing a tuition check. After all, FAAs won't know about your problem unless you tell them. Some even welcome the opportunity to discuss aid packages and explain how the family's expected contribution was calculated. At the same time, families can help FAAs understand what circumstances are impacting on their ability to pay.

The Professional Judgment Process

As schools grow tired of "let's make a deal," they're beginning to formalize their "professional judgment" process. Over half now have written policies, and stick to them. After all, if aid administrators start increasing Pell awards willy-nilly, the Department of Education's Inspector General might start sniffing around, and remove their discretionary ability. At one university, for example, too many students knew which counselors would be most sympathetic to their cause, and would schedule appointments accordingly. To correct the imbalance, the school now has a formal appeals process. Here's how it handles dependency status:

First, students complete a standard form which asks them to:

- Identify the location of their parents and describe their last contact.
- Explain why they should receive a waiver. Expect this to be open-ended—schools don't want students to parrot back some approved definition of "unusual circumstance."
- Describe how they've been self-supporting (and for how long).
- Provide statements of support from two responsible adults aware of their situation (HS counselor, social worker, clergy member, etc.).
- Provide copies of any relevant court documents.

Next, two counselors review the forms independently and render judgment. If counselors vary in their decision, a third counselor will break the tie. Students unhappy with the decision may request an interview with the financial aid director. Finally, the financial aid director reviews the decision to make sure the process remains consistent. In subsequent years, students simply submit a letter saying "the situation has not changed."

As we move further away from "Ozzie and Harriet" families of the 50s, schools are seeing more blended families, and students raised by grandparents or unwed parents. Accordingly, schools may grant "independent" status based on these "unusual" living circumstances. Or, they may ask, "What is the family unit?" And agree to disregard parental income in favor of the income of whomever is supporting the student (for example, the grandparent). Unfortunately, some students try to declare "independence" simply to enhance eligibility for assistance, so colleges have been forced to dig deeper into your personal situation to make it more difficult for phony "independent" students to slip through. A simple disagreement with your parents over issues totally unrelated to college attendance won't suffice.

The Lesson?

If you feel the college should change any part of your award letter—the expense budget, your family contribution, or the mix of aid—then call the office. But do so with sound reasons and documentation, maybe even a monthly cash flow statement showing all your income, as well as your fixed and flexible expenses. And don't try to "cut a deal." FAAs are professionals who must stick to certain budget goals—they won't increase your award without good cause. So before you bully your way in demanding a recount, document your case carefully and remember, you catch more Drosophila Melanogaster with honey than with vinegar.

CHAPTER 10

■ ■

UNCLE SAM

Meet Your Uncle—Uncle Sam

For many students, applying for financial aid represents their first encounter with Uncle Sam. One thing will become apparent very quickly. Getting things from Uncle Sam is no more pleasant than giving him things, like your money at tax time. Here is what you should expect:

Uncle Sam likes forms. Lots of forms. Most have an awkward layout, an illogical sequence, and poorly written instructions.

Uncle Sam makes a sharp distinction between "authorizations" and "appropriations." Authorizations earn Uncle a lot of good will, without costing him a penny. So before you get excited about a new $10 billion student aid program, look to see how much money has actually been appropriated (spent) for it.

Uncle loves semantics and fine distinctions. His authorization bill may promise a chicken in every pot. But the enabling legislation may define "chicken" as "any part of the bird," a claw, a feather... Or the definition may emphasize the avian nature of a chicken. The operative word then becomes "bird" and any bird can be substituted for a chicken—pigeon, crow...

Uncle is a social engineer. After redefining chicken, he will turn his attention to the pot. He may rule that anyone who owns a pot large enough to hold a chicken is too rich to qualify for a fowl. Only owners of small pots can get birds—the smaller the pot, the bigger the bird will seem.

Uncle's promises don't hold for very long. Any program can be modified, filibustered, or rescinded near election time when it becomes important to hold down expenses and balance the budget.

Uncle likes to arm wrestle with himself. If the Administration doesn't like what Congress has mandated (or vice versa), it will miss dead-lines, base its case on budget figures that have already been rejected (but not yet replaced), blow smoke over the issues, hold up regula-tions, or tie up appropriated funds.

Uncle's timing does not correspond to the academic cycle. When you want to start planning for next year, Uncle is not ready. By the time he can tell you what he will do for you, you've already made your plans.

But when all is said and done, Uncle Sam is still your main source of aid—nearly 25 million awards worth nearly $95 billion is awarded to 10.8 million students. Warts or no warts, you had better learn to live with him.

More Money, More Complexity

One of our nation's top worries is that a good college education is becoming too expensive. Accordingly, Uncle Sam has attacked the problem from two sides: tax initiatives to benefit middle income students and budget initiatives to benefit the most needy. The end result? A cobbled together package that requires advanced legal and accounting skills to decipher. The first part of this Chapter focuses on federal student aid. The second part explains how the IRS can become your new best friend.

Program	Level of Study Under-grad	Grad	Need-Based Yes	No	Part-Timers Yes	No	Need Analysis
Pell Grant	X		X		X		FM
Stafford Loan	X	X	X			X	FM
Unsub. Stafford	X	X		X		X	FM
PLUS Loan	X			X		X	none
SEOG	X		X		X		FM
Work-study	X	X	X		X		FM
Perkins Loans	X	X	X		X		FM
ACG/Smart	X		X		X		FM

The Big Seven Today

Most of Uncle's student aid flows through seven gigantic programs. Three are student based—Pell Grants, Family Education Loans (Stafford and PLUS), and Direct Student Loans (Direct Stafford and Direct PLUS). You apply for assistance under these programs and the money comes to you.

The other four programs—Supplemental Educational Opportunity Grants (SEOG), Academic Competitiveness Grants (ACG) and SMART Grants, Work-Study and Perkins Loans—are campus-based. This means Uncle funds the programs, but gives the money to the colleges to dispense in accordance with federal guidelines. Most of the money goes to full- and half-time students, however, a small sum will go to part-time students.

Uncle also funds several smaller programs, for example, AmeriCorps, LEAP (Leveraging Educational Assistance Partnership), and TEACH Grants.

Useful Phone Contacts

For information about federal programs, call the Federal Student Aid Information Center, 800/4-FED-AID, from 8am to midnight, EST, seven days a week (TTY: 800/730-8913). Trained staff can help you:

- Complete the FAFSA
- Check on the status of your FAFSA
- Make corrections to your Student Aid Report (SAR)
- Request a duplicate SAR
- Explain Expected Contribution, and
- Answer questions about eligibility.

You may also request Uncle's free book, *Funding Education Beyond High School*. (Blind and visually-impaired students may request audio highlights of the book on a compact disc.) The number is NOT to be used for financial counseling, to interpret policy, or to expedite application processing.

Useful Web Contacts

Students.Gov (www.students.gov) was designed to be a 24/7 "Student Gateway to the U.S. Government." Its collection of (commercial and governmental) sites helps students find a job (or internship), e-file taxes, plan vacations, register to vote, buy postage stamps, and plan and pay for a college education.

Student Aid on the Web (studentaid.ed.gov) focuses on federal resources, including links to:

- *FAFSA on the Web* (www.fafsa.ed.gov) which lets you submit your FAFSA electronically.
- *Completing the FAFSA* (studentaid.ed.gov/students/publications/completing_fafsa/index.html) which provides very detailed FAFSA instructions, in English or Spanish.
- *Funding Education Beyond High School: The Guide to Federal Student Aid* (studentaid.ed.gov/students/publications/student_guide/index.html) which answers all your basic questions about federal student aid, in English or Spanish. Blind and visually-impaired students can hear highlights at www.FederalStudentAid.ed.gov/audio.

Information for Financial Aid Professionals (IFAP) *Library* (www.ifap.ed.gov) is for people who work in the student aid field, or families with an interest in the nitty-gritty of student aid regulations, including all of Uncle's "Dear Colleague" letters and "Negotiated Rulemaking" sessions.

College.gov (www.college.gov) is a new site, still being developed by the Department of Education. It is intended to be the federal government's main source for information about planning, preparing and paying for college.

Pell Grants

These make up Uncle's largest gift program. In 2009/2010, over $18 billion in Pells will be dispensed to 5.7 million students. The average award is around $3,150, and most recipients come from families with incomes under $40,000. You may receive a Pell for up to 18 semesters of undergraduate education. And, students who are accelerating completion of their degrees by enrolling year-round may receive up to two Pell awards in an academic year.

Pell Grants are the foundation of need-based student aid. For 2009/2010, the President has budgeted for maximum grants of $4,800 which will cover around 75% of tuition and fees at a typical four-year public university. The minimum Pell equals 10% of the maximum Pell funded for that year. Students who are eligible for a Pell that is between 5% and 10% of the maximum Pell shall receive the minimum (10%) Pell. Students eligible for less than 5% receive nothing.

The maximum authorized Pell was scheduled to increase to $6,000 in the 2009/2010 award year, and $8,000 in 2014/2015. But remember, there is a big difference between "authorized limits" and "funded limits"—each $100 increase in the maximum Pell costs the government nearly $600 million.

How large a Pell will you get? It varies with your expected family contribution and your student status. If you are a part-time, half-time or three-quarter time student, you receive 25%, 50% or 75% of your award, respectively.

Uncle publishes tables with exact levels of Pell funding, but to get an estimate, if your cost of college exceeds the maximum Pell (e.g., $4,800), just subtract your EFC from the maximum grant. For example, assuming an award range of $480 to $4,800, an EFC of $1,000 translates into $3,800 for full-time students (and $1,900 for half-time students). An EFC of $4,500 rounds up to $480 (but nothing for a half-time student). And an EFC of 4600 gets you nothing, regardless of your enrollment status.

For Whom the Pell Tolls

You apply for a Pell by completing the FAFSA. Make certain to go this route, even if you know you aren't eligible. Colleges and the states expect you to do so and won't consider you for other awards until they know your Pell status. The only way for them to know your Pell status is by seeing results from your FAFSA.

Federal Student Loans

Uncle Sam runs two parallel student loan programs:

Federal Family Education Loans: Subsidized Staffords, Unsubsidized Staffords and PLUS. These loans are made by commercial lenders.

William D. Ford Federal Direct Student Loans: Direct Subsidized Staffords, Direct Unsubsidized Staffords, and Direct PLUS. These loans are made by Uncle Sam.

Interest rates, loan limits, fees, deferments, cancellations, and forbearance terms are essentially the same. Repayment options vary slightly. The main difference, as far as the student is concerned, is who lends them the money. So why are there two programs? Politics, as usual. There is an ongoing disagreement between elected officials over who best can run the programs—private lenders or Uncle Sam (with help from private contractors). Can you borrow under both? No! Your college will tell you which it prefers. And despite alarming headlines concerning the tightening student loan market, federal Stafford and PLUS student loans will be readily available. Private loans are a different story. As noted in Chapter 7, they could be more difficult (or more expensive) to obtain depending on your family's credit rating.

Stafford Loans

Formerly called Guaranteed Student Loans, the program was renamed in honor of retired Senator Robert T. Stafford (R-VT). Stafford Loans are low-interest loans to undergraduate and graduate students enrolled at least half-time. They are available to all families without regard to financial need. Next year, students will receive over $74 billion in student loans; the average subsidized Stafford will be around $3,900 and the average unsubsidized Stafford will be around $4,800.

Which Stafford Loan is for you?

Students with financial need receive subsidized Staffords—Uncle pays the interest while they are in school and during deferments.

Students without financial need receive unsubsidized Staffords— interest accrues while they are in school and during any deferments.

Students with partial financial need receive a combination of the two.

Loan Limits:

Dependent Undergraduates: Freshmen may borrow up to $3,500 per year. Sophomores may borrow $4,500 per year. Juniors, seniors and fifth-year undergrads may borrow $5,500 per year. If a student is borrowing under both the subsidized and unsubsidized program, these annual limits each increase by $2,000. For example, a freshman who receives a $1,500 subsidized Stafford may borrow an additional $4,000 under the unsubsidized program for a total of $5,500. The maximum undergraduate loan amount is $31,000 (of which no more than $23,000 can be subsidized).

Independent Undergraduates and Dependent Students Whose Parents Cannot Borrow under the PLUS program: Freshmen may borrow up to $3,500 per year. Sophomores may borrow $4,500 per year. Juniors, seniors and fifth-year undergrads may borrow $5,500 per year. If a student is borrowing under both the subsidized and unsubsidized program, these annual limits each increase by $6,000 for freshmen and sophomores and $7,000 for juniors, seniors and fifth-year undergraduates. The maximum an independent student (or, a dependent student whose parents cannot borrow under the PLUS programma) may borrow during his or her undergraduate years is $57,500 (of which no more than $23,000 can be subsidized).

Graduate Students may borrow up to $8,500 per year. If a student is borrowing under both the subsidized and unsubsidized program, this limit increases by $12,000 per year to a maximum of $138,500 (of which no more than $65,500 can be subsidized). This limit includes any money borrowed as an undergraduate.

Additional Limits: Students in health-related fields may borrow up to $224,000. Also, in no case may a Stafford Loan exceed the cost of attendance at your school minus any other financial aid you receive.

Prorated loan limits: Borrowing limits are prorated for programs of less than a full academic year, e.g., students attending the equivalent of 1/3 a year are eligible for 1/3 the maximum annual loan amount.

Origination Fee and Insurance/Default Fees. Lenders may subtract a small origination and insurance/default fee. A few lenders will waive these fees, or refund them during repayment saving you up to $1,000.

The origination fee is supposed to be phased out by 2010.

Minimum Annual Repayment. $600.

Years to Repay. 5 to 10.

Interest Rate. The interest rate on subsidized loans is now fixed at 6% and will decrease to 5.6% for loans disbursed after July 1, 2009; 4.5% for loans disbursed after July 1, 2010 and 3.4% for loans disbursed after July 1, 2011. The interest rate on unsubsidized loans is 6.8%.

Tip: If you have an unsubsidized loan, don't let the interest capitalize; instead, pay the interest while you're in school. The charges are minimal, and you'll save hundreds of dollars during repayment. Also, if your income is below the caps described later in this Chapter, you can deduct the interest payments from your AGI saving you tax dollars as well. And if the deduction lowers your AGI to under $50,000, you might now be qualified for the simplified, asset-free, version of the Federal Methodology. The result? Extra need-based aid next year.

Interest Subsidy. In the subsidized program, Uncle Sam pays interest on the loan while the student is in school and during deferments, including a six-month grace period after the student completes his or her studies. In the unsubsidized program, students may forgo making payments, but interest continues to accrue while they are in school and during deferments, including the grace period.

Deferments. Deferments are granted whenever a student is enrolled at least half-time. Deferments are also authorized for periods of unemployment or economic hardship, as well as active-duty service in the military (or National Guard) during time of war or national emergency.

Forbearance. If unanticipated problems affect your ability to repay the loan, and you do not qualify for deferment, lenders may grant forbearance—permitting (1) the temporary cessation of payments, (2) an extension of time for making payments, or (3) smaller payments than were scheduled. Typical reasons for forbearance: unemployment, poor health, personal problems or underemployment. Interest continues to accumulate during forbearance.

Cancellation. Under certain circumstances, your loans can be canceled. Usually these circumstances are unpleasant things like death or permanent disability. In addition, there is a growing recognition that high debt levels affect career choices—the higher your debt, the less likely you are to work in a non-profit or public service field. So now there are some other cancelation (and forgiveness) options as well:

- Up to $5,000 in loans may be canceled for teaching for five consecutive years in a school serving low-income families. This amount may be increased to $17,500 for those who work in low-income areas teaching reading, math, science or special ed.

- A portion may also be canceled for working in areas of "National Need" (as defined by Uncle Sam), for example, child-welfare workers and civil legal assistance attorneys.

- In the Direct Student Loan program, the government will forgive the balance of your loans if you have been repaying them for 10 years while working in a public service job (for example, law enforcement, social work, public health, or public education).

Who Makes Loans? Private lenders—Banks, Credit Unions, Insurance Companies. Also Uncle Sam, for students attending Direct Lending schools. If you can't find a lender, contact your college's financial aid office for recommendations.

Entrance Counseling. Before you may receive any Stafford money, you must go through "Entrance Counseling" to learn about your responsibilities as a borrower. Some schools let you complete this requirement online. Other schools insist on an in-person interview.

PLUS Loans

PLUS loans are not need-based, so they can be used to cover expected family contribution. Creditworthy parents may borrow up to the student's total cost of attendance less any aid received. Next year, the government estimates the average PLUS will be about $11,300. They can be a good alternative to private loans—but, first, look at the offered interest rates.

If a parent is deemed uncreditworthy, the student may borrow additional money under the unsubsidized Stafford program; freshmen and sophomores get an extra $6,000; juniors and seniors, an extra $7,000 (these amounts correspond to the higher borrowing limits for independent undergraduates).

Graduate students are also eligible for PLUS loans, however, they must first file a FAFSA and apply for a Stafford loan.

Origination Fee and Insurance/Default Fees. Lenders may subtract a 3% loan origination fee and a 1% insurance/default fee. If your loan comes from Uncle, you pay a combined 4% instead.

Interest Rate. The interest rate for Direct PLUS is 7.9%. The interest rate for FFEL PLUS loans is 8.5%.

Interest Subsidy. There is no interest subsidy to borrowers.

Repayment begins within 60 days of disbursement and extends from 5 to 10 years. Borrowers may, however, choose to defer payments for up to six months after the student ceases to be enrolled at least half-time. Under certain circumstances, loans can be deferred, postponed, canceled or considered for forbearance. Usually these circumstances are unpleasant things like death, permanent disability, or economic hardship.

Who Makes Loans? Private lenders—Banks, S&Ls, Credit Unions, some states, and Uncle Sam, for students attending Direct Lending schools.

Supplemental Educational Opportunity Grants

Uncle will give the colleges $757 million for SEOGs next year. Colleges must match 25% of this money with funds of their own.

Size of awards. From $100 to $4,000 per year of undergraduate study. Over 1.29 million students receive average grants of $764.

Criteria for Selection. Need and fund availability. Be smart. Apply early. Priority goes to those receiving Pells.

Work-Study

Uncle gives colleges nearly $1 billion for work-study each year. Colleges are supposed to match a portion of this money with funds of their own.

Eligibility. Undergraduate and graduate students. 800,000 students receive an average of $1,478 each.

Criteria for Selection. Need and fund availability. Work-study students are more likely to stay in school and graduate with less debt. Be smart. Apply early.

Program Description. On- and off-campus employment, however, work-study employment may not involve political or religious activity nor may it be used to replace regular employees. The recipient's salary must at least equal minimum wage, and the student cannot earn more money than their award stipulates. Thus, if you receive a $1,000 award, your employment lasts until you earn $1,000 and then it terminates for that academic year.

Schools may use this money to fund community service jobs as well, including projects that will prepare communities to cope with emergencies and natural disasters.

Perkins Loans

The college acts as lender, using funds originally provided by the federal government. Uncle adds about $65 million for loan forgiveness. Colleges must match a portion of this money with funds of their own. Thanks to these new infusions, and money that has been paid back by past borrowers, colleges now control a multi-billion dollar Perkins "revolving fund."

Eligibility. Undergraduate and graduate students. 500,000 students receive an average of nearly $2,200 each.

Criteria for Selection. Need and fund availability. Be smart. Apply early.

Loan Limits: *Undergraduate*: $5,500 per year to a maximum of $27,500. *Graduate students:* $8,000 per year to a maximum of $60,000 (less any Perkins money borrowed as an undergraduate).

Minimum Annual Repayment. $480.

Interest rate. 5%.

Interest Subsidy. Student pays no interest while in school or during a 9-month grace period following graduation.

Repayment. 10 years. Under certain circumstances, loans can be deferred, postponed or considered for forbearance. Usually these circumstances are unpleasant reasons like death, permanent disability, or economic hardship.

Loan Cancellation. Loans can be forgiven or canceled if you do worthwhile things after graduation, like serve in the Peace Corps, work as a public defender (or prosecutor) or teach low-income, high-risk students.

Academic Competitiveness Grants and SMART Grants

The federal budget for 2009 includes $710 million for these two grant programs. States and colleges will be responsible for helping to identify eligible students—as many as 730,000 students could qualify.

Academic Competitiveness Grants (ACG) award up to $750 to first-year Pell-eligible recipients and $1,300 to second-year Pell-eligible recipients provided these students maintain at least a 3.0 GPA and complete a "rigorous secondary-school program of study" that prepares them for college, for example, four years of English, three years of math, three years of lab science (biology, chemistry, physics), three years of social science, and one year of a foreign language.

National Science and Mathematics Access to Retain Talent (SMART) Grants will award up to $4,000 per year to Pell recipients in their third and fourth years of college. The average award is $3,176. To receive SMART funds, students must major in math, science, computer science or certain foreign languages (those deemed critical to national security) and they must maintain a 3.0 GPA in that major. If the school doesn't offer science majors, students must take courses that are equivalent to those of a science major.

TEACH Grants

Teacher Education Assistance for College and Higher Education Grants will award up to $4,000 per year (to a maximum of $16,000 for undergraduates and $8,000 for graduate students) to students completing the coursework necessary to begin a career in teaching.

You begin the process of applying for a TEACH Grant by indicating your interest in teaching when you complete the FAFSA. Like the other campus-based programs, the federal government gives money to the colleges to dispense. Next year, $114 million will be awarded to 41,000 recipients, for an average award of $2,780.

Recipients must have at least a 3.25 GPA and agree to serve as a full-time teacher for at least four years in a high-need school within eight years of completing their course of study. Furthermore, they must teach Math, Science, Foreign Language, Special Ed, or some other subject deemed "high need" by the federal, state or local government. Students who do not fulfill their obligation must repay their TEACH Grant with interest as though it was an unsubsidized Stafford.

On Defaulting

Uncle Sam punishes colleges for the behavior of their scofflaw graduates. Schools with high default rates (25% +) for three years running may become ineligible for federal funds altogether. No Perkins money. No Stafford money. No Pell money. No any kind of federal student aid money. The national default rate is currently about 4.6% per year, ranging from 2.4% at non-profit private colleges to 4.3% at public colleges to 8.2% at for-profit proprietary schools. It may pay you to ask schools for their default rate before you apply.

Uncle can also punish defaulters, as he should, since in our book, defaulters eclipse even the most parasitic protozoa! He can notify credit bureaus which will damage your credit rating. He can withhold your tax refunds until your loan is repaid. He can take you to court. He can garnish up to 15% your wages (and fine employers who don't follow through). And he has access to the "new hires" database used to track down "deadbeat dads."

Loan Repayment Options

Borrowers who face larger payments than they can initially handle under regular repayment, may want to use an alternate plan, either Extended Repayment, Graduated Repayment, or an Income-Based Repayment. Under these plans, your monthly payments will be smaller but the total amount you repay much greater than under standard (10-year) repayment.

Uncle currently runs two parallel sets of repayment plans, one under Federal Family Education Loan (FFEL), the other under Federal Direct Student Loan (FDSL). For more information, check with Uncle Sam or the institution that gave you your loan.

To help you decide which repayment plan is best for you, try using *FinAid's* online loan calculators: www.finaid.org/calculators.

Standard Repayment

Students pay a fixed annual amount over a fixed period of time, not to exceed ten years.

Graduated Repayment

Borrowers must repay the loan within ten years, however, payments start small when income is low, and increase over time, while income also rises. Students sometimes have the option of making interest-only payments for the first few years.

Extended Repayment

Students with debts over $30,000 may extend repayment for up to 25 years and choose between a fixed or graduated repayment schedule.

Income-Sensitive Repayment

This option is available only under FFEL. Students work with their lender to establish a more flexible repayment schedule than the ones above. For example, students may choose to repay from 4% to 25% of their gross monthly income. Payment amounts may be adjusted annually to reflect current income and future earning potential. The repayment period equals ten years, however, it can be extended up to five years if repayment amounts are insufficient to repay the loan within the designated time frame.

Income Contingent Repayment

This option is available only with FDSL. Uncle has developed a complex formula for determining repayment rates; they vary based on your income and the size of your loan. For example, a single borrower with an income of $25,000 would begin repaying a $15,000 loan at $114 per month while a borrower earning $40,000 would repay that same loan at $145 per month.

After 25 years, a borrower who has been repaying faithfully, but has not yet retired the loan, will have the rest of his or her debt forgiven. On the downside, the IRS will count this unpaid amount as in-kind (taxable) income. Parents may not use this option to repay their PLUS loans.

Income-Based Repayment

Beginning July 1, 2009, all students will be able to take advantage of a third form of income-based repayment. In this new plan, a student's monthly loan payment will be limited to 15% of their discretionary income, or 15% of the amount by which the student's adjusted gross income exceeds 150% of the poverty line, divided by 12. Got it? The government will forgive any remaining balance after 25 years of repayment. Borrowers who are using one of the other income-based repayment plans may switch to this one. For more information, visit IBRInfo.org.

Borrower Bonuses

Private lenders must charge all borrowers the same upfront fees, however, some will reward students who repay their loans faithfully. They might:

- Give you one year, interest-free.
- Lower your interest rate by 2% after receiving 48 on-time payments
- Refund your loan origination fee.
- Lower your interest rate an additional .25% if you repay using automatic (electronic) monthly bank transfers.
- Lower your interest rate simply for having more than $7,500 in loans.

Before you take out a student loan, make certain your lender offers these bonuses; otherwise, keep looking. A student with $10,000 in Stafford loans could save over $1,000.

Tip: To benefit from these opportunities, set up overdraft protection on your checking account so you're sure not to miss an automatic payment due to "insufficient funds."

Of course, all of these borrower bonuses may come to an end, as the government continues to reduce lender subsidies. Also, the plans outlined above present a general overview of loan repayment options. Exact details vary depending on the nature of your debt. Besides, by the time you begin repayment, all of these choices will probably be obsolete! For current information, contact your lender.

Some state provide perks, as well. "Vermont Value" gives students annual rebates equal to 1% of the principal balance each year (on a $5,000 Stafford loan, students would receive $475 over 10 years). Maine cuts borrowers' interest rate by 3% after 36-months of on-time payments.

Loan Consolidation

Borrowers with multiple federal loans may consolidate (aka refinance) their loans, and take advantage of the graduated and extended repayment plans just described. Sometimes they qualify for borrower bonuses, as well.

Interest Rate. The interest rate on consolidation loans equals the weighted average of all your loans rounded up to the nearest 1/8% with an 8.25% cap. It is fixed at this rate for the life of the loan.

Eligible Loans. You may consolidate all federal loans—Stafford, Perkins, PLUS, Nursing and Health Professional Student Loans (HPSL). Married couples may no longer consolidate their individual loans into a joint loan.

Interest Subsidies. If your consolidation loan contains subsidized loan money, you might retain the interest subsidy benefit on that portion of your consolidated loan during deferments.

Deferment is allowed (1) while in school at least half-time, (2) while pursuing a graduate fellowship program or rehabilitation training program for persons with disabilities, (3) up to three years for unemployment or economic hardship, and (4) up to three years for active-duty military service. Deferment periods are not included in the number of years allowed for repayment.

If you choose to consolidate a Perkins loan, you lose out on its myriad deferment and cancellation options.

Years to Repay. 10 years for loans under $7,500; 12 years for loans between $7,500 and $9,999; 15 years for loans between $10,000 and $19,999; 20 years for loans between $20,000 and $39,999; 25 years for loans between $40,000 and $59,999; and 30 years for loans larger than $60,000. Yikes!

For more on FFEL Consolidation, contact your current lender. For more information on Direct Consolidation, call 800/557-7392 or visit www.loanconsolidation.ed.gov.

Loan Serialization

Students with multiple loans of the same type but from different lenders may be able to "collapse" or "serialize" their loans to create a single monthly payment. Technically, the loans remain separate, but now you're writing just one check a month without going through the hassle of consolidation (and possibly losing out on the borrower bonuses described above). Check with your lenders to see if they can offer you this option.

AmeriCorps

Participants receive a minimum wage stipend of up to $9,300 plus a $4,725 credit per year of full-time service (for up to two years). They may use the credit at any college or graduate school, or to pay down outstanding student loans. Furthermore, the money does not affect their eligibility for other federal student aid. Currently, about 50,000 students serve in 450 different programs with Uncle providing most of the funding, but states and nonprofits doing the hiring. Prime projects are those that address unmet needs in education (assisting teachers in Head Start), the environment (recycling or conservation projects), human services (building housing for the homeless) or public safety (leading drug education seminars).

Interested students should apply directly to a funded program (for a list, visit www.AmeriCorps.gov, 800/94-ACORPS).

While AmeriCorps is small in scope, its real importance has been to focus attention on our county's extensive network of service programs. With AmeriCorps adding new structure, and a solid core of workers, these programs have become a magnet for corporate money as well as for volunteers with only an hour to spare. The funded projects have brought huge economic benefits to the communities in which they operate as well as a heightened sense of personal and social responsibility for the AmeriCorps participants.

Despite the fact that this has been a highly and widely praised public service program, and very popular with Governors of both political parties (who have seen the programs work in their states) there are still a few Congressional critics who want to snuff it out saying the government has no business creating a Department of Good Deeds. Accounting squabbles and claims of financial mismanagement have plagued AmeriCorps in past years, but the Bush Administration supports the program, so for now, it lives.

LEAP

Leveraging Educational Assistance Partnership provides states with $66 million for need-based grants for low-income students. Many states would not be able to operate their need-based grant programs without federal support, however, states must match these grants dollar-for-dollar.

The maximum LEAP Grant is $12,500.

Reauthorization of the Higher Education Act

The Higher Education Act (which establishes the main federal student aid programs) expires every five years. The last reauthorization was supposed to occur in 2003. Instead, Congress has passed a dozen short-term extensions, as well as a variety of smaller pieces of legislation. Finally, in August, 2008, after five years of deliberation, the new 1,158-page "Higher Education Opportunity Act" was approved overwhelmingly by the House and Senate, and promptly signed into law by President Bush. According to the

Senate's summary of the bill, it focuses on five major areas:
1. Holding colleges more accountable for their costs;
2. Simplifying the application process for federal financial aid;
3. Curbing unethical practices in the student loan marketplace;
4. Expanding aid for the neediest students and members of the military;
5. Expanding college access for students with disabilities

In addition, in the past year, both sides of the aisle worked together to pass (1) the "College Cost Reduction and Access Act," to boost federal student aid programs by more than $20 billion; and (2) the "Ensuring Continued Access to Student Loans Act" to ensure the availability of federal student loans despite the current upheaval in the credit market. This edition of *Don't Miss Out* incorporates all three of these higher education bills.

Highlights from the College Cost Reduction and Access Act

Here are a few highlights of the College Cost Reduction and Access Act, as passed in September, 2007:

- Increase in the size of Pell Grants from $4,310 to $4,800 (with additional increases by 2012-2013).
- Introduce a new grant (TEACH Grants) worth $4,000 per year to assist students who are planning to become teachers.
- Reduce the interest rate on Stafford Loans from 6.8% to 6% for loans disbursed after July 1, 2008, 5.6% for loans disbursed after July 1, 2009, 4.5% for loans disbursed after July 1, 2010 and 3.4% for loans disbursed after July 1, 2011.
- Introduce a new income-based loan repayment option.
- Introduce a new loan-forgiveness option for public-service employees.
- Increase income protection allowances in the need-analysis formula beginning in 2009-2010.
- Standardize treatment of 529 plan assets and income.
- Expand the definition of Independent Student to include "emancipated minors" and unaccompanied youths who are homeless, or at risk for homelessness.

Highlights from the Continued Access to Student Loan Act

Here are a few highlights of the Continued Access to Student Loan Act, as passed in May, 2008:

- Increase Stafford loan limits by $2,000 per year.
- Give parent borrowers the option to delay repaying PLUS loans.
- Expand eligibility for ACG and SMART Grants.
- Creates a Lender of Last Resort program.

Highlights from The Higher Education Opportunity Act of 2008

Pell Grants and ACG/SMART Grants

- Increase the maximum authorized Pell from $4,800 to $6,000 for 2009 and to $8,000 for 2014.
- Increase the minimum Pell from $400 to 10% of the maximum grant.
- Place an 18-semester limit on Pell eligibility.
- Enable low-income students to receive Pell Grants year-round.
- Expand eligibility for ACG and SMART Grants.

Stafford/PLUS/Perkins Loans

- Increase Perkins loan limits for undergraduates from $4,000 to $5,500 and for graduate students from $6,000 to $8,000. Increase aggregate loans limits for undergraduates from $20,000 to $27,500 and for graduate students from $40,000 to $60,000.
- Allow service members to defer payments, interest-free, on Federal Direct Loans while they are on active duty.
- Expand federal loan forgiveness for students who become civil legal aid lawyers, prosecutors, public defenders, teachers, and other public-service professions.
- Require colleges that identify "preferred lenders" to place at least three lenders on the list, and clearly explain to students why the college believes the lender is offering attractive terms and conditions.
- Prohibit lenders from offering gifts to college officials as a condition of making student loans.

Free Application for Federal Student Aid

- Simplify the FAFSA, without reducing its ability to identify students with financial need.
- Introduce EZ-Fafsa (a shortened version of the FAFSA) for low-income students.
- Phase out the paper FAFSA

College Costs

- Provide in-state tuition for members of the Armed Forces and their dependents who have lived in a state for more than 30 days.
- Provide more transparency about college costs by publishing detailed college pricing data on the Department of Education's website.
- Encourage states to maintain high levels of higher education funding.
- Require colleges with the greatest cost increases to submit reports to the Secretary of Education explaining why their costs have risen, and what steps they are taking to hold costs down.

Tax relief For Education Expenses

Tuition Tax Credits

Education can be the "Continental Divide" between those who will prosper economically and those who will not. Unfortunately, many families feel priced out of college, hence, the push to make middle-income tuition-payers the big tax-relief winners.

For more details on all types of education-related tax benefits, read the official IRS publications. In reviewing these sites, remember they are valuable for their factual information, not their consumer insights:

1. *Tax Information for Students* at www.irs.gov/individuals/students/index.html; or

2. *Tax Benefits for Education* at www.irs.gov/pub/irs-pdf/p970.pdf

The Hope Credit

The Hope Credit allows taxpayers to claim a maximum annual credit of $1,800 per student for tuition expenses paid on behalf of the taxpayer, the taxpayer's spouse, or a dependent for the first two years of college; 100% of the first $1,200 of tuition, and 50% of the next $1,200. That $1,200 figure will be indexed for inflation. To qualify, the student must be enrolled at least half-time.

The Lifetime Learning Credit

The Lifetime Learning Credit allows taxpayers to claim an annual credit equal to 20% of up to $10,000 in total tuition expenses. Unlike the Hope credit, this is a "per taxpayer" maximum, rather than a "per student" maximum. Also, part-timers are eligible, so are working-adults taking classes to improve their job skills. There is no limit to the number of years you may claim this credit.

Phaseouts and Restrictions

These credits will be phased out for single filers with incomes between $48,000 and $58,000, and joint filers with incomes between $96,000 and $116,000. Income levels are indexed annually for inflation.

You can only use one of these credits per student, per year, however, you can claim the Hope credit for one student's expenses and the Lifetime Learning Credit for another's. In other words, parents with incomes under $96,000 could take advantage of the Hope credit for their college Freshman and the Lifetime Learning credit for their college Junior, for a maximum total credit of $3,800.

If your family's income is too high to claim these credits, consider letting your child claim them on his or her tax return. This is possible only if the parents forego claiming that child on their return—you'll have to evaluate the benefit for yourself, however, in most instances, if the student has sufficient taxable income, the value of the tax credit outweighs the dependency exemption.

To claim your credit, simply file IRS Form 8863 with the rest of your 1040 tax return. Note: The FAFSA collects data on the size of your tuition credits, and the Federal Methodology provides offsets for them. Otherwise, these credits would increase available income, which would increase EFC, and decrease eligibility for aid. . .certainly not the tax writers' intent.

Tax Deductions

(Temporary) Deduction for Higher Education Expenses

Itemizers and non-itemizers alike with incomes under $130,000 ($65,000 for single filers) can deduct up to $4,000 per year in tuition expenses from their AGIs; families with incomes between $130,000 and $160,000 (or singles with incomes between $65,000 and $80,000) can deduct $2,000. In previous years, this deduction has been allowed to expire, however, most experts expect the provision to continue to be extended, at least until the whole hodge-podge of education-related tax breaks is simplified.

This deduction is to benefit families with incomes too high to qualify for the Hope or Lifetime Credit; in fact, you can't claim this deduction for expenses that you use to qualify for the Hope or Lifetime credit.

Deduction for Student Loan Interest

You may deduct up to $2,500 per year in interest paid on "qualified education loans." This definition includes commercial education loans, but not loans from people related to the taxpayer. The deduction will be phased out for single filers with incomes between $55,000 and $70,000 and joint filers with incomes between $115,000 and $145,000. Income levels will be indexed annually for inflation.

Tax Credits vs. Tax-free Savings

The IRS says, "no double benefits." If you pay a portion of your college bills using earnings from a tax-advantaged Section 529 Plan, or Coverdell Education Savings Account, you can receive an education tax credit or deduction only on family contribution that is in excess of those earnings.

Example One: Your family income is $80,000, your first year of college costs $15,000, and you receive no financial aid. If you take $12,600 in earnings from a Section 529 Plan, and $2,400 from a regular savings account, you can receive an $1,800 Hope tax credit.

Example Two: Your family income is $130,000 (too high to qualify for a Hope or Lifetime Learning Credit), your Junior year of college costs $19,000, and you receive no financial aid. If you take $15,000 in earnings from your Coverdell Account, and $4,000 from a regular savings account, come tax-time, you can deduct that $4,000 from your adjusted gross income. If you take $19,000 from your Coverdell Account, but only $15,000 of that amount represents earnings, you can still deduct $4,000 from your AGI. (This assumes the deduction for higher education expenses is extended.)

Example Three: Your family income is $52,000, your first year of college costs $20,000, and you receive $5,000 in need-based student aid. If you pay the balance using $6,000 in earnings from your Coverdell Account and $9,000 from a regular savings account, you can choose whether to take a Hope Credit (worth $1,800) or a $4,000 tax deduction (worth around $1,120). In this case, the tax deduction might actually be the more advantageous option since it would lower your AGI to under $50,000, possibly qualifying you for additional need-based student aid next year—remember, the Federal Methodology ignores assets of families with incomes under $50,000 who are eligible to file a 1040A or 1040EZ. Of course, the IRS may remove this little loophole by the time you file your taxes. (Again, this assumes the deduction for higher education expenses is extended.)

For more information on tax-free withdrawals from Coverdell Education Savings Accounts and Section 529 Savings Plans, see Chapter 8. For more information on employer-provided education tax benefits, see Chapter 12.

Good Politics or Good Policy?

Naysayers call it Torture By Taxation—these policies benefit families who could have (and would have) sent their kids to college anyway, rather than those most in need. They drown the system in added complexity. And they give people tax breaks only if they spend money in ways that Uncle deems desirable. On the flip side, the system used to be so full of disincentives to save or borrow for college, if this hodge-podge gets more families to assume responsibility for tuition payments, we'll take it!

On the Horizon

Government estimates show that 27% of tax filers who are eligible for a tuition tax break do not claim one on their tax returns. Accordingly, many in Congress want to consolidate all of these tax incentives into one simpler program—for example, a tax credit of up to $3,000 per year per student, with a lifetime maximum of $12,000 per student. The income phaseout level might begin at $60,000 (or $70,000) for singles and $120,000 (or $140,000) for couples. And for families with incomes too low to benefit, a portion of the credit would be refundable (like the earned-income credit).

Will this actually happen? It will probably be up to the next Administration to decide.

CHAPTER 11

▪▪▪▪▪▪▪▪▪▪▪▪▪▪▪▪▪▪▪▪▪▪▪

THE STATES

State-Funded Student Aid Programs

All states maintain extensive programs of grants, fee reductions and loans. Based on information from the National Association of State Student Grant and Aid Programs (NASSGAP), we estimate that next year over 4 million students will receive over $7.1 billion in need-based state grant aid and $2.8 billion in non-need-based grant aid. States award another $2.3 billion in loans and work-study. Also from NASSGAP:

States making over 50,000 awards: New York, Florida, Georgia, Texas, Illinois, Pennsylvania, California, Ohio, Illinois, Michigan, Minnesota, North Carolina, Kentucky, New Jersey, Virginia, South Carolina, Tennessee, Oklahoma, Puerto Rico, Washington, Indiana, Wisconsin Massachusetts, Maryland and New Mexico—in that order.

States spending over $100 million on student aid: New York, California, Florida, Texas, New Jersey, Pennsylvania, Georgia, Illinois, Indiana, Michigan, Minnesota, North Carolina, South Carolina, Ohio, Virginia, Tennessee, Washington, Kentucky, Oklahoma, Louisiana, Massachusetts, Maryland, Wisconsin and Connecticut—in that order.

States giving awards to at least 30% of their students: Georgia (72.54%), Alaska (71.4%), Kentucky (63.6%), South Carolina (62.9%), Nevada (60.7%), New Mexico (57.6%), Oklahoma (56.6%), Florida (46.2%), Puerto Rico (44%), Minnesota (43.7%), Ohio (41.6%), Tennessee (41.2%), Nebraska (40.2%), West Va. (40%), Illinois (39.5%), Michigan (38.1%), Pennsylvania (37.8%), New Jersey (37.7%), New York (37.5%), Vermont (36.4%), Maine (33.6%), North Carolina (32.6%), Virginia (31.8%) and Washington (31.5%).

States awarding average need-based grants of at least $2,000 per recipient: Mississippi ($3,909), California ($3,766), New Jersey ($3,725), Indiana ($3,375), Texas ($3,330), Iowa ($3,020), Pennsylvania ($2,712), Illinois ($2,613), New York ($2,590), Washington ($2,518), West Virginia ($2,488) and Maryland ($2,243).

Eligibility for State-Based Student Aid

States determine eligibility for need-based aid in one of three ways: (1) Most use only the federal methodology (or a modified version of the federal methodology); (2) Some rely on their own system; (3) About a dozen rely on their own system for some awards, and the federal methodology for other programs.

So, how do you know which forms to file? In most instances, to qualify for state-based aid, you must file Uncle Sam's FAFSA. Some states might ask you to use the College Board's PROFILE, and finally, some states have their own applications. Important: Many states have noted that using the federal methodology to determine eligibility means more students are qualifying for aid. Unfortunately, state grants are not usually entitlement programs, so when the money runs out, too bad. Again, apply early!

A Summary of State Programs

The following summary table describes state programs other than state participation in federal programs like the Stafford and PLUS loans. With regard to Stafford and PLUS loans, most states have a guaranteeing agency to administer loans. Here is an explanation of the table's columns:

Column 1—In-State Study. These are need-based grants, generally restricted to undergrads. Many of these grants are funded with help from Uncle's Leveraging Educational Assistance Partnership (LEAP) program.

Column 2—Some Other States. Some states provide a bit of need-based assistance to residents attending schools out-of-state.

Column 3—Merit Programs. Three types of programs: (1) Those based on financial need that require you to meet some academic threshold to be eligible; (2) Those based on academic accomplishment that require you to demonstrate financial need to qualify for a monetary award—also called "merit within need"; and (3) Those based solely on academic accomplishment, with no regard to your finances. *Funding for merit-based programs (and "merit-within need" programs) is growing faster than funding for need-based programs because states don't want their best students defecting to other states.*

Column 4—Special Loans. These are separate from federal programs. They carry low interest rates and in some cases, are available to out-of-state students attending school in the underwriting state. For example, Massachusetts offers (need-based) no-interest loans with a 10-year repayment period.

Column 5—Loan Forgiveness. To increase the supply of teachers, nurses and doctors, many states have instituted loan programs with "forgiveness" features if the students actually end up in classrooms or medical practice. If the students don't work in state, they must repay the aid. Some programs limit benefits to students who work in a shortage area. This could mean a certain specialty or subject area. It could also mean a geographic area like a rural part of the state, or an inner-city. At least 35 states also get money for loan forgiveness from Uncle's "National Health Service Corps." For more information, you'll have to contact your state's Department of Health Services, or Department of Public Health.

Column 6—Tuition Equalization. These states offer awards to reduce the difference between in-state public and private college tuition.

Column 7—Minority Group Programs. Beneficiaries must usually be African-American, Latino or Native American—Eskimo, Indian or Aleutian.

Column 8—Work-Study. State-operated programs similar to the federal work-study or cooperative education programs.

Column 9—Veterans. Special benefits to state residents who served in the Armed Forces, usually during times of hostilities. For more information, you may have to contact your state's Department of Veteran's Affairs.

Column 10—National Guard. State educational benefits for serving in the state's National Guard. These are in addition to federal benefits.

Columns 11,12, 13. Special benefits to state residents who are dependents of deceased or disabled veterans, POWs, MIAs, or police/firefighters killed on duty.

Column 14—Military Dependents. Dependents of military personnel stationed within the state may attend in-state universities at in-state rates. (New federal legislation makes this a national requirement.)

Column 15—Tuition Savings Plans. All 50 states have tax-advantaged savings programs to encourage early college planning. No two states offer the same terms, and most welcome out-of-state participation, so shop around for the best deal! Prepaid Plans (P) let parents make a lump sum investment (or periodic payments) to guarantee tomorrow's tuition (room and board) at today's prices. The guarantee is usually good at any of the state's public or private colleges. Increasingly, they are good out-of-state, as well. Savings Plans (S) offer no guarantees, but usually invest more aggressively, and offer special sweeteners.

For more information, see "Section 529 Plans" in Chapter 8; for details (and plan comparisons), check www.collegesavings.org and www.savingforcollege.com.

Innovative State Programs

No two states have the same programs. Here are some you should ask about. Your questions might lead you to little-known opportunities.

Reciprocal Arrangements I

Students living near a state's border can sometimes study in the adjoining state at discounted tuition rates. Sometimes this means students actually pay less by going out-of-state.

Reciprocal Arrangements II

Study out-of-state at reduced rates. In some instances, you'll only receive a discount if your major is not offered in state. Such arrangements are coordinated by multi-state consortia:

| | 1. In-State Study | 2. Some Other States | 3. Merit Programs | 4. Special Loans | 5. Loan Forgiveness | 6. Tuition Equalization | 7. Minority Gp Prgrms | 8. Work Study | 9. Veterans | 10. National Guard | Dependent of | | | 14. Active Duty | 15. Tuition Savings Plan |
											11. Disabled Vet	12. POW or MIA	13. Police/Fireman		
Alabama	X		X			X				X	X	X	X	X	P/S
Alaska	X			X	X				X	X	X	X	X	X	S
Arizona	X									X	X	X	X	X	S
Arkansas	X		X		X		X			X	X	X	X	X	S
California	X				X								X	X	S
Colorado	X		X						X	X	X	X	X	X	P/S
Connecticut	X	X	X			X	X			X	X	X	X	X	S
Delaware	X	X	X	X	X	X				X	X	X	X	X	S
DC	X	X	X			X								X	S
Florida	X		X		X	X	X	X	X	X	X	X	X	X	P/S
Georgia	X		X		X	X				X			X	X	S
Guam						X								X	
Hawaii	X					X				X				X	S
Idaho	X		X		X		X	X		X		X	X	X	S
Illinois	X		X		X		X			X				X	P/S
Indiana	X	X	X			X	X	X		X	X	X	X	X	S
Iowa	X				X	X				X				X	S
Kansas	X		X		X		X	X		X			X	X	S
Kentucky	X		X			X		X		X	X	X	X	X	P/S
Louisiana	X		X							X				X	S
Maine	X	X			X		X			X			X	X	S
Maryland	X	X	X		X					X			X	X	P/S
Massachusetts	X	X	X	X	X	X				X	X	X	X	X	P/S
Michigan	X		X	X				X	X	X	X	X	X	X	P/S
Minnesota	X		X	X					X	X	X	X	X	X	S
Mississippi	X		X		X		X			X		X	X	X	P/S
Missouri	X		X							X	X		X	X	S
Montana	X			X			X	X	X	X	X	X	X	X	S
Nebraska	X						X		X	X	X		X	X	S
Nevada	X		X				X	X		X	X		X	X	P/S
New Hampshire	X	X	X		X					X	X			X	S
New Jersey	X		X	X	X	X				X			X	X	S
New Mexico	X		X		X	X	X	X	X	X	X	X	X	X	S
New York	X		X		X					X	X		X	X	S
North Carolina	X		X			X	X		X	X	X	X	X	X	S
North Dakota	X		X		X		X		X	X	X	X	X	X	S
Ohio	X		X		X	X				X	X	X	X	X	P/S
Oklahoma	X		X			X				X		X	X	X	S
Oregon	X		X		X					X			X	X	S
Pennsylvania	X				X				X	X	X	X	X	X	P/S
Puerto Rico	X									X				X	
Rhode Island	X	X								X	X		X	X	S
South Carolina	X		X		X	X				X	X	X	X	X	P/S
South Dakota			X							X	X	X		X	S
Tennessee	X		X		X	X	X			X			X	X	P/S

| | 1. In-State Study | 2. Some Other States | 3. Merit Programs | 4. Special Loans | 5. Loan Forgiveness | 6. Tuition Equalization | 7. Minority Gp prgrms | 8. Work Study | 9. Veterans | 10. National Guard | Dependent of | | | 14. Active Duty | 15. Tuition Savings Plan |
											11. Disabled Vet	12. POW or MIA	13. Police/Fireman		
Texas	X			X	X	X	X	X	X	X		X	X	X	P/S
Utah	X	X	X		X		X			X				X	S
Vermont	X	X								X	X			X	S
Virgin Islands	X													X	
Virginia	X		X			X	X			X	X			X	P/S
Washington	X		X					X	X	X	X	X	X	X	P
West Virginia	X	X	X		X	X				X	X		X	X	P/S
Wisconsin	X	X	X	X			X			X				X	S
Wyoming	X									X				X	S

- *The Western Interstate Commission for Higher Education:* Alaska, Arizona, California, Colorado, Hawaii, Idaho, Montana, Nevada, New Mexico, North Dakota, Oregon, South Dakota, Utah, Washington and Wyoming. For information, contact WICHE, 3035 Center Green Drive, #200, Boulder, CO 80301, 303/541-0200, www.wiche.edu.

- *The Southern Regional Education Board:* Alabama, Arkansas, Delaware, Florida, Georgia, Kentucky, Louisiana, Maryland, Mississippi, North Carolina, Oklahoma, South Carolina, Tennessee, Texas, Virginia and West Virginia. For information, contact SREB, 592 10th St., NW, Atlanta, GA 30318, 404/875-9211, www.sreb.org.

- *The New England Regional Student Program* covers Connecticut, Maine, Massachusetts, New Hampshire, Rhode Island and Vermont. For information, contact the New England Board of Education, 45 Temple Place, Boston, MA 02111, 617/357-9620, www.nebhe.org.

- *Midwestern Higher Education Compact:* Illinois, Indiana, Iowa, Kansas, Michigan, Minnesota, Missouri, Nebraska, North Dakota, Ohio, South Dakota and Wisconsin. For information, contact MHEC, 1300 S. Second Street #130, Minneapolis, MN 55454, 612/626-8288, www.mhec.org.

Reciprocal Arrangements III

WICHE offers a second program in which undergrads pay reduced tuition at any of 135 participating schools in the region. The reduced rate equals resident tuition plus 50%; a large savings over non-resident rates. Graduate and professional students may study outside their home state and pay in-state tuition in certain fields of study, www.wiche.edu.

Private School Grant Programs

Nearly thirty-percent of all need-based state grant aid goes to students attending in-state private institutions.

Brain Drain, Brain Gain

Nebraska officials once said they were making an all-out effort to keep bright students from leaving the state for more "cosmopolitan and less topographically-challenged places." They would offer merit awards to students who promise to earn degrees in high-demand fields, and remain Cornhuskers for at least three years after graduation.

Arkansas displays a large "First Choice Arkansas" tagline on its higher education web site and awards Governor's Distinguished Scholarships worth $10,000 each to its best students who stay in-state.

Maine wants to give tax credits of up to $5,000 per year for ten years to students who stay and work in state. The money may be used to help repay student loans.

Kentucky First Scholarships would forgive one year of college tuition for every year that a student works in Kentucky after graduation.

Merit Money

Arkansas, Florida, Georgia, Idaho, Kentucky, Louisiana, Michigan, Mississippi, Missouri, Nevada, New Mexico, South Carolina, Tennessee, and West Virginia are all doing more to keep high-ability students in state. They've created very generous merit aid programs that ignore financial need, and sometimes let recipients choose between in-state public or private schools. When state budgets get tight, however, some policy makers rethink their largesse. Here's why: Most merit awards are tied to a percentage of college costs, so when states increase tuition (which is common during tough economic times), they also increase their budget for merit aid. To get program costs under control, some states are moving toward fixed awards that don't necessarily increase with tuition.

Discounts for Senior Citizens

Most of our states give tuition discounts to seniors. Some states waive tuition entirely. See Chapter 23 for more information.

Tuition Freezes

In response to the public outcry over years of double-digit tuition increases, many states are feeling pressured to freeze tuition, or at least limit increases to the rate of inflation, or gains in median state income. Illinois and Georgia take a different approach—these states want to freeze tuition for each incoming class for four years so students have some sense of what their total cost will be. These states also hope the freeze will encourage students to graduate on time since they would face hefty tuition increases if they linger for additional years.

Dual Enrollment

More than twenty states, including Minnesota, Washington, Georgia, Tennessee, Utah and Missouri, allow high school students to take classes at local community colleges and count them toward high school graduation. State officials say this lets high school juniors and seniors get a more rigorous education and earn a year or two of college credit at the same time.

More Money for Part-timers

Many states are providing more money to part-time students, to improve the educational opportunities for working adults and single parents, for example the HEAPS (Higher Education Adult Part-time Student) grant program in West Virginia and the "Parents as Scholars" program in Texas.

Graduation "Efficiency"

Some states are cracking down on the number of credits you may take at subsidized, in-state rates. Why? Too many students are taking too many extra courses and spending too many years in college. These states are fed up, and think they've found ways to get students through college more quickly, thereby solving their classroom capacity problems and saving everyone a bit of money.

Some states impose a four-year limit on state-aid. Pennsylvania gives grants worth $700 per graduating student directly to colleges that graduate at least 40% of their in-state students within four years. Florida would require students to pay out-of-state tuition on excess credits. And Texas hopes to discourage dawdling by giving $1,000 rebates to students at public universities who take no more than 3 credits in excess of the number required for graduation.

Lottery-Financed Scholarships

With other resources drying up, an increasing number of states are betting on lotteries to finance (mostly) merit-based programs, for example Florida, Georgia, Kentucky, Nebraska, Oregon, South Carolina, and West Virginia. Here are some standouts:

Georgia: *Helping Outstanding Pupils Educationally* (HOPE) was the first large-scale, state-based merit award program. Through HOPE, every Georgia high school graduate can receive free tuition at one of Georgia's public universities, or up to $3,500 for a private, in-state school. To qualify, college-bound students must maintain a 3.0 GPA in their high school courses; Vo-tech students must earn a 3.2 GPA. Students must hold a 3.0 GPA while in college to continue receiving money. HOPE is funded by the Lottery for Education. Call 800/546-HOPE, www.gacollege411.org.

New Mexico's Lottery Success Program will pay tuition (beginning in the second semester) for students who earn at least a 2.5 GPA during their first semester at an in-state public university.

Indiana wants to use money from the Hoosier Lottery to fund $6,000 scholarships for bright students from families with incomes under $60,000.

Tennessee will give $4,000 awards to applicants with at least a 3.0 GPA (or a 21 on the ACT).

Tobacco Tax

South Dakota is using an increased tax on tobacco products to finance an "education enhancement fund" which will provide college scholarships.

Tennessee wants to triple the cigarette tax and use the proceeds to cap tuition increases and boost its top merit-based award to $4,000.

Nevada, South Dakota and **Michigan** are using a multi-billion dollar legal settlement with tobacco companies to finance merit-based awards.

Community College Partnerships

Many states encourage partnerships between two- and four-year colleges to help make the transition seamless. Sometimes students are promised admission to the four-year school. Sometimes they are guaranteed that their course credits will transfer. Sometimes they're offered additional aid opportunities. And sometimes they just get guidance on course selection.

Community Service Programs

States were way ahead of the community service bandwagon. All fifty have ties to AmeriCorps and some also fund their own projects. To find your State Commission on National Service and receive a list of funded programs, contact AmeriCorps, 202/606-5000, www.cns.gov.

Finish What You Start

Nationally, around 20 million people in the work force have earned some college credits, but no degree. Several states are planning to offer financial incentives to woo those students back to school, for example, by offering awards of $500-$2,500. Part-time students are sometimes eligible. In Kentucky it's called "Project Graduate;" in Ohio, it's "Complete to Compete;" in New Mexico, it's the "Graduation Project;" and in Philadelphia, it's "Graduate! Philadelphia." (Yes, we know Philadelphia is not a state.)

State Standouts

There's lots of action on the state level—some of which will result in important new programs (and some which will fizzle).

California: Cal Grants promise needy-state residents free tuition at in-state public universities, or an equivalent amount of money for use at in-state private universities. To qualify, students must meet certain income criteria; for example, in 2008/2009, a family of four must have had an income under $76,400 and assets of less than $59,100. For some Cal Grant awards, students must also have a minimum high school GPA of 3.0.

Arkansas Academic Challenge Scholarships, **Indiana** 21st Century Scholars and **Oklahoma**'s Promise. They all have similar themes: States give scholarships or pay in-state tuition for low-income students who make certain commitments, for example, maintain a minimum GPA in college prep courses and pledge not to use drugs, or engage in criminal activities. The theory behind this performance-based tuition waiver is that some students drop out because they perceive high school as a dead end. But, if you promise them a college education (assuming they stay out of trouble and meet admission standards), you'll see a huge increase in achievement.

District of Columbia: DC residents have little to choose from in the way of "in-state" public universities. To compensate, they may now receive up to $10,000/year (with a $50,000 lifetime cap) to cover the difference between in- and out-of-state tuition rates at any public university in the country. Alternatively, DC residents may receive annual grants of $2,500 (with a $12,500 lifetime cap) to help pay tuition at private colleges in DC, Virginia or Maryland, or historically-black colleges nationwide. Contact the DC-TAG Program, 202/727-2824, www.tuitiongrant.washingtondc.gov.

Kentucky: *Kentucky Educational Excellence Scholarships* (KEES) allow high school students to earn college scholarships based on their year-end GPA. Annual awards range from $125 to $500 with $125 going to those with GPAs of 2.5 and $500 to those with a perfect 4.0. Students can also earn bonus awards for good ACTs—$36 for a "15" up to $500 for a "28."

Louisiana: *START Smart* (Student Tuition Assistance and Revenue Trust) lets participants save at their own pace. The money is managed by the State Treasurer and invested in Vanguard funds; the state adds an annual incentive ranging from 2% to 14% of the amount deposited during the calendar year. For depositors with AGIs under $30,000, that match would be at 14%. For those with AGIs over $100,000, that match would be at 2%. Families may deduct up to $4,800 in deposits from their Louisiana state income tax.

Ohio: *The Ohio GI Promise* will make all veterans "honorary Ohioans" and allow them to attend Ohio schools at in-state tuition rates. This means their benefits under the new, Post 9/11-GI Bill (see Chapter 13) should cover the full cost of their education. Of course, Ohio also hopes they'll stick around after graduation, and will link them up with mentors to help them find jobs and ease their transition to civilian life.

Texas: *Good Neighbor Scholarships* for students residing in the Western Hemisphere (countries other than Cuba or the US).

Texas: *B-On-Time* incentives would forgive student loans for Texans who graduate on time (from in-state schools), and maintain a 3.0 GPA.

Virginia: *Two-Year College Transfer Grant* of up to $2,000 per year (for up to three years) to state residents who have completed their associate degrees at a Virginia two-year public institution and are now enrolled in a Virginia four-year school (public or private).

Directory of State Higher Education Agencies

wdcrobcolp01.ed.gov/Programs/EROD/org_list.cfm

To see what your home state offers, go to the above web site and scroll down to "State Higher Education Agency" for links to your home state; or write to the following addresses. (No information for Nevada, sorry!)

Alabama
334-242-1998
AL Comm. on Higher Ed.
Box 302000
Montgomery, AL 36130

Alaska
800-441-2962
Comm. on Postsecondary Ed.
PO Box 110505
Juneau, AK 99811

Arizona
602-229-2500
Comm. for Postsecondary Ed.
2020 N. Central Avenue, #550
Phoenix, AZ 85004

Arkansas
501-371-2000
Dept. of Higher Education
114 E. Capitol St.
Little Rock, AR 72201

California
888-224-7628
Student Aid Commission
PO Box 419027
Rancho Cordova, CA 95741

Colorado
303-866-2723
Comm. on Higher Ed.
1380 Lawrence St. #1200
Denver, CO 80204

Connecticut
860-947-1800
Department of Higher Ed.
61 Woodland Street
Hartford, CT 06105

Delaware
302-577-3240
Higher Ed. Commission
820 N. French Street, 5th fl
Wilmington, DE 19801

District of Columbia
202-727-6436
Education Supt. Office
441 4th St NW #350N
Washington, DC 20001

Florida
850-410-5200
Student Fin. Assistance
1940 N. Monroe St., #70
Tallahassee, FL 32303

Georgia
770-724-9000
Student Finance Comm.
2082 E. Exchange Pl., #230
Tucker, GA 30084

Hawaii
808-956-8213
Postsecondary Ed Comm.
2444 Dole Street, Room 209
Honolulu, HI 96822

Idaho
208-334-2270
State Board of Education
PO Box 83720
Boise, ID 83720

Illinois
847-948-8500
Student Assistance Comm.
1755 Lake Cook Road
Deerfield, IL 60015

Indiana
317-232-2350
Student Assistance Comm.
150 West Market St., #500
Indianapolis, IN 46204

Iowa
515-725-3400
College Student Aid Comm.
200 10th St., 4th fl.
Des Moines, IA 50309

Kansas
785-296-3421
Board of Regents,
1000 SW Jackson St. #520
Topeka, KS 66612

Kentucky
502-696-7200
Higher Ed. Assistance Auth.
PO Box 798
Frankfort, KY 40602

Louisiana
225-922-1012
Office of Student Fin. Assist.
PO Box 91202
Baton Rouge, LA 70821

Maine
207-623-3263
Finance Authority of Maine
Box 949
Augusta, ME 04332

Maryland
410-260-4500
MD Higher Ed. Commission
839 Bestgate Rd. #400
Annapolis, MD 21401

Massachusetts
617-994-6950
Dept. of Higher Education
One Ashburton Place, #1401
Boston, MA 02108

Michigan
800-642-5626 x37054
Student Fin. Services Bureau
PO Box 30047
Lansing, MI 48909

Minnesota
651-259-3501
Office of Higher Ed.
1450 Energy Park Dr., #350
St. Paul, MN 55108

Mississippi
601-432-6647
Inst. of Higher Learning
3825 Ridgewood Road
Jackson, MS 39211-6453

Missouri
573-751-2361
Dept. of Higher Education
3515 Amazonas Drive
Jefferson City, MO 65109

Montana
406-444-6570
Comm. of Higher Education
46 Last Chance Gulch
Helena, MT 59620

Nebraska
402-471-2847
Postsecondary Ed. Comm.
PO Box 95005
Lincoln, NE 68509

New Hampshire
603-271-2555
Postsecondary Ed. Comm.
3 Barrell Court #300
Concord, NH 03301

New Jersey
609/588-3226
Student Assistance Authority
4 Quakerbridge Plaza, Bx 540
Trenton, NJ 08625

New Mexico
505-476-6500
Comm. on Higher Ed.
1068 Cerrillos Road
Santa Fe, NM 87505

New York
518-473-1574
Higher Ed. Services Comm.
99 Washington Ave.
Albany, NY 12255

North Carolina
919-549-8614
State Ed. Assistance Authority
PO Box 13663
Research Triangle , NC 27709

North Dakota
701-328-4114
Student Financial Asst. Prgm.
600 East Boulevard Ave. #215
Bismark, ND 58505

Ohio
614-466-7420
OH Board of Regents
PO Box 182452
Columbus, OH 43218

Oklahoma
405-225-9100
State Regents for Higher Ed
655 Research Pkwy. #200
Oklahoma City, OK 73104

Oregon
541-687-7400
Student Assistance Comm.
1500 Valley River Dr., #100
Eugene, OR 97401

Pennsylvania
717-787-5041
Office of Higher Ed
333 Market Street, 12th fl.
Harrisburg, PA 17126

Rhode Island
401-736-1100
Higher Ed. Authority
560 Jefferson Blvd., #100
Warwick, RI 02886

South Carolina
803-737-2260
Higher Ed. Commission.
1333 Main Street #200
Columbia, SC 29201

South Dakota
605-773-3455
Board of Regents
306 E Capitol Ave., #200
Pierre, SD 57501

Tennessee
615-741-3605
Higher Ed Commission
404 James Robertson Pkwy, #1900
Nashville, TN 37243

Texas
512-427-6101
Higher Ed. Coord. Board
Box 12788, Capitol Station
Austin, TX 78711

Utah
801-321-7103
State Board of Regents.
60 South 400 West
Salt Lake City, UT 84101

Vermont
802-655-9602
Student Assistance Corp.
10 East Allen Street
Winooski, VT 05404

Virginia
804-225-2600
Council of Higher Ed
101 North 14th St., 9th fl.
Richmond, VA 23219

Washington
360-753-7800
Higher Ed. Coord. Board
917 Lakeridge Way
Olympia, WA 98504

West Virginia
304-558-0699
Higher Ed. Policy Comm.
1018 Kanawha Blvd E, #700
Charleston, WV 25301

Wisconsin
608-267-2206
Higher Ed. Aids Board
131 W. Wilson Street #902
Madison, WI 53703

Wyoming
307-777-7763
Comm. College Commission
2020 Carey Ave., 8th fl.
Cheyenne, WY 82002

CHAPTER 12

■ ■

LETTING THE BOSS PAY FOR IT

OK. You are willing to pick up a little maturity along with your education. You are willing to invest some extra time into earning a baccalaureate. And you want to start your professional career without the staggering burden of student debt. What can you do? You can investigate two major alternative methods of financing an education: (1) Letting the boss pay for it; or (2) letting the military pay for it.

Chapters 12 and 13 cover both of these "employee" tuition plans—those found in corporate offices and those sponsored by the US Military.

Company Tuition Aid

Once upon a time you could go to work for a company that had a tuition reimbursement plan, take college courses on your own time, and let the employer foot the bill. Then the IRS decided this was too good a deal. It ruled that courses had to be job-related to qualify as a benefit. Courses not job-related, but paid for by the employer, had to be declared as taxable income. That ruling pulled the rug out from what had promised to become a major alternative program for young people. The reason: Jobs at the bottom are often so narrowly defined that few courses required for a degree could pass the "job-related test." Why would a shipping clerk need a course in American History?

Congress eventually brought back the exclusion for non job-related tuition benefits (Section 127 of the tax code), but limited the exclusion to $5,250 per year and restricted the benefit to undergraduate courses. Unfortunately, the rule was made subject to annual renewal, and was thus tied up in budgetary rigmarole until half-way through each academic year. Students, meanwhile, could do little other than keep their fingers crossed that the exclusion would be extended and applied retroactively.

Finally, in 2001, the exclusion was made permanent and extended to include graduate education. Of course the $5,250 limit hasn't increased in nearly 25 years, so the benefit doesn't go as far as it used to.

There's nothing in the law to prevent companies from paying tuition tabs over $5,250, it's just that employees will owe tax on the excess; all in all, a pretty sweet benefit.

Smart Workers Work Smarter

Of course, if your employer does reimburse you for tuition, he or she may do so with strings attached. For example, you may have to stay with your generous firm for a set number of years after you graduate, usually one year for each year you receive assistance. Or you might have to maintain a certain grade point average while in school, generally a "B." These requirements are only fair—after all, employers help employees with their education because it's good for the company, not just good for the employee.

Some companies have added loan repayment plans to their recruitment arsenal. UPS, for example, desperately needs part-timers (to fill all those night shifts) so it offers these employees up to $3,000 per year for tuition (to a max of $15,000), plus up to $2,000 per year in forgiveable loans (to a max of $8,000). UPS has also persuaded nearly 200 partner universities to defer charging students until the end of the semester when the students receive this "Earn and Learn" subsidy, www.upsearnandlearn.com.

Even the federal government is getting into the act, offering civilians (in select occupations, and in exchange for a three-year job commitment) up to $10,000 per calendar year in loan repayment to a maximum of $60,000.

While many corporations offer tuition assistance programs, it's surprising how few employees take advantage of this largesse. Intel, for example, spends $25 million each year on tuition reimbursement programs—but only about five percent of its employees participate.

Reimbursement for job-related courses (i.e., those for which you could have deducted the expenses from your taxes) continues to be deductible without limitations.

Cooperative Education

Co-op education combines formal studies with an off-campus job related to your major. The money you earn will range from $2,500 to $15,000 per year; in some cases, enough to cover all your college costs. In some schools, practically the entire student body participates in cooperative education. Examples: Northeastern University (MA) and GMI Engineering & Management Institute (MI).

There are three common methods for rotating between school and work:

- **The alternating method.** Under this method, you are a full-time student for a semester, then you work for a semester, with the cycle repeating itself until you graduate—usually in five years.

- **The parallel method.** Here you attend classes part time and work between 15 and 25 hours a week. You may be a student in the morning and a worker in the afternoon, or vice versa. This method, too, may require five years for degree completion.

- **Extended day method.** The student works full-time and attends school in the evening.

Recent surveys done by the National Commission for Cooperative Education and The Cooperative Education and Internship Association present some interesting (and encouraging) cooperative education statistics: Nearly 500 colleges participate in co-op, as do over 50,000 employers ranging from large corporations to small businesses, government agencies and non-profit organizations.

Employers like co-op, considering it, in the Wall Street Journal's words, "a source of realistic, work-oriented, future full-time employees." In fact, there are over 250,000 undergraduate placements each year (as well as 40,000 graduate student placements)—these students earn $1.3 billion annually. After graduation, over 60% of all co-op students accept permanent jobs with their co-op employers.

Cooperative Education Resources

1. *The Best of Co-op,* published by the National Commission for Coopera-tive Education. Read it online at www.co-op.edu, or write to the Commission at 360 Huntington Avenue, 384CP, Boston, MA 02115.

2. *NCCE Scholarship Program.* The National Commission for Cooperative Education also sponsors a $4.5 million scholarship program—$6,000 (renewable) merit awards to high school seniors and transfer students planning to participate in co-op education.

3. *Your Home State.* Most states have work-study or co-op programs. If your counselor doesn't have the address for your state's Co-op Educa-tion Center, get the information from your state agency (Chapter 11).

4. *The Cooperative Education and Internship Association* web site includes links to a variety of co-op resources, and a list of colleges that offer co-op, www.ceiainc.org.

5. *Your College.* Over 500 colleges have co-op programs. If the financial aid office doesn't have the information you need, try career services, or ask if there's a separate co-op office on campus.

6. *The Federal Government* also sponsors co-op, with Uncle himself serving as the employer. *Studentjobs.gov* (studentjobs.gov), has pulled together information on federal co-op, as well as government fellow-ships, grants, internships and ideas for resume building.

7. *Co-op Handbook.* Northeastern University's web site contains a terrific collection of co-op resources including an online co-op handbook, www.coop.neu.edu/students/handbook.html.

Internships

It can be hard to draw a clear line between cooperative education and internships. Here are two general distinctions:

- Co-op participants alternate between formal studies and work throughout their college career, while internships often last only one semester or one summer break.

- Co-op participants always get a paycheck; interns may or may not. The average wage for paid internships is $16 per hour, however, in many instances, the more "desirable" the internship, the less the pay. Tip: If you're spending your time making the office coffee, ask for a project that will bring you more professional experience (and contacts), or go to Starbucks, and earn a real paycheck.

Even if unpaid, the internship can still be of (future) value. In a recent survey by the National Association for Colleges and Employers, employers identified internship programs as an effective method for recruiting new college graduates for full-time positions—they offer full-time jobs to nearly two out of three of their interns, and over 31% of their new hires come directly from their own internship programs. For more information, visit the Association's web site, www.naceweb.org.

And what are the best ways to find internships?

- Attend career fairs
- Visit your on-campus career center
- Ask your professors about possible contacts

I'M GOING TO COLLEGE LEMONADE

$1,500

OR
BeST OFFer

CHAPTER 13

■ ■

PUTTING ON THE UNIFORM

Don't overlook the military! You can pick up tuition dollars before you enter the service, while in uniform and after being discharged. There are programs for active duty personnel and programs for Reservists. And there are programs for officers and programs for enlisted people.

Military tuition benefits are dispensed with no reference to financial need. But they are not free. At a minimum you'll have to get a haircut, salute superior officers and give a few years of your time. The U.S. Armed Forces have collaborated on a web site that answers your questions (oh-so-objectively), about whether the military is for you, myfuture.com.

Usually when there's a slow economy and decline in private-sector hiring, each service branch easily its meets recruiting goals. But the continuing conflicts in Iraq and Afghanistan (no matter what the state of the economy) is putting real stress on the all-volunteer system, especially the Army. Patriotic pride is no longer enough. Parents are clearly worried about war, and wary of having their sons and daughters enlist.

Pentagon brass is doing its part to help fill up the slots—pushing for better pay, bigger signing bonuses and re-enlistment bonuses, mortgage assistance and most recently, the Army's $20,000 "Quick Ship" bonus for signees willing to leave for basic training within 30 days. There are also increased tuition benefits (for new recruits and as a retention tool). Just don't look for mention of these education incentives in new ad campaigns. High-priced consultants say the promise of money-for-college belittles the value of military service and recommend a more heroic pitch that also reassures nervous parents about the character-building benefits of military service. (For example, "There's strong, and then there's Army-strong.")

Nevertheless, recruiters say that prospects ask more questions about education benefits than anything else. And no wonder. Tuition assistance is plentiful, but the array of benefits is very confusing, and ever-changing. This chapter covers programs to consider before you enter the service, while you're in the service, and after you leave the service.

For More Information

For more information on all-things-military, visit "Military.Com," www.military.com, an extensive career and education resource center from a privately-funded company targeting the military community.

Before Entering Service

Military Academies

Free tuition, room and board, and a military commission (and service requirement) at graduation. Not bad, however, the academies are extremely competitive. Good grades, athletic excellence and demonstrated leadership in extracurricular activities are in demand. So are superb health and solid SAT scores. You should have 600+ on the math portion and combined scores of 1200 or more. Contact the academies during your junior year of high school. Most appointments are made by U.S. Representatives and Senators. Tell your elected officials about your interest. Make sure they open a file on you in their offices. Keep feeding that file with your achievements. Also add recommendations from people who are deemed important by the elected officials.

- **Army:** Admissions Office, US Military Academy, 606 Thayer Road, West Point, NY 10996, 800/822-USMA, www.usma.edu.
- **Air Force:** Director of Cadet Admissions, US Air Force Academy, Colorado Springs, CO 80840, 800/443-9266, www.usafa.af.mil.
- **Navy:** Candidate Guidance, US Naval Academy, Leahy Hall, Annapolis, MD 21402, 800/638-9156, www.usna.edu.
- **Merchant Marines:** Admissions, US Merchant Marine Academy, 300 Steamboat Road, Kings Point, NY 11024, www.usmma.edu.
- **Coast Guard:** Admissions, US Coast Guard Academy, 15 Mohegan Avenue, New London, CT 06320, 800/883-USCG, www.cga.edu

ROTC Scholarships

The military has one-, two-, three- and four-year ROTC scholarships which pay up to full tuition. You also receive $300 to $500 per month in (tax-free) spending money. Furthermore, ROTC schools frequently offer additional incentives ranging from $1,000 'Leadership' awards to free room and board.

A combined 1100 on the Math/Verbal sections of the SAT (24 ACT) will enhance your chances for an ROTC scholarship. So will a varsity letter and membership in the National Honor Society. Nearly all scholarship winners are in the top 25% of their HS class; most are class officers and captains of varsity athletic teams. About 70% of the awards go to students planning to major in science or technology fields like math, physics or engineering.

Application should be made by December 1 of your senior year (the Army has an early application option with a July 15 deadline). There might be an interview. Before the interview, brush up on current events. Also, be ready to give your reasons for seeking a military career. An interest in the physical sciences, engineering or nursing will help.

If you're already a college freshman or sophomore, and your school offers ROTC, you can still apply for a two- or three-year award, no matter what your major.

ROTC is not offered at all colleges. The services will provide you with a list. You may use your award at any college on that list assuming you are able to secure admission (something you must do on your own).

For more information on general recruiting and ROTC (including extra sweeteners):

- **Army,** 800/USA-ROTC, www.goarmy.com/rotc
- **Air Force,** 800/423-USAF, www.afrotc.com
- **Navy,** 800/USA-NAVY, www.navy.com/careers/nrotc
- **Marines,** 800/MARINES, www.usmc.mil

The Regular ROTC Program

This is not a scholarship. Students join the program in their freshman year, at colleges that offer ROTC. For two years they march and salute for free. In their junior and senior years, they do get paid: from $450 to $500 per month.

ROTC-Coop Education Combination

The Army reserves co-op positions for some ROTC cadets in nearby Army installations. These positions, which provide added earnings, may also lead to federal employment after you have served on active duty.

One-Shot Programs

Sometimes financial aid is used to recruit people with specific skills. For example, in past years the Air Force has a "College Senior Engineer Program" for students in electrical, nuclear, astronautical and aeronautical engineering while the Navy's "Baccalaureate Degree Completion Program" paid a bonus to qualified technical majors.

Military Medical Programs

See Chapter 20

In-Service Educational Benefits

Commissioned Officer

Each year, the services select hundreds of officers to attend grad schools. The chosen officers receive full pay and allowances and have all their educational expenses met while pursuing their master's degree or doctorate.

Off-Duty Programs

All services encourage off-duty course work, with the services paying 100% of tuition costs up to $250 per credit hour and a maximum of $4,500 per year. Through arrangements with accrediting institutions, such off-duty courses can be accumulated to gain credit for associate, baccalaureate or even master's degrees. If you are extremely ambitious, and want to take more than 18 credits per year, you can usually apply for a waiver to exceed the $4,500 reimbursement limit.

1. *Concurrent Admissions Program (ConAP).* More than 1,800 participating colleges. For more information, contact Servicemembers Opportunity Colleges, 1307 New York Ave., NW, 5th floor, Washington DC 20005, 800/368-5622, www.soc.aascu.org/ConAP.

2. *eArmyU.* Traditional classrooms aren't always flexible enough to incorporate erratic military schedules. In response, the Army is promoting more portable online learning, www.eArmyU.com.

3. *DANTES.* The Defense Activity for Non-Traditional Education Support (DANTES) Distance Learning Program is primarily for military personnel whose schedules or duty locations do not permit traditional classroom attendance. The DANTES web site contains a great deal of information on distance learning, as well as a course catalogue of nationally-accredited distance learning degree programs, www.dantes.doded.mil.

Reserve Duty Programs

Through the National Guard and Army Reserves, you can receive up to $11,412 in education benefits under the Montgomery GI Bill. As an alternative, reservists who have been called to active duty since 9/11 may qualify for even more money under the Reserve Education Assistance Program (REAP)—up to $38,016 (the amount varies depending on the length of activation). Reservists may receive an additional amount through the "Kicker" (up to $12,600 for enlistment in certain specialties) as well as cash bonuses of up to $8,000 for completing advanced training. 800/USA-ARMY, www.goarmyreserve.com.

Select Army, Air Force and Coast Guard Reservists may also receive up to $250 per credit hour in tuition assistance to a max of $4,500 per year.

Loan Repayment Options

The Navy, National Guard, Army and Army Reserves also offer repayment on federal student loans. In the Army Reserve and National Guard, you may have up to $10,000 forgiven at the rate of 15% or $1,500 per year, whichever is greater. As an incentive for enlistment in selected skills, the Army Reserves will double those amounts to $20,000 in total loans, forgiven at the rate of 15% or $3,000 per year, whichever is greater.

In the Navy and Regular Army you may have up to $65,000 forgiven at the rate of 33 1/3% or $1,500 per year, whichever is greater.

After Service Benefits

The Montgomery GI Bill (www.gibill.va.gov)

While on active duty, the soldier, sailor, or airman allocates $100 per month (to a maximum of $1,200) to an educational fund. At the end of a two-year enlistment, the Veteran's Administration contributes $37,428; at the end of a three- or four-year enlistment the VA contributes $46,356. After you leave the military, your money will be paid directly to you in monthly installments for each month you're enrolled in college.

For example, if you enlisted for three or four years and qualified for $47,556 ($46,356 + $1,200), you would receive $1,321 per month for 36 months to help you pay your educational costs. If you enlisted for less than three years, your monthly payment would be $1,073 per month. If your school year has nine months, this income stream should cover your full four years. *Students who contribute an additional $600 during active duty can receive an "Increased Benefit Option" of $5,400.*

For more information, and future rate increases, visit the official GI Bill Web Site, www.gibill.va.gov. Rates are adjusted each October.

For students who score well on the Armed Forces Qualification Text, the Army sweetens the pot with "kickers" for enlisting in critical "Military Occupation Specialties." This could bring your total fund to over $73,000 for a four-year enlistment. The Army calls this bonus "The Army College Fund." Call 800/USA-ARMY for more information. The Navy, Coast Guard and Marine Corps offer similar-sized bonus college funds.

Post-9/11 Veterans Educational Assistance Act of 2008 (www.gibill.va.gov)

Beginning August 1, 2009, there will be a new, "Post-9/11 GI Bill" for reservists, veterans and active-duty personnel who have served on active duty for at least 90 days since September 11, 2001. Benefits are payable for a total of 36 months, which translates to 4 years of college (assuming a 9-month academic year), and are available for up to 15 years after your last discharge or release from active duty. Unlike the Montgomery GI Bill, there are no enrollment fees. You will be eligible for three main types of benefits, based on your length of service (see chart on next page):

- Up to full tuition and fees, not to exceed the most expensive in-state public university. This money will be paid directly to your school.
- A monthly housing allowance for students who are *not* on active duty and who are attending college at least half time. The allowance equals the basic housing allowance paid to a military E-5 with dependents in the same zip code as your school. This money will be paid directly to you. (Distance learners do not qualify for this allowance.)
- Up to $1,000 per year for books and supplies for students who are *not* on active duty. This money will be paid directly to you.

Length of Service	% of Maximum Benefits
At least 36 months	Full benefits*
Between 30 and 36 months	90% of the maximum benefits
Between 24 and 36 months	80% of the maximum benefits
Between 18 and 24 months	70% of the maximum benefits
Between 12 and 18 months	60% of the maximum benefits
Between 6 and 12 months	50% of the maximum benefits
Between 3 and 6 months	40% of the maximum benefits

*You will also receive full benefits if you served at least 30 days and were then discharged due to a service-connected disability.

Yellow Ribbon Program

The "Yellow Ribbon GI Education Enhancement Program" might provide you with additional funds if you qualify for full GI Bill benefits, and you choose a school that exceeds the maximum "allowable" cost. Check with your school to see if it will be participating in this program.

Dependent Education Benefits

Details are still being worked out, but it looks like service members with at least six years of active duty (who agree to serve on active duty for at least four more years) will be able to transfer their Post 9/11 GI Bill tuition benefits (but not the housing allowance) to a spouse or dependent child.

Which GI Bill is Better?

Many people were troubled that the Montgomery GI Bill did not provide enough money to cover the cost of education today, and was causing veterans to limit their college choices to community colleges. So Congress increased the Montgomery GI Bill payout and created the Post-9/11 GI Bill. There is some debate as to whether this new, more generous bill will really change enrollment patterns, since veterans often cite convenience rather than cost as the primary reason for choosing a college. But you will have to evaluate your own situation to determine which plan is best for you.

For example, if you want to pursue an online degree, or attend school only part-time, you will not receive a housing allowance, so the Montgomery GI Bill might be your better choice. If you want to transfer your benefit to a college-age dependent (see above), or attend a pricier school, and live on campus, then opting for the Post-9/11 Bill will be your smarter move.

Benefits for Military Dependents

Most states have aid programs for Veterans and their dependents. See Chapter 11 and write to your state's Office of Veteran Affairs. In addition, here are some scholarship programs specifically for you:

All

ThanksUSA Scholarships. Undergraduate scholarships of $1,000 for the (dependent) children and spouses of active duty military personnel. By May 15. ThanksUSA Scholarship Program, Scholarship America, One Scholarship Way, Box 297, St. Peter, MN 56082, www.thanksusa.org.

Army

Army Emergency Relief. Scholarships for unmarried children of active duty, retired, or deceased soldiers. By March 1 to Army Emergency Relief, 200 Stovall Street, Alexandria, VA 22332, www.aerhq.org.

Air Force

Air Force Aid Society. Need-based grant program for dependent sons and daughters of active duty, retired or deceased Air Force; spouses of active duty members; and surviving spouses. Must attend college full-time. 3,250 grants of $2,000/year. By mid-March. Air Force Aid Society, Education Assistance, 241 18th Street, #202, Arlington, VA 22202, www.afas.org.

Navy/Marines

Dependent's Scholarship Program. More than 75 Navy-oriented organizations offer aid to dependent sons and daughters of Navy, Marine Corps, and Coast Guard members. Information from *Need A Lift? (see below)*

Benefits for the Families of Former Military

Nearly every military association sponsors student aid programs for the children of its members. For a comprehensive list, see *Need a Lift?* from The American Legion, free download at www.needalift.org. For example:

AMVETS Memorial Scholarship. Ten awards of $1,000/year based on need and academic achievement. Applicants must be AMVETS members, or the child or grandchild of an AMVET member and have exhausted all government financial aid. By April 15. Send SASE to AMVETS National Headquarters, attn. Scholarships, 4647 Forbes Blvd., Lanham, MD 20706, www.amvets.org.

Reserve Officers Association. Henry J. Reilly Memorial Scholarships for dependents of Association members; 35 for graduate students, 75 for undergrads. From February 1 to April 10. For additional information, send SASE to Scholarship Fund, ROA, One Constitution Ave., NE, Washington, DC 20002, www.roa.org.

Military Officers Association of America. Interest-free loan for undergraduate dependent children of active duty, reserve or retired military personnel (officer or enlisted). Up to $4,000/year, renewable for up to five years. Also, several grant programs ranging from $1,000 to $4,000. By March 1. Apply online, www.moaa.org.

CHAPTER 14

■■■■■■■■■■■■■■■■■■■■■■■

PRIVATE SOURCES WITH
FEW STRINGS

AXA Achievement Scholarship

AXA Achievement Scholarship (in association with *U.S. News & World Report*). Fifty-two (non-renewable) $2,000 - $25,000 scholarships to high school seniors, one from each state, the District of Columbia and Puerto Rico. For more information and an application, www.axa-achievement.com.

BrainStorm USA

National Scholarship Program, "Dare to Dream, Expect to Succeed." Scholarships awarded each quarter. 8800 Roswell Road, #200, Atlanta, GA 30350, 800/595-5561, www.brainstormusa.com

Coca-Cola Scholars Foundation, Inc.

250 merit-based scholarships per year (137,000 applicants): 50 awards are for $5,000/year, renewable for 4 years. 200 are for $2,500/year, renewable for 4 years. An additional 400 (non-renewable) $1,000-$2,000 scholarships per year for students attending 2-year institutions. By October 31. For more information, or to apply online, www.coca-colascholars.org, 800/306-COKE..

Elks National Foundation

Most Valuable Student Award. Nearly 500 awards, ranging from $1,000 to $15,000 per year. HS senior, Scholarship, leadership, and financial need. Application online or from local Elk Lodge, www.elks.org/enf.

Hattie M. Strong Foundation

Interest-free loans for final year of college of up to $5,000. Repayment based on monthly earnings after graduation. Applications available between 1 Jan. and 15 May. Hattie M. Strong Foundation, 1620 Eye St., NW, Suite 700, Washington, DC 20006, www.hmstrongfoundation.org.

Hitachi Foundation

The Yoshiyama Award recognizes outstanding community service and is accompanied by a gift of $5,000 disbursed over two years with no restrictions. Nominees need not be college-bound. By April 1 to Yoshiyama Award, 1215 17th Street, Washington, DC 20036, (202) 457-0588, www.hitachifoundation.org/yoshiyama.

Pickett & Hatcher Educational Fund, Inc.

Low interest loan to undergrads in fields of study *other than* law, medicine, or the ministry. Up to $22,000 total (over 4 years). Interest rate equals 2% while in school, 6% during repayment. No fees. Based on scholastic ability, character, financial need. Pickett & Hatcher Educational Fund, P.O. Box 8169, Columbus, GA 31908, www.pickettandhatcher.org.

Product-Sponsored Scholarship Contests

Keep your eyes open. Companies often put their contest notices in with the Sunday newspaper ads (alongside their product coupons).

Sallie Mae Unmet Need Scholarship Program

Scholarships range from $1,000 to $3,800 and may be used to meet the need of full-time undergraduate students whose aid packages fall short by $1,000 or more. To qualify, family income must be below $30,000. By May 31. For application, The Sallie Mae Fund, www.thesalliemaefund.org.

Target All-Around Scholarships

One $25,000 award; Over 600 $1,000 awards to high school seniors or college students (up to age 24) who are active community service volunteers. By 1 November. Applications available at Target stores, or online, www.target.com/community.

USA Today

Twenty awards worth $2,500 each. Leadership, academic achievement is important. USA Today, 1000 Wilson Blvd., 10th fl., Arlington, VA 22229, allstars.usatoday.com.

US Bank's Internet Scholarship Program

30 awards of $1,000 each (14,000 applicants). By Feb. 1. You can only apply online, www.usbank.com/studentloans.

Walmart

Thousands of awards, $1,000 each. Application from your local Walmart store, or www.walmartfoundation.org.

CHAPTER 15

■■■■■■■■■■■■■■■■■■■■■■■■

MONEY IN YOUR COMMUNITY

Most communities offer scholarship help to their young citizens. The grants vary in size from $100 to several thousand; they are usually circumscribed in their geographic coverage and you must learn about them yourself. There is no central registry. Read your local newspaper carefully, especially the page devoted to club and community affairs. Visit your Chamber of Commerce. It might keep track of local business and corporate scholarships. Also visit the American Legion Post. The legionnaires take a special interest in helping people with their education. And finally, ask your high school counselor! This chapter gives you some examples.

Your Community

Look for scholarship bulletins from civic associations, businesses, PTA chapters, social and professional clubs, fraternal organizations, patriotic and veterans organizations. Some communities do very well by their students. For example, Washington Metropolitan Scholars (www.wmscholars.org, part of the legacy of journalist Carl Rowan) awards scholarships each year in amounts ranging from $4,000 to $80,000 to some of the Washington DC area's brightest low-income (mostly African-American) students. In addition to private donors in your community, you should look toward larger local foundations. There are over 400 community funds nationwide which award in excess of $100 million to education projects annually.

Your High School

Many high schools have information clearinghouses that work in conjunction with the guidance office. Students (and parents) may attend college financing workshops; they receive help with filing aid applications; they have access to current financial aid literature, ALL FOR FREE! Some schools have even created foundations to provide "last dollar scholarships" for students with exceptional financial need. Examples: The Scholarship Fund of Alexandria (VA), I Know I Can, Columbus (OH).

"I Have A Dream"

Once upon a time, the very-wealthy Eugene Lang promised scholarships (and counseling) to an entire 6th grade class at his former school in East

Harlem. In 1986, he created the "I Have A Dream" foundation to help other people start similar projects. The Foundation now helps support projects in 16 states, serving 4,000 students. While many sponsors have had great success getting at-risk students through high school and into college, others have found that money alone isn't enough to compensate for missing parents, missing discipline, and missing expectations. They've also learned it takes many volunteers to keep Dreamers on track. Alas, students can't apply for this assistance; they can only hope someone will adopt their class (and at $500,000 to $1 million/class, plus a 12-15 year commitment) benefactors are hard to find), www.IHAD.org.

Corporate Generosity

Corporate America is jumping on the "I Have a Dream" bandwagon—for example, Pepsi's "The Pepsi Challenge" provided support and scholarships for "at-risk" students at selected schools across the country. Similarly, *The Washington Post* gives students at Eastern High School (Washington, DC) $500 for college for each semester they get all As and Bs. *Post* staffers serve as mentors and almost 30 colleges offer matching grants, www.washpost.com/community/education/ehsp.shtml.

Dollars for Scholars™

Dollars for Scholars is a national network of more than 1260 community-based, volunteer-operated scholarship foundations affiliated with *Scholarship America*. Last year, chapters awarded nearly $36 million to over 38,000 students. All funds are distributed by a local awards committee to students of the community. Ask your counselor if your community has a chapter, or check www.scholarshipamerica.org.

Community Service Scholarships

If you have demonstrated a solid commitment to serving your community, you may be able to turn your good deeds into college scholarship money. For more information on both of these programs, contact your guidance counselor, or your principal.

Comcast Leaders and Achievers

This award recognizes high school seniors for their community service, positive attitude and leadership qualities with $1,000 awards. Must be nominated by your high school principal, www.comcast.com.

Prudential Spirit of Community Awards

These $1,000 awards (plus an expense-paid trip to Washington, D.C.) go to two students per state who have demonstrated "exemplary, self-initiated community service." Also, 10 National Honorees receive an additional $5,000. Schools may nominate one honoree for every 1,500 students, so tell your counselor of your good work, www.prudential.com/spirit.

Finding the Perfect Project

If you are still looking for that perfect volunteer project, the Internet has two solid information clearinghouses, IdeaList (www.idealist.org) and ServeNet (www.servenet.org). If you'd prefer a concentrated 4-8 week summer program, try one of the following:

- Global Routes (www.globalroutes.org) or Global Works. (www.globalworksinc.com) for international hot spots in Africa, Asia and Latin America.

- Amigos de las Americas (www.amigoslink.org) for Latin American adventures.

- Where There Be Dragons (www.wheretherebedragons.com) for rugged Asian learning adventures—think Mongolia rather than Tokyo.

- The Student Conservation Association (www.theSCA.org) or Habitat for Humanity (www.habitat.org) for something stateside.

These international programs usually charge $2,000-$7,500 and combine the service experience with a little recreation and sight-seeing. Part of this fee might be tax-deductible.

Community Service Programs

The Corporation for National Service funds about $800,000 worth of opportunities through a variety of umbrella programs—AmeriCorps, National Service Trust, Learn and Serve America, Vista, Senior Corps, State Commission Grants and the National Civilian Community Corps. Positions are further distributed across 2,000 organizations nationwide (see Chapter 10), rewarding volunteers for their work on education, environmental and public safety projects.

While each community is free to run its own program, there are several common threads. In general, volunteers work in teams of 5-10 people from a wide variety of backgrounds (this racial, ethnic, and economic diversity is at the heart of most programs—everyone benefits from the experiences and perspectives of their fellow participants). In exchange for service, they receive a living allowance (ranging from $100 to $180 per week), and a bonus upon completion of their service commitment. Bonuses range up to $4,725 per year of full-time service to a maximum of $10,000. Some programs don't require you to use the bonus for education expenses; others give smaller bonuses to the non-college bound. In general, the higher the weekly stipend, the lower the year-end education bonus.

Here are some sample programs:

City Year

Founded in Boston in 1988, City Year now has over 1,000 corps members (aged 17 - 24) in sites across the country and South Africa. While City Year's primary focus is on improving the lives of children, corps members also renovate housing and beautify urban spaces. Workers earn a weekly stipend, health insurance, a cell phone service contract, and an education bonus at the end of 10-months. They also receive college and career counseling, meet regularly with community and business leaders, and get the chance to earn their GEDs (if they have not yet graduated from high school). Contact: City Year, 287 Columbus Avenue, Boston, MA 02116, 617/927-2500, www.cityyear.org.

Public Allies

Ten-month program designed and run by young people for young people who want to help solve some of our nation's most pressing social problems. Currently, more than 200 "Allies" between the ages of 18 and 30 receive a stipend ($1,300 to $1,800 per month, plus health insurance and $4,725 education bonus) while working on projects in public safety, education, human needs and the environment. Highly competitive. Public Allies, 611 N. Broadway., #415, Milwaukee, WI 53202, www.publicallies.org.

Teach For America

Recent college grads spend two years teaching in under-resourced urban and rural public schools nationwide earning $25,000 to $44,000 per year, plus up to $6,000 for transitional expenses and a $4,725 education bonus. Very competitive with 18,000 applicants for 2,900 new teaching spots. Late October and early February deadlines. 315 W. 36th St., New York, NY 10018, 800-832-1230, www.teachforamerica.org.

YouthBuild USA

Rehab abandoned housing, or build new housing for homeless, disabled and low-income individuals. Contact: YouthBuild USA, 58 Day Street, Sommerville, MA 02144, www.youthbuild.org.

Resources

1. *Corporation for National Service.* To learn more about funded community service programs in your state, search at www.nationalservice.gov.

2. *National Association of Service and Conservation Corps.* More than 110 youth corps programs operate in 41 states and the District of Columbia. Most operate year-round, and allow participants to improve life-skills (budgeting, parenting, personal health) earn GEDs, and prepare for future employment, www.nascc.org.

3. *Americorps Alums.* If you aren't sure if a year of public service is for you, ask an AmeriCorps alum, www.americorpsalums.org. Find out whether climbing corporate ladders might be easier after a few years of climbing rickety wooden ones, with a bucket of paint in your hand.

4. *Idealist on Campus* educates students about community service, www.idealist.org.

CHAPTER 16

■■■■■■■■■■■■■■■■■■■■■■■

ARE YOUR PARENTS ELIGIBLE?

You may be eligible for considerable financial assistance courtesy of your parents' employers or membership affiliations. Locating these opportunities requires a systematic approach and considerable parental cooperation. This chapter reviews some questions to ask, and provides samples of the kind of information you will uncover. Remember, these are only a few of the many opportunities.

Where Do Your Parents Work?

Parents should ask their company's benefits manager about education-related employee perks—loans, scholarships and savings plans. More and more organizations are using education perks to build goodwill and foster employee loyalty.

Loans

A growing number of large companies make it easier for employee children to receive low cost loans. The companies put up a reserve against loan defaults, then hire outside firms to administer the program and find banks to act as lenders. To find out if your company has such a plan, ask the employee benefits coordinator.

Scholarships

Many companies sponsor scholarships for employee children as part of their fringe benefit programs. Unfortunately, these scholarships count as taxable income unless they are awarded selectively (to less than ten percent of eligible students) and continue, even if the employee leaves the job.

Merit scholarships. Approximately 2,600 renewable, need-based awards (ranging from $500 to $4,000) sponsored by over 300 corporations for employee children who are Merit Program Finalists, www.nationalmerit.org (Chapter 18).

General scholarships for employee children. Most awards range from $1,000 to $2,500. Some companies manage their own programs; others partner with an outside organization. For example, Scholarship America manages scholarship programs for over 1,100 companies, distributing over 76,000 scholarships each year worth over $171 million, www.scholarshipamerica.org.

Collegiate-based Scholarships. Many colleges offer scholarship money to children of ministers and other clergy (also, to children of alumni, and to children of staff and faculty from colleges with which they have reciprocal arrangements).

Savings Plans

Ask your company's employee benefits coordinator about any special savings programs. More and more employers support and encourage their employees' efforts to save for college. Here are some examples:

Contributory Accounts. These work much like retirement accounts with companies matching their employee's contributions.

Educational Savings Plans. Using payroll deductions, employees stash money into a company-managed educational fund. These may be matched, or not, depending on the generosity of the employer.

Free Advice

Some companies don't provide you any extra money, but they will include free or discounted college advice as part of your benefits package. And sometimes good advice is worth more than a $500 employer match.

University Employee

The Tuition Exchange is a reciprocal scholarship program for dependents of faculty and staff employed at over 585 participating institutions. For school list, and additional information, contact The Tuition Exchange, 1743 Connecticut Ave., NW, Washington DC 20009, 202/518-0135, www.tuitionexchange.org.

Military Service

If either of your parents served in the US Armed Forces, get a copy of *Need A Lift?* $3.95 from The American Legion, Attn: Emblem Sales, PO Box 1050, Indianapolis, IN 46206, 888-453-4466, or, print for free at www.needalift.org. Also re-read Chapter 13.

Federal Employees

The Federal Employee Education and Assistance Fund awards 400+ merit-based scholarships ranging from $500 to $7,500 to civilian federal employees and postal workers and their dependent family members. Send SASE by late March to FEEA Fund Scholarship Award, 8441 W. Bowles Ave., #200, Littleton, CO 80123, or online at www.feea.org.

Public Educators

The Horace Mann Scholarship Program awards over 35 scholarships each year in amounts ranging from $500 to $5,000 to public educators' children. Must have at least a "B" average. Apply by mid-Feb. Online applications are available in early September, www.horacemann.com.

September 11 Funds

Many organizations have set up funds to help families that were directly affected by the September 11, 2001 attacks on America. For example, Scholarship America is administering the Families of Freedom Fund which will award a total of $100 million in post-secondary assistance through the year 2030, www.FamiliesOfFreedom.org.

Are Your Parents Members of...

A Trade Group or Association?

Employees of member firms may be eligible. Examples: *National Continental Association of Resolute Employers*; *National Office Products Association*; *National Association of Tobacco Distributors*. Addresses in Gale's *Encyclopedia of Associations.*

You might also search the Web. Through its "Gateway to Associations," The American Society of Association Executives (asaecenter.org/Directories/AssociationSearch.cfm) represents about 10,000 different associations.

A Patriotic/Civic/Fraternal Association?

Among many organizations making awards to members and members' children: *Knights of Columbus; Elks Club; United Daughters of the Confederacy*; Even the *Society for the Preservation of Barber Shop Quartets* has sixteen scholarships.

Again, you'll find addresses in Gale's *Encyclopedia of Associations,* or at asaecenter.org/Directories/AssociationSearch.cfm.

A Union?

Unions sponsor over $4 million in scholarships. To link to your union's national page, go to the AFL-CIO Web site, www.aflcio.org/aboutus/unions.

Examples: AFSCME, American Federation of Teachers, Fire Fighters, Airline Pilots, Bricklayers, Teamsters, Letter Carriers, Postal Workers, Nurses, Machinists, Mine Workers, etc.

Of course, with over 38,000 local unions in the United States, it can take some digging. Don't limit yourself to the AFL-CIO's main links, be sure to contact your local union as well.

Also, check the Union Plus Scholarship Program. It is for union members and their dependent children. Awards range form $500 to $4,000, www.unionplus.org/benefits.

CHAPTER 17

■ ■

MONEY FROM YOUR
AFFILIATIONS

Your background, employment record, religion, and nationality as well as your membership in clubs and associations may be the key to financial opportunity. Here, as in the previous chapter, you will have to develop a systematic search strategy.

The Affiliation Matrix

The questions below will help you build your own affiliation matrix:

Question. Could any of my past jobs lead to a financial aid award? (Rule out baby-sitting for grouchy Mrs. Grumpelstein).

Answer. Check with the personnel office of your present or former employers.

Question. What about my future career ? Any hope for a scholarship if I become an engineer?

Answer. See Chapters 20 and 21 for some ideas. Also, search the Web (starting at the American Society of Association Executives site, asaecenter.org/Directories/AssociationSearch.cfm) and Gale's *Encyclopedia of Associations* (in the reference room of your public library) for addresses of professional associations that match your interests.

Question. How about my clubs?

Answer. Check with chapter/club president or faculty adviser.

Question. What about my religious affiliation? Does my denomination sponsor aid awards?

Answer. See your minister, priest, or rabbi or write to the national organizations sponsored by the denomination. Search the Web or Gale's *Encyclopedia of Associations*.

Question. How about my ancestry or my nationality?

Answer. Write to the organizations serving your ancestry or your nationality. Search the Web or Gale's *Encyclopedia of Associations*.

What will you find? You can strike pay dirt or you can strike out. But even if you find nothing, there is a reward. You will develop good research skills and learn to use your computer for something other than e-mail, chatrooms and games (even better, you become reacquainted with the library which had greatly missed your patronage).

Examples: Jobs You Have Held

Caddie

Evans Scholars Foundation. Golf caddies receive one-year, renewable full-tuition scholarships. Students must be of outstanding personal character, require financial assistance, have at least a "B" in their college-prep classes and have caddied regularly at a WEA-sponsored club for at least 2 years. By September 30. Scholarship Committee, Western Golf Association/ Evans Scholars Foundation, 1 Briar Road, Golf, IL 60029, 847/724-4600, www.evansscholarsfoundation.com.

Fast Food Worker

McDonalds and Burger King both have demonstrated serious commitments to higher education. For example, McDonalds provides scholarships worth $1000 - $5000.

Newspaper Carrier

Thomas Ewing Education Grants for former *Washington Post* carriers; 33 awards ranging from $1000-$2000. Other papers have similar awards.

Examples: Clubs

Boy Scouts

The National Eagle Scout Association lists a variety of scholarships available to Eagle Scouts. The awards are worth $1,000 to $12,000 per year; www.nesa.org to download an application. By Jan. 31. For programs for other scouts and explorers, send SASE to Boy Scouts of America, 1325 Walnut Hill Ln., Irving, TX 75015, www.scouting.org.

Girl Scouts

Girl Scout Scholarships. For a list of scholarships for Girl Scouts, send a SASE to Membership and Programs, Girls Scouts of the USA, 420 Fifth Avenue, New York, NY 10018. Or view online, www.girlscouts.org/ program/gs_central/scholarships.

Boys & Girls Club

Youth of the Year Competition. Five $10,000 awards for regional winners with an additional $15,000 for the national winner. For more information, contact your local Boys & Girls Club, www.bgca.org.

DECA: An Association of Marketing Students
Must be member of high school DECA chapter, have financial need and an interest in marketing or distribution. Information from chapter advisor or www.deca.org.

4-H Clubs & Future Homemakers of America (FHA)
Scholarships for current or former 4-H members who have won state honors. 250 awards ranging from $750 to $1,500. Contact your State 4-H leader or county 4-H agent, www.4husa.org.

Examples: Ancestry and Nationality

National Society Daughters of the American Revolution
Various scholarships programs for children of DAR members. By Feb. 15. SASE for an application packet from Office of the Committees, NSDAR, 1776 D Street, NW, Washington DC 20006, www.dar.org.

Descendants of Signers of the Declaration of Independence
Must be able to prove direct lineal descent to a signer of the Declaration of Independence and be a member of the Descendants of the Signers. Requests not naming an ancestor signer will not receive a reply. Annual grants average $1,500. By Jan. 15, www.dsdi1776.com.

Italian
UNICO National, 271 US Highway 46W, #A108, Fairfield, NJ 07004. $1,500 each year for four years. Applicant must reside in community with UNICO chapter. By April 15, www.unico.org.

Japanese
Japanese American Citizens League, 1765 Sutter Street, San Francisco, CA 94115. Entering freshmen, undergraduate, graduate. 30 awards averaging $2,000 per year. Special awards for Performing arts, Creative arts, Law. For more information, send SASE. Apply by March 1, www.jacl.org.

Polish
Grants Office, The Kosciuszko Foundation, 15 East 65th Street, New York, NY 10021-6595. Polish Studies, music, voice, and others. Mainly specialized, graduate and postgrad study awards. Domestic deadline is Jan. 15. Exchange program deadline is Nov. 15. Summer Session in Poland deadline is April 15, www.kosciuszkofoundation.org.

Membership Organizations
Chinese-American Foundation, Danish Brotherhood of America, Lithuanian Alliance, Polish Falcons, Daughters of Penelope, Order of AHEPA, Sons of Norway, Sons of Poland, many others. Addresses of all these

organizations may be found in Gale's *Encyclopedia of Associations*. An increasing number may also be found on the Infobahn. Get started using a good search engine, or try the American Society of Association Executives site, asaecenter.org/Directories/AssociationSearch.cfm).

Examples: Denomination

Catholic

Knights of Columbus, Pro Deo and Pro Patria scholarships. 62 awards of $1,500 based on academic excellence. Applicant or applicant's father must be member of the Columbian Squires or Knights of Columbus. Must be used at a Catholic college. By March 1. Sponsors other scholarships, as well. Director of Scholarship Aid, Knights of Columbus, 1 Columbus Plaza, Box 1670, New Haven, CT 06507, 203-752-4000, www.kofc.org.

Christian Scientist

Grants as well as low-interest loan program, up to $6,000/year. Repayment starts six months after graduation. Loans are interest-free to Christian Scientist nurses if they achieve Journal listing. By August 1. The Albert Baker Fund, 777 Campus Commons Road, #165, Sacramento, CA 95825, abf@albertbakerfund.org, www.albertbakerfund.org/funding.htm.

Jewish

Up to $10,000/year for 2 years of graduate work leading to a career in Jewish Community Center work. Involves a 3 year (post-graduation) work commitment in any North America center. By Feb. 1. Write Scholarship Coordinator, JCC Association, 520 8th Avenue, New York, NY 10018, www.jcca.org.

Lutheran

The Aid Association for Lutherans (AAL), and the Lutheran Brotherhood have merged their operations, resulting in Thrivent Financial for Lutherans. For current information visit www.thrivent.com or call 800/THRIVENT.

Presbyterian

$1 million awarded annually to undergraduate and graduate members of the Presbyterian Church. Grants as well as low-interest loans and special minority awards. Financial Aid for Studies, Presbyterian Church in the USA, 100 Witherspoon St., Louisville, KY 40202, www.pcusa.org/financialaid.

United Methodist

Loans and scholarships for US citizens who have been active, full members of the United Methodist Church for at least one year prior to submitting application. More information from your church, www.umc.org.

CHAPTER 18

■■■■■■■■■■■■■■■■■■■■■

MONEY FOR BRAINS
AND TALENT

Standardized tests are now optional at many colleges, including some of the country's top schools, like Wake Forest, Bates, Middlebury and Holy Cross. Nevertheless, the SAT remains a national industry. The money spent designing tests, administering tests, scoring tests, taking tests, teaching test skills, coaching test takers, disseminating test results, selling the names and scores of test takers to eager college recruiters, interpreting scores, analyzing scores, publicizing scores, and writing about the test, pro and con, places the SAT somewhat behind the automobile industry but far ahead of the horseradish crop as a contributor to our gross national product. Each year, the nationwide panic among little Fermat wanabees (and their parents), causes test prep enrollments and our country's GNP to soar!

Unfortunately, this testmania has no rational underpinnings. Many argue that the SAT is not an intelligence measure. It is not an aptitude measure. It is not a predictor of academic success. And getting high scores isn't always important for gaining college admission. It's only verifiable characteristics are: (1) test scores correspond quite closely to family income—the higher the income, the higher the scores; and (2) it thrives on criticism. The more it is attacked and exposed, the more it gains in universality and acceptance.

Nearly as many students now take the lower-profile ACT. And while this test has generally been viewed as fairer and more straightforward, studies show that disparate scores point to similar gender, race and income biases.

SATs: Now and Forever?

So why does the SAT (and ACT) survive? Simple. Rampant grade inflation means 40% of all college-bound students have "A" averages, so admission officers (and award-givers) say they need other criteria to help them sort out the most "meritorious." Furthermore, the impersonal nature of standardized tests makes them an easy-to-use crutch when rendering difficult (and unpopular) decisions concerning admission and merit aid.

But don't let this outburst scare you away. High test scores have a direct impact on your family budget. They can cost you money or they can make money for you.

High Test Scores Can Cost You Money...

Suppose you live in a school district which emphasizes test teaching. That emphasis will raise scores. And higher scores cause property values to soar because parents from everywhere now want to move to your district so the smarts rub off on junior. Your $120,000 home with a swampy basement, shaky foundation, and indigenous population of overweight termites is suddenly worth $220,000, a nice increase that could add $5,000-$6,000 to your family contribution. Frankly, we think enterprising real estate firms should underwrite SAT prep courses. It could be their smartest investment.

...Or Make You Money

Now that we have learned how SATs can cost you money, let's see how they can make you money. Here is what good scores can do:

1. Qualify you for a National Merit Scholarship.

2. Push you over the eligibility cutoff for increasingly-plentiful collegiate academic scholarships—the higher your score, the greater your award.

3. Give you bargaining power when negotiating the content of an aid package (including need-based aid). Your good scores make you more valuable to the school because they help raise the average for the entire entering class.

The hard way to raise SAT scores is to find an error in the test and appeal it. Although recently two students requested that their exams be re-scored by hand leading to a wave of College Board mea-culpas, a class-action suit, and a $3 million settlement—widespread scanning problems had caused nearly 4,500 SATs to be under-scored, some by as many as 450 points.

An easier way is to take a good SAT prep course—but take it for the practical reasons listed above and not for any mythological reasons like, "test prep makes you smarter." If an $800 investment in a SAT prep course yields a $5,000 no-need scholarship, renewable for four years, you have done far better with your money than the shrewdest Wall Street stockbroker.

Average SATs are 502 (Verbal/Critical Reading) and 515 (Math). Average ACTs are 21.1 (out of 36). The most lucrative awards usually go to students with SAT scores over 1100, or ACTs over 23. The College Board has also released statistics on the new writing section of the exam; the average score is 494, with girls scoring 13 points higher than boys.

The New, New SAT

A few years ago, the College Board developed a completely revised SAT format in an effort to better measure student achievement rather than abstract reasoning skills. Students no longer have to suffer with Column A < = > Column B Quantitative Comparisons or ridiculous : relationship ::

Analogy : Questions. But they do have to answer multiple-choice grammar questions, write an original essay, and be comfortable with a slightly-higher level of mathematical concepts, for example absolute value and radical equations (as well as other Algebra II-level teachings). The top combined score has increased from 1600 to 2400.

With some high school curriculums skewed to teach to the test, one hopes that these changes will encourage a greater emphasis on writing skills and higher-level math. But critics, and cynics, worry that the new test will do little more than reward (thus encourage) bland, formulaic writing, and that test prep companies will emerge as the biggest beneficiaries, with wealthier students gaining an even greater edge.

And now, studies are showing that this new (longer, more expensive) exam is no better than the old one at predicting college success (as measured by first-year college grades), although the writing portion does a little bit better than the math and verbal sections.

The ACT has also added a writing test, however, this portion of the exam is optional. Some colleges will ask students to take it; other colleges might decide it's not necessary or prefer to administer their own.

SAT Prep Courses

The College Board claims the elimination of gimmicky questions like Quantitative Comparisons and Verbal Analogies makes this new format less coachable. But it will take a few more years before there is enough data to judge any differences in student performance. In the meantime, few people dispute that SAT coaching can improve your scores (if only because they force you to practice, practice, practice). Students who already have a strong vocabulary, who read with perception and think logically, will benefit from taking sample tests. Students who are a little unsteady in these areas, will benefit from learning good SAT test-taking skills. And, beginning with the Class of 2010, students may choose which of their SAT scores to submit. In other words, schools will now see only your best effort, not your shaky first effort.

Two national organizations are Kaplan (www.Kaptest.com, 800/KAP-TEST) and the Princeton Review (www.princetonreview.com, 800/2REVIEW). Their "teaching" styles are very different and they have no great love for each other, but they both have great track records for raising scores. Call the above numbers for the nearest test center.

Currently, most students taking test prep courses come from wealthier school districts (and families), thus furthering the correlation between high scores and high income. Fortunately, cost should not be a barrier to solid coaching, and you have no excuse not to work on pumping up your scores:

1. Both Kaplan and Princeton Review have free online help as well as reduced-cost programs and scholarships for low-income students.

2. Many high schools feel pressured to produce students who score well on tests and now sponsor their own (free) test prep classes.

3. Local test prep services can get good results and are less expensive.

4. There are free and low cost ($50 - $150) online courses at www.number2com or www.studyhall.com.

5. If you're really disciplined, several publishers produce test prep books and CD-Roms for "self-study." Despite its former claim that the test isn't coachable, The College Board is one of the largest publishers (and promoters) of self-study materials. Hmmm.

6. The College Board web site gives samples of actual essays, representing a variety of writing styles, including commentary, so you can see the difference between a top score (of "6") and a low score (of "1"). Be sure to understand this scoring criteria and practice composing clear, persuasive passages every time you write—whether it's a school assignment, a personal journal or an email to friends.

At the very least, buy (or borrow) a copy of The College Board's "Official SAT Study Guide" with eight official practice tests. It's important that you prep for the test using authentic questions. If you've been polishing your skills online, it's also important that you take at least one practice exam in a setting that simulates actual test conditions—complete with timer, paper and pencil. At three hours and 45 minutes, the SAT is a real endurance test with just two short breaks and very little time (25 minutes) to compose a thoughtful, well-organized essay.

With a little effort, average students can increase their scores by 100-150 points, enough to put them over the threshold for most academic awards. (Note: If your scores increase by too much, say 350 points or more, the test-makers launch an automatic investigation into your newfound brilliance.)

Where Are the Rewards for the Bright?

The A's & B's of Academic Scholarships (see last page) describes 100,000 academic awards offered at 1200 colleges; awards that range from $500 to $40,000 per year. Most of these awards are not based on financial need.

Your home state (see Chapter 11) is also likely to offer awards based on achievement—part of their effort to keep bright kids from moving away.

Finally, many private scholarships are reserved for students with extraordinary abilities. You can usually link up (1) via competitions, or (2) through recommendations of teachers, coaches, and bandmasters. In following this route, make certain the honor you're applying for isn't going to cost you a fortune. Some companies would love to make a profit off your achievement. They buy mailing lists of good students (e.g., those with B+ averages or better) and try to sell them everything from $50 books featuring (surprise) their very own biography and photo, to $750 trips to Washington to hobnob with the political elite.

Art and Photography

The Scholastic Art Awards. 1200 national award recipients. Grades 7-12. By November 1, The Scholastic Art & Writing Awards, 557 Broadway, New York, NY 10012, www.artandwriting.org.

Arts (Dance, Film, Music, Theater, Visual Arts, and Writing)

Arts Recognition & Talent Search (ARTS) awards from $100 to $10,000 in scholarships and identifies talented students to colleges which, in turn, award over $3 million in additional awards to ARTS applicants. Also, the chance to be named a Presidential Scholar in the Arts. $25-$40 fee (may be waived in hardship cases), Oct. 1 deadline. National Foundation for Advancement in the Arts, 444 Brickell Ave., #P-14, Miami, FL 33131. 800/970-ARTS, www.ARTSawards.org.

Brains

1. *National Merit® Scholarship Program.* The Merit program selects about 34,000 high-scorers as "Commended Students" and another 16,000 as "Semifinalists" based on the PSAT/NMSQT exam taken no later than the Junior year of HS. Approximately 8,200 become Finalists and receive either (1) a $2,500 National Merit Scholarships; (2) a Corporate-sponsored Merit Scholarship; or (3) a College-sponsored Merit Scholar-ship. Corporate sponsors also provide 1,500 scholarships each year to non-Finalists. Get the *PSAT/NMSQT Official Student Guide* from your counselor or the National Merit Scholarship Corp., 1560 Sherman Ave., #200, Evanston, IL 60201, www.nationalmerit.org.

2. *National Honor Society.* 200+ scholarships ranging from $1,000-$2,500 for National Honor Society members. Nominations through HS. Late Jan, www.nhs.us.

3. *Mensa Scholarships.* Awards to $1,000. By Jan. 15. For an application, www.mensafoundation.org. If you have doubts about whether you're Mensa material, try "The Mensa Workout" at www.mensa.org.

4. *Phi Theta Kappa, the International Honor Society of the Two-Year College.* Members who plan to pursue a baccalaureate degree are eligible for Senior Institution Transfer Scholarships, available at over 650 four-year colleges. Last year, 13,000 Society members received over $36 million. For a copy of the Phi Theta Kappa Scholarship Directory, write PTK, The Center for Excellence, 1625 Eastover Drive, Jackson, MS 39211, or read it online at www.ptk.org.

5. *REACH Program (Rewarding Achievement).* A group of philanthropists has teamed up to offer New York City students (at 31 schools) cash rewards for doing well on AP Exams. Students receive $1,000 for a top score of "5," $750 for a "4," and $500 for a "3." The selected schools primarily serve students from low-income, minority backgrounds. There are similar opportunities in other cities.

Contests

There are nearly 100 national contests—spelling bees, math bees, history bees, geography bees, etc. Be forewarned, however, in going for the honey, do it because you enjoy the competition and not because of the prize money. In some cases, millions of students compete for a handful of awards. Ask your counselor for current program announcements or check the list of approved student contests maintained by the National Association of Secondary School Principals, www.principals.org. Examples:

1. *National Spelling Bee* sponsored by E.W. Scripps Company. Eight million students compete for $50-$30,000 awards, www.spellingbee.com.

2. *The National Geography Bee* is sponsored by the National Geographic Society. Top prizes (to fourth- through eighth-grade participants) are three college scholarships worth $25,000, $15,000 and $10,000. Register by mid-October, www.nationalgeographic.com/geobee.

Drama

Thespian Society. Members-only scholarships through HS chapter.

Leadership & Brains

1. *Wendy's High School Heisman Award.* For scholarship, citizenship and athletic ability. 1020 state finalists, 102 state winners, 12 national finalists. By October 1, www.wendysheisman.com.

2. *Principal's Leadership Award (PLA).* 100 scholarships ranging from $1,000 to $12,000. Applications sent to HS principal in October. December deadline. Administered by National Association of Secondary School Principals, www.principals.org.

3. *U. S. Senate Youth Program.* 104 $5,000 scholarships to elected student officers plus an expense-paid week in Washington, DC in early March. Selections by state. Contact your HS principal or the William Randolph Hearst Foundation, 90 New Montgomery St., #1212, San Francisco, CA 94105. (800) 841-7048, www.ussenateyouth.org. Fall deadlines.

4. *Truman Scholars.* Up to $30,000 over 2 years. 70-75 awards. Must show outstanding potential for leadership in government and public service and be nominated by your college in your junior year. Award winners must work in public service for three of seven years following completion of their graduate school program. By early Feb. Truman Foundation, 712 Jackson Pl., NW, Washington, DC 20006, www.truman.gov.

5. *Jack Kent Cooke Scholars.* $30,000 awards for community college students who plan to transfer to a four-year college. For application and information, 800/498-6478, www.jackkentcookefoundation.org.

Math, Engineering and Natural Sciences

Barry M. Goldwater Scholarship. For outstanding college sophomores and juniors who plan to pursue careers in math, engineering or the natural sciences. Up to $7,500/year for one or two years. Up to 300 awards—one scholarship to a resident of each state, with additional scholars-at-large. Applicants are nominated by their college. By February 1. Contact your campus faculty representative, or www.act.org/goldwater.

Music

Competitions and Awards. $750,000 of competitive award opportunities ranging from $400 to $10,000. For a copy of the current awards chart, contact the National Federation of Music Clubs HQ, 1336 N. Delaware St., Indianapolis, IN 46202, www.NFMC-music.org.

Oratory & Essays

Large awards. Lots of competition. The American Legion, Optimist International and Civitan all sponsor contests (example: about 25,000 students compete for a top prize of $18,000 in the American Legion's Oratorical Contest). Contact your local club for more information.

And try googling "essay contest" and "college scholarship"—new ones pop up every year (www.google.com). For example, the American Foreign Service Association awards $750 - $2,500 for an essay on the role of the Foreign Service in today's world, www.afsa.org. Looking for something frothier? How about $1,000 from the Cat Writers Association of America (www.catwriters.org) for a purrfect composition, or an equally-meaty bone from the Dog Writers Association of America (www.dwaa.org)?

Of course you should write your admission essays first since, in the long run, they are more important; however, you might be able to re-tool one of them for a scholarship contest (or vice-versa).

Presidential Scholars

Presidential Scholars. No application. Approximately 120 students selected from high scorers on the SAT and ACT. Also 20 students picked for achievement in the arts, as identified by the Arts Recognition & Talent Search (see above). A four-day visit to Washington and a handshake from the President, www.ARTSawards.org.

Writing

1. *The Scholastic Writing Awards.* 1200 national award recipients. Grades 7-12. 300 awards. By Nov. 1. Scholastic Writing Awards, 557 Broadway, New York, NY 10012, www.artandwriting.org.

2. *Young Writers Contest.* Scholarships range from $1,000 to $10,000. Write and submit a first person, 1200 word story about a memorable or moving experience you have had. November Deadline. Guideposts, 16 E 34th St., 21st fl., New York, NY 10016, www.guideposts.com.

3. *National Federation of Press Women,* Small cash awards for female members of their school newspaper staff. National Federation of Press Women, Box 5556, Arlington, VA 22205, by May 1 www.nfpw.org.

CHAPTER 19

■■■■■■■■■■■■■■■■■■■■■■■■

MONEY FOR ATHLETES

Athletic scholarships are not limited to those with prowess in the big sports—there is scholarship money for gymnastics, lacrosse, bowling, archery, fencing, rowing, synchronized swimming, skiing and volleyball.

All-star athletes don't need this book. They need an (unofficial) agent who can sort through all the offers, enticements, contracts and gifts that come their way. They might need a mechanic, too, to advise them on the relative merits of a Porsche vs. a Mercedes.

This chapter is for the better-than-average athlete with varsity potential in major and minor sports. What's available for this athlete? Here is the situation in a nutshell: There is considerable financial aid at most colleges for students who are good, but not necessarily great, athletes. This aid is either "reserved" for athletes (through designated scholarships) or awarded on a preferential basis as part of the aid packaging process. Division I and II schools award over $14 billion in athletic scholarships each year to a total of 123,000 students. This sounds like a lot until you realize that 4.3 million boys and over three million girls participate in high school sports.

The key to receiving an athletic award is your determination to market your own talents. You must contact the appropriate college coaches and get them to shepherd your admission and financial aid requests through the bureaucracy of the admission and financial aid offices. College coaches, if convinced of your potential contribution, will take an active role in facilitating your requests. Some schools even have admission reps whose main responsibility is to coordinate referrals from the athletic department.

On Your Mark, Get Set, Go!

An increasing number of high schoolers are using personal trainers (at $40-$80 an hour) to gain an extra edge in making the team and winning athletic scholarships. Unfortunately, they're also getting so wrapped up in individual achievement that they're forgetting about the team! Here is a (less costly, more sensible) approach to marketing your talents:

1. Start early. Discuss with your counselor the range of colleges for which you are academically qualified; remember, most colleges, even the country's most elite liberal arts colleges, reserve spots ("tips") for good athletes who might not be admitted based on academic criteria alone.

2. Talk to your coach about the quality of athletic programs for which you might qualify. Don't sell yourself short—colleges need backups as well as starters. Visit www.ncaasports.com for coverage of all 81 NCAA championships, and learn which schools are strong in each sport.

3. Narrow your college list to a manageable size, taking into consideration the quality of athletic and academic programs and your "fit" with them. You *don't* want to be a four-year bench-warmer; you *do* want to be challenged by the school's academic program (but not overwhelmed).

4. Research coach names at each college on your list. Best source: your high school athletic director's copy of *The National Directory of College Athletics* (separate editions for men and women). Do a follow-up call to the athletic department to verify this name, and make certain the coach is still at the school and coaching your sport.

5. Draft a personal letter to each coach. This letter should include a profile of your academic interests and achievements. The letter's main part, however, should be a detailed discussion of your athletic accomplishments and be supported by statistics, clippings, letters earned, records, and honors. Include mention of any camps or clinics you've attended, and if appropriate, a videotape of yourself in action. (Keep it to ten minutes, look enthusiastic, start with skills, move on to "game" highlights and make certain you're easily identifiable.) If your real value to the team is as a leader and motivator rather than a top scorer, make that clear. (Have you won any awards for sportsmanship?) Lastly, indicate you will need financial aid.

6. As an alternative, visit *The National Directory of College Athletics* web site, www.collegiatedirectories.com, for e-mail addresses of college coaches in your sport. Then send a polite note, accompanied by a description of your athletic accomplishments, and maybe a link to your own Web site so coaches can learn more, and see you in action.

7. If your approach elicits interest, ask your high school coach to follow up with a letter of recommendation or a phone call. You should also send the college a schedule of your games in case recruiters are nearby. Participating in multi-team tournaments and competitive summer (sports) camps can be especially fruitful, and efficient, since several college reps are likely to be there (observing) at once.

8. Now you must decide where to apply. Few coaches will take an interest in you unless your initial letter is followed by a formal application. And remember, as with any other application, apply as early as possible.

9. After applying, stay in touch with the college coaches. Ask about the status of your application and request for financial aid. If possible, visit the college and sell yourself as a person and as an athlete. Get to know the coach, and make certain his or her coaching philosophy is compatible with your style!

Counting Noses

The number (and size) of athletic scholarships varies widely by sport and the formulas can get complicated.

In some sports, schools must impose an actual head count. For example, the NCAA allows a school to offer 12 women's volleyball scholarships which it must spread over four years of recruits, which translates to an average of three awards per year. (And could be less if the school opts not to fund all 12 awards.)

In other sports, they may split scholarships between many more athletes—room and board to one student, books and fees to another. Stretching awards like this might mean your award is worth only $1,000 - $4,000.

And, one last dose of reality—athletic scholarships are guaranteed for one year only. They may be renewed for an additional four years, but they may also be canceled or reduced. That's between you and your coach!

NCAA Division I

Division I Football Bowl Subdivision schools (formerly Division I-A) can have up to 85 football players on scholarship.

Division I Football Championship Subdivision schools (formerly Division I-AA) are limited to the equivalent of 63 football scholarships.

Division I men's basketball may award 13 scholarships; women's basketball gets 15; women's gymnastics, 12; women's tennis, 8; women's volleyball, 12. Schools may not split any of these grants.

Men's sports which may split scholarships are: baseball, 11.7 awards; cross country/track, 12.6; fencing, 4.5; golf, 4.5; gymnastics, 6.3; lacrosse, 12.6; rifle, 3.6; skiing, 6.3; soccer, 9.9; swimming, 9.9; tennis, 4.5; volleyball, 4.5; water polo, 4.5; and wrestling, 9.9.

Women's sports and their equivalency levels are: archery, 5; badminton, 6; bowling, 5; crew, 20; cross country/track, 18; fencing, 5; field hockey, 12; golf, 6; lacrosse, 12; rugby, 12; skiing, 7; soccer, 14; softball, 12; squash, 12; swimming, 14; synchronized swimming, 5; team handball, 10; and water polo, 8.

NCAA Division II

All sports are subject to an equivalency test rather than a head count:

Men's sports: baseball, 9; basketball, 10; cross country/track, 12.6; fencing, 4.5; football, 36; golf, 3.6; gymnastics, 5.4; ice hockey, 13.5; lacrosse, 10.8; rifle, 3.6; skiing, 6.3; soccer, 9; swimming, 8.1; tennis, 4.5; volleyball, 4.5; water polo, 4.5; and wrestling, 9.

Women's sports: archery, 5; badminton, 8; basketball, 10; bowling, 5; crew, 20; cross country/track, 12.6; fencing, 4.5; field hockey, 6.3; golf, 5.4; gymnastics, 6; ice hockey, 18; lacrosse, 9.9; skiing, 6.3; soccer, 9.9;

softball, 7.2; squash, 9; swimming, 8.1; synchronized swimming, 5; team handball, 12; tennis, 6; volleyball, 8; and water polo, 8.

NCAA Division III, NAIA

NCAA Division III: Since aid is unrelated to athletics, there is no limit on how many student-athletes can receive financial assistance, however, the NCAA closely monitors whether or not gift aid to athletes exceeds gift aid to non-athletes with similar financial need—it's OK for athletic ability to provide an edge in the admission process, but not the financial aid process.

NAIA: There are no scholarship limits, but most schools have limited funds.

Additional Financial Aid

The NCAA has ruled that student-athletes who receive athletic scholarships may receive additional forms of financial aid as well, for example, Pell Grants or miscellaneous institutional grants for which athletic participation is not a requirement. The total aid package may not exceed the school's full cost of attendance—tuition, fees, room, board, books as well as travel and miscellaneous expenses. Furthermore, the NCAA has approved a proposal that would allow students to receive merit-based aid without counting against the team's scholarship limits as long as students have completed at least one year of college and carry at least a 3.3 GPA.

Gender Equity: Slowly But Surely

"No person in the United States shall, on the basis of sex, be excluded from participation in, be denied the benefits of, or be subjected to discrimination under any education program or activity receiving federal financial assistance." That's the text of Title IX of the Education Act of 1972 and any school that receives federal money, which means virtually every school in the country, must comply. And not just when it comes to sports.

Title IX Crash Course

The Education Department's Office of Civil Rights has a three-prong test to determine whether athletic programs satisfy Title IX: (1) Schools must have roughly the same proportion of female athletes as female undergraduates; OR (2) Schools must demonstrate a history of expanding athletics opportunities for the under-represented gender; OR (3) Schools must fully accommodate the interests and abilities of the under-represented gender.

In addition, colleges must award the same proportion of athletic scholarships to women athletes as there are women participating in varsity sports.

Critics claim that at some schools, Title IX compliance has led to the elimination of men's athletic teams. But Title IX compliance does not require schools to meet any quotas; rather, schools that choose to eliminate men's teams have opted to demonstrate compliance by using the clearest of the above-described tests—proportionality—and don't have large-enough athletic budgets to do so by simply adding women's teams.

To emphasize this point, the government issued clarification on Title IX compliance, emphasizing (1) that "each of the three prongs is an equally-sufficient means of complying with Title IX" and (2) that "nothing in Title IX requires the cutting or reduction of teams to demonstrate compliance, and the elimination of teams is contrary to the spirit of Title IX." And, in fact, there has been a net gain of 70 men's teams over the past 15 years.

Take the Money and Run (or Row)

Of course, if schools were to trim just a bit of fat from their football programs, Title IX compliance would be a breeze! Instead, with their huge rosters, and highly-paid coaching staffs, football has been unscathed by Title IX. So why does a sport with a maximum of 22 starters (excluding special teams) need 85 full scholarships? And a roster much larger than any NFL team? Schools are ever hopeful they'll win the big Bowl Game (or Final Four) jackpot, so they continue to pump up their big money sports (football and basketball) and deal with Title IX in other ways: adding women's sports, dropping men's sports (golf, wrestling and gymnastics have been the hardest hit), adding women's athletic scholarships, limiting the number of non-scholarship athletes on team rosters, turning men's varsity teams into clubs—all to help even out the numbers. Women's crew has been the biggest beneficiary of Title IX largess since it is one of the few women's sports with a large enough team to offset men's football—in fact, participation has doubled over the past ten years.

Why is it so important that women get a fair shake in college sports? It goes beyond fun and games. Sports teach discipline, teamwork and leadership. And statistically, women who play sports are more (professionally) successful than women who don't. They have higher graduation rates, and a better chance of avoiding abusive relationships.

Academic Eligibility

To play your sport at a Division I or II school, you must have your eligibility certified by a central clearinghouse—the NCAA wants to make certain all student-athletes are exactly that, and has instituted minimum academic requirements for athletes.

Students who plan to compete at Division II schools must have a GPA of at least 2.0 in 14 core (college prep) academic courses; a combination of math, English, social science, natural or physical science, foreign language or non-doctrinal religion/philosophy. Furthermore, they must have a combined SAT score of 820 or an ACT composite score of 68. Beginning August 1, 2013, the number of required core courses will increase to 16. (Most Division II prospects are already exceeding that number.)

Students who plan to compete at Division I schools must complete 16 academic courses (from the subjects listed above). Furthermore, to help crack down on post-high school "Diploma Mills," students must complete at least 15 of these courses within the traditional eight semesters (four years) of high school. Students who need extra time to complete more than one of their core courses may apply for a waiver, and extend their high school careers. Students must also meet the NCAA's sliding scale of acceptable GPA/test scores. For example, if they squeak in with the minimum SAT score of 400 or ACT composite score of 37, they must have a GPA of at least 3.55 in their core curriculum. If their SAT/ACT composites are 1010/86 or higher, they can get away with a GPA as low as 2.0. *Note*: In calculating these qualifying test scores, the NCAA is currently excluding scores on the new writing portion of the SAT, and looking only at your combined total on the Critical Reading (formerly "Verbal") and Math sections of the exam.

After dozens of top students were denied eligibility due to taking "offbeat" courses, the NCAA is expanding approved course lists to bring them in line with already-established standards for HS graduation. Furthermore, the NCAA will modify course requirements for (documented) LD students to include some special-education classes. You can check approved course lists online at www.ncaaclearinghouse.net.

The NCAA Eligibility Center

If a school wants to recruit you, it will verify your eligibility status (and your amateurism status) from a central NCAA Eligibility Center. Registration costs $50, however, students who qualify for a fee waiver for the SAT/ ACT may also receive a fee waiver for the Eligibility Center. If you attended more than one high school, each school will need to submit your official transcript. *Note: Eligibility certification has no bearing on your admission to a particular Division I or II institution.*

Register online at **www.ncaaclearinghouse.net**. For more information, call 877/262-1492.

Graduation Success Rates and Academic Progress Rates

Don't let headlines scare you, or cause you to think that athletes are held to lower academic standards than non-athletes. Most of the abuses you read about are restricted to big name (Division I) men's football, baseball and basketball programs. In fact, the average Graduation Success Rate (GSR) shows that 77 percent of student-athletes graduate within six years; a higher rate than their more-sedentary classmates. (Note: GSR is a little different than the federal government's published graduation rate in that GSR accounts for outgoing transfer students who leave in good academic standing as well as incoming transfer students who graduate on time.) The fact is, most student-athletes have a higher graduation rate than other students and fare better economically in the job market.

Nevertheless, the NCAA keeps pushing proposals that would penalize teams that perform poorly in the classroom. The latest plan measures the Academic Progress Rate (APR) of each sports program at every Division I school. The formula is a little complicated: Scholarship student-athletes can receive two points each term—one point for meeting academic eligibility standards and a second point for remaining at the school. The team's APR is then determined by dividing the total points earned by the total points possible and multiplying the result by 1000.

Individual sports programs must maintain an APR of at least 925 or risk losing up to 10% of their scholarships for a year. (A 925 APR correlates to a 60% graduation rate.) APRs will be based on four years of data, so one "bad" year shouldn't have much impact on a program's total score.

The NCAA is continuing to refine its APR methodology to ensure that programs won't be punished for players who leave school early as a result of circumstances beyond the school's control, like illness or a death in the family or early departure for the pros. Assuming these departing-players would have been academically-eligible to remain on the team, schools will no longer lose retention points for these cases.

Doonesbury has already spoofed the concept, suggesting that some scholarships might start going to "academic ringers"—scrawny bench sitters whose only job is to maintain good grades and graduate on time.

Our advice: Find out the APR of any program that interests you to be sure it's over 925 (scores are posted on the NCAA's web site, www.ncaa.org). Unless you're planning to play one of the big-money sports—men's football, baseball or basketball—your program is probably in good shape.

Division II is implementing a similar measurement, but it goes a little further—its "Academic Success Rate" (ASR) measures graduation rates of all student-athletes including those who do not receive athletic scholarships.

New Standards?

The NCAA is constantly tinkering with eligibility requirements, in an effort to keep the STUDENT in student-athlete. Stay alert.

Recruiting Violations

The NCAA publishes hundreds of pages of rules and regulations. Violating one can quickly turn you into an "ineligible" athlete. For an overview of recruiting guidelines, read the *Guide for the College-Bound Student-Athlete* (see resource list). Or, you can read ALL the rules online, www.ncaa.org.

When should you start worrying about do's and don'ts? As soon as you become a "Prospective Student-Athlete" (which happens when you start ninth-grade), although you don't need to become obsessive until you are a "Recruited Prospective Student-Athlete." This occurs the moment a college coach (or representative of the school's "athletic interests") contacts you or a family member about participating in athletics at that college. "Contact" means providing you (or a family member) with an official visit, calling you more than once, or visiting you anywhere other than the college campus.

Commercial Scouting Services and Agents

Colleges often pay services to help them find top-notch athletes. These services go around the country evaluating talent and selling this data to colleges, usually in the form of videotapes and ratings booklets. You, however, are not likely to have any contact with these services. Why? In an effort to stem the perception that college teams are little more than feeders for professional teams, the NCAA keeps tightening recruiting regulations and limiting the type of contact a coach may have with prospects.

As for agents, be careful. You can jeopardize your college eligibility by speaking to an unauthorized rep, by speaking to an authorized rep outside the approved contact period, or by agreeing to professional representation while still in HS or college (even if "the deal" doesn't become effective until after you finish college).

The Pros and Cons of Exposure Services

Exposure (or placement) services, represent the student in their search for athletic scholarships. These services can cost from $400 to $1,500 (or higher), and generally just follow the nine steps outlined previously. In other words, you can probably "sell" yourself and save the fee. Also, some college coaches say they're skeptical of organizations that claim they can do more for a student than his or her high school coach—after all, your coach is the person who should be most familiar with your abilities.

On the flip side, some exposure services are good and many students and schools are pleased with their results. From the student's perspective, it's an easy way to get their athletic profile sent to as many as 800 colleges. Students can then just sit back and wait for nibbles. From the school's perspective, since athletes pay the fee, the school is getting perfectly good, free information on hundreds of potential student-athletes. These services are most useful for students who participate in "minor sports" (regardless of the school) or who are interested in smaller, less athletically-prominent schools (regardless of the sport).

If you decide to use a placement service, ask your high school coach about services that specialize in your sport, or check into the online placement services listed below.

If you still have questions, call the NCAA. It can't make endorsements, but it can steer you clear of shady businesses. Also, if you use a placement service, be careful about how it determines your fee. The NCAA prohibits them from receiving money based on the value of your scholarship.

Putting Your Profile on the Web

Online placement services are increasingly popular. For a fee ranging from $29 to $595, they let you post an athletic profile (and sometimes a 'highlights' video) where it's available to hundreds of college coaches. Of course, there are no guarantees. And many college coaches still prefer to identify new talent in person (at summer sports camps and HS competitions), or rely on referrals from HS coaches. Here are some online options:

- PrepStar, prepstar.com
- Scout USA, www.scoutusa.com
- College Prospects of America, www.cpoa.com

Locating Scholarships in Your Sport

Sports Careers

The NCAA awards more than $1 million to student-athletes who are pursuing an athletics-related career or post-graduate program. Four programs are for postgraduates; one is for undergraduates. Request information from the NCAA, PO Box 6222, Indianapolis, IN 46206, www.ncaa.org.

Sports and Brains

1. *Got Milk?* The American Dairy Farmers and Milk Processors award 25 $7,500 scholarships each year. SAMMY (Scholar-Athlete Milk Mustache of the Year) winners are judged on academic and athletic excellence, leadership and community service, sammy.bodybymilk.com

2. *ESPN* awards. 8 $2,500 scholarships based on academic achievement, sports participation and community service. 860/585-2000 x3999.

References for Further Reading

1. The NCAA publishes stiff rules on recruiting. Learn them! Get a free copy of the *Guide for the College-Bound Student-Athlete* from NCAA Publishing, 800/638-3731, or read it online at www.ncaa.org.

2. NAIA schools, National Association of Intercollegiate Athletics, 1200 Grand Blvd., Kansas City, MO 64106, www.naia.org.

3. For more information on competing at the junior college level, write to the National Junior College Athletic Association, 1755 Telstar Drive, #103, Colorado Springs, CO 80920, 719/590-9788, www.njcaa.org.

4. *The Women's Collegiate Athletic Scholarship Guide* from the Womens Sport Foundation, Eisenhower Park, East Meadow, NY, 11554, 800/227-3988, WomensSportFoundation.org.

5. In your enthusiasm for playing college sports, be sure you don't do anything dangerous, like experiment with steroids or other banned substances. For detailed information on dietary supplements, visit the *National Center for Drug Free Sport*, www.drugfreesport.com.

Chapter 20

■ ■

Money for Health Careers

As a budding nurse or doctor or therapist, don't limit your reading to this chapter, or you will never blossom into a nurse or doctor or therapist. For instance, you can benefit from all the major federal student aid programs (Chapter 10). And you can get money from your home state (Chapter 11) if you enter a medical field in which it believes it has a shortage.

Federal Support for the Health Professions

Uncle Sam pours great amounts of money—almost a half billion dollars per year—into the training of health professionals. The assistance programs fall into two broad categories: Individual-based programs which fund students, and school-based programs which fund schools (the schools, in-turn, parcel some of the money out to students).

The nursing shortage is especially acute, which is why there are expanded grants and loan repayment for nursing education.

Individual-Based Programs

Individual-based programs are fairly easy to locate. You apply directly to Uncle Sam or through the school you plan to attend. One bit of advice: You will gain an advantage over fellow applicants if you indicate a willingness to practice in a "shortage area." Don't worry about what a shortage area is. Its definition and location will change several times between the time you apply and the time you graduate. What's important to know is that "shortage areas" are a big thing at the Department of Health & Human Services. It has "primary medical care shortage areas," "dental manpower shortage areas," "rural dental shortage areas," "vision care shortage areas," "podiatry shortage areas," "pharmacy shortage areas," "psychiatric shortage areas," even "veterinary care shortage areas."

Bureau of Health Professions

For more information on Uncle's individual-based health care programs, visit the Bureau of Health Professions at bhpr.hrsa.gov/dsa. For example:

National Health Service Corps Loan Repayment Program. In exchange for providing primary care in federally-designated health profession shortage areas, the program will repay up to $50,000 in education loans for a minimum 2-year commitment. The program is open to primary care physicians (family medicine, OB/gyn, internal medicine, pediatrics, general psychiatry), mental health care clinicians (psychiatrists, psychologists, family counselors and clinical social workers), nurse practitioners, midwives, dentists, dental hygienists and physician assistants. By late March. NHSC Loan Repayment Program, 800/638-0824, nhsc.bhpr.hrsa.gov.

National Health Service Corps Scholarship Program. The NHSC will pay tuition, fees, books and supplies, plus stipend (c. $1,100 per month) for up to four years. This very-competitive program is open to US citizens enrolled in a fully-accredited medical school, dental school, family nurse practitioner program, nurse midwifery program or physician assistant program. For each year of support, you owe one year of full-time clinical practice in high-priority health professions shortage areas. Minimum 2 year obligation. If you fail to comply with the terms of your contract, the penalty equals three times the cost of your scholarship, plus interest. The scholarship is tax exempt; the stipend remains taxable. NHSC Scholarship Program, 800/638-0824, nhsc.bhpr.hrsa.gov/join_us/scholarships.asp.

Primary Care Loan. Students in allopathic or osteopathic medicine may borrow up to the cost of attendance. Interest equals 5% and begins to accrue following a one-year grace period after you cease to be a full-time student. Deferment options of up to four years. Must practice in primary health care until the loan is repaid. Apply through school, bhpr.hrsa.gov/dsa/pcl.htm.

Nursing Scholarship Program. Tuition, fees and monthly stipend of c. $1,200. Priority goes to those with a "zero" expected family contribution (from the FAFSA), very competitive. By late June, 877/464-4772, bhpr.hrsa.gov/nursing/scholarship.

Nursing Education Loan Repayment Program (NELRP) helps nurses repay educational loans in exchange for service in eligible facilities located in areas experiencing a shortage of nurses. For two years of service, the NELRP will pay 60% of the participant's loan balance; for a third year of service, NELRP will pay an additional 25% of the loan balance. By early-March. Nurse Education Loan Repayment Program, 877/464-4772, bhpr.hrsa.gov/nursing/loanrepay.htm.

Nursing Student Loan Program. Long-term, low-interest loan to full- and half-time nursing students. Apply through school.

Health Professions Student Loan. Long-term, low-interest, need-based loans. Must practice in primary care. Apply through school.

Exceptional Financial Need Scholarships. All tuition plus stipend. Good for one year only. At year's end, participants have priority for a NHSC Scholarship. Must practice in general dentistry or primary care medicine for five years after residency. Apply through school.

Scholarships and Loans for Disadvantaged Students (SDS and LDS Programs). Scholarships and low-interest loans for full-time, financially-needy students from disadvantaged backgrounds who are enrolled in health professional and nursing programs. Apply through school's financial aid office.

National Institutes of Health

Medical researchers at NIH can qualify for up to $35,000 in loan forgiveness, and an extra amount to cover federal and state income taxes that result from these repayments, 866/849-4047, lrp.info.nih.gov.

Commissioned Officer Student Training & Extern Program (COSTEP)

For graduate awards, students must complete one year of medical, dental, veterinary school. For undergrad awards, students must complete two years in a dietary, nursing, pharmacy, dental hygiene, medical laboratory technology, therapy, sanitary science, medical records, engineering, physician's assistant, or computer science field. Student must return to studies following completion of COSTEP assignment. Serve as an extern in various divisions of the US Department of Health and Human Services during school breaks of 31-120 days duration. Ensign's pay during work phases, about $2,500 per month. COSTEP, 800/279-1605, www.usphs.gov/student.

School-Based Programs

School-based programs are something else. Here, the available dollars go directly to schools, and usually become part of the faculty payroll (Reason: Medical faculties are so high-priced, without federal aid to help pay their salaries, schools would have to foot the bill alone. To do this, they would have to raise tuition so high, no student could afford to enroll). Your challenge is to look for funded schools and negotiate with the Dean for some of the spoils. Or at least to take advantage of any extra student aid dollars. Ask your intended school about these secret pots of money.

State-Based Programs

Many states have loan repayment programs (some of which are funded by the National Health Service Corps, nhsc.bhpr.hrsa.gov). For a listing, check out the financial aid section of the American Medical Colleges web site, www.aamc.org/students/financing.

Military Medical and Nursing Programs

Armed Forces Health Professional Programs

Health Professions Scholarships for medical, dental, veterinary, psychiatric nurse practitioner, optometry and psychology students. Tuition, fees and

$1,907 monthly stipend (adjusted each July). Additional sign-on bonus for certain medical and dental students of up to $20,000. Service obligation.

Health Professional Loan Repayment Program (HPLRP). Depending on branch of service, up to $38,000 per year in educational loans for officers serving up to four years on active duty in designated specialties

Financial Assistance Program. Residency training for graduate physicians, endodontists, periodontists, orthodontists and oral surgeons. More than $28,000 per year plus $1,907 monthly stipend (adjusted each July). Service obligation.

Each branch of the service has its own point of contact:

- **Army:** Medical Department, 800/USA-ARMY, www.goarmy.com/amedd/index.jsp.
- **Navy:** Medical Command, 301/319-4118, www.navy.com/healthcareopportunities.
- **Air Force:** Dir. of Health Professionals, 800/443-4690, www.airforce.com/education/healthcare.

ROTC Nurse Program (Army, Navy, Air Force)

Students at approved nursing schools affiliated with an Army, Navy, or Air Force ROTC unit. 2, 3, 4 year scholarships; tuition, textbooks, and fees, plus a monthly stipend. Service obligation.

- **Army,** Army ROTC, www.goarmy.com/rotc/nurse_program.jsp.
- **Navy,** 800/NAV-ROTC, www.nrotc.navy.mil.
- **Air Force,** HQ AFROTC, 866/423-7682, www.afrotc.com.

Navy-Specific Programs

For more information on the following programs, contact the Navy Medical Command, 301/319-4118, www.navy.com/healthcareopportunities.

1. *Navy Health Services Collegiate Program.* Up to $180,000 to finish graduate school in the form of a monthly salary and housing allowance.
2. *Navy Nurse Candidate Program.* $10,000 upfront plus $1,000 per month for 24 months for nursing school.

Army-Specific Programs

HQ, US Army Recruiting Command, Health Services Division, 1307 Third Avenue, Fort Knox, KY 40121, 800/USA-ARMY, www.goarmy.com/amedd/index.jsp

1. *Specialized Training Assistance Program (STRAP).* Monthly stipend for students and residents in designated specialties including nursing (specialties are identified every two years). $1,600+/month (adjusted each July). Recipients serve two years in the Reserve component of the Army Medical Department for every year or partial year they receive the stipend.

2. *Health Professional Loan Repayment Program (HPLRP).* Army will repay up to $50,000 in educational loans for officers serving in designated specialties in the Reserves—$20,000 in each of the first two years, and $10,000 in the third year.

3. *Health Professions Special Pay.* Annual bonus to health care professionals in designated specialties (specialties are identified every two years) who join the Army Reserve. Bonuses vary from $5,000 to $10,000 per year for up to 3 years. Also, Active Duty bonuses from $6,000 to $14,000 per year, depending on the specialty.

4. *Army Nurse Candidate Program.* Bonus money for undergraduates pursuing nursing degrees: $5,000 when enterng the program, another $5,000 at graduation, plus $1,000 per month during enrollment.

Uniformed Services University of the Health Sciences

Fully-accredited federal school of medicine and graduate school of nursing. Request catalogue, from Admissions Office, 4301 Jones Bridge Rd., Bethesda, MD 20814; 800/772-1743, www.usuhs.mil.

F. Edward Hebert School of Medicine. This tuition-free institution's main emphasis is on training medical officers for the Army, Navy and Air Force. While enrolled, students serve on active duty as Reserve commissioned officers in grade O-1 with full pay and allowances. Civilian and uniformed services personnel are eligible for admission. Seven year service obligation, exclusive of internship, residency or other service obligations.

Graduate School of Nursing. Offers degrees in Nurse Anesthesia, Psychiatric Mental Health Nurse Practitioner, Family Nurse Practitioner and Perioperative Nursing.

Private Programs

Dental Assistant

American Dental Assistants Assoc., From $500-$5,000. By Jan. 31. Juliette A. Southard/Oral-B Laboratories Scholarship Program, ADAA, 35 E. Wacker Drive, #1730, Chicago, IL 60601, www.dentalassistant.org.

Dental Hygienist

American Dental Hygienist Association. For enrolled dental hygiene students. Up to $1,500. Also, 25 $1,000 scholarships. By May 1. ADHA, 444 N. Michigan, #3400, Chicago, IL 60611, www.adha.org.

Dentistry

American Dental Association, 80 awards of up to $2,500. By June 15. ADA Foundation, 211 E. Chicago Ave., Chicago, IL 60611, www.ada.org.

Medical and Biological Sciences

Medical Fellows Program. $27,000 annual stipend plus $11,000 research allowance. By January 7. Howard Hughes Medical Institute, 4000 Jones Bridge Rd, Chevy Chase, MD 20815, www.hhmi.org.

Medicine and Dental

MedAchiever (up to $375,000) and *DentalAchiever* (up to $275,000). The interest rate during repayment equals the 3-month LIBOR (London Interbank Offered Rate) plus 4%-7% (depending on credit history). 25 years to repay. Also, loans of up to $15,000 to help out during your residency, 800/KEY-LEND, www.key.com.

Medical School Loans from SallieMae. Up to $250,000. The interest rate equals the Prime plus 1.25% if you use a direct repayment plan; otherwise it equals the Prime plus 2%. Dental school loans, too, www.salliemae.com.

Medicine, Nursing and Therapy (Occupational and Physical)

DAR Scholarship Committee. Scholarships for students sponsored by their local DAR chapters. Amounts range from $500 to $5,000. Applications from DAR Scholarship Committee, 1776 D St. NW, Washington, DC 20006. Send SASE for listing of awards, or read them online, www.dar.org.

Nursing (Advanced)

Nurses Educational Funds, Inc., Scholarship for registered nurses, $2,500-$10,000. GRE or MAT scores required. By March 1. Nurses' Educational Funds, 304 Park Ave. South, 11th Floor, New York, NY 10010, 212/590-2443, www.n-e-f.org.

Physician Assistant

Physician Assistant Foundation, 40-50 awards ranging from $2,000 to $5,000 for student AAPA members. By 15 Jan. Also, for a brochure listing financial assistance sources, write American Academy of Physician Assistants, 950 N. Washington Street, Alexandria, VA 22314, www.aapa.org.

Surgical Technology

Association of Surgical Technologists, Awards range from $500 to $2,000. By April 1. Association of Surgical Technologists, 6 West Dry Creek Circle, Littleton CO 80120, www.ast.org.

Therapy

AMBUCS, Physical, Occupational, Hearing Audiology and Speech Language Pathology. 400 awards per year, $500-$1,500 juniors, seniors and graduate student scholarships. Apply by April 15, www.ambucs.com.

Therapy (Respiratory)

American Respiratory Care Foundation, $1,000-$3,500. 9425 N MacArthur Blvd., #100, Irving, TX 75063, by late May/June, www.aarc.org.

CHAPTER 21

■■■■■■■■■■■■■■■■■■■■■■

MONEY FOR OTHER CAREER INTERESTS

The best way to capitalize on your career interest is through cooperative education (Chapter 12). The next best way is to enroll in a school with a strong reputation in your career field (e.g., Agriculture—*Iowa State*; Hotel Management—*Cornell*). Strong departments usually attract scholarship funds. These funds may not start flowing until you declare a major, but if you're fairly certain of your career, you should inquire about endowed scholarships now—especially if your interest is accounting, engineering, nursing, or anything related to computers.

The third—and hardest method—is to look for portable scholarships to fund your major at any accredited school. The following list is illustrative, rather than complete. To dig for additional awards, contact professional associations which serve these careers—you'll find them listed in Gale's *Encyclopedia of Associations* at your public library. You can also search the web. About 10,000 associations have sites linked to the American Society of Association Executives, www.asaenet.org.

Most organization hope you'll do your research (and apply) online. But if you don't have Internet access, always enclose a self-addressed, stamped business-size envelope (SASE) with your written request.

Accounting
1. *AccountingMajors.com.* Provides links to nearly 20 scholarship sources exclusively for accounting majors as well as a listing of awards offered by state CPA societies, www.accountingmajors.com.
2. *National Society of Accountants.* 40 $500-1,000 awards; one $2,000 award. Undergrads only. B+ GPA. By Mar. 10. Must be a US or Canadian citizen attending a US school majoring in accounting. Nat'l Society of Accountants Scholarship Foundation, 1010 N. Fairfax St., Alexandria, VA 22314, www.nsacct.org.

Architecture
American Institute of Architects offers undergrad and graduate scholarships from $500-$2,500. Obtain applications through an accredited school. or local AIA chapter. For state and local contact information contact AIA, Scholarship Programs, 1735 New York Ave., NW, Washington, DC 20006, www.aia.org.

Art & Architecture

Cooper Union (New York City). Extremely competitive admissions. All admitted students receive a full scholarship for the duration of their study.

Education

Phi Delta Kappa. Awards ranging from $500 - $1,000. For HS seniors planning on a teaching career. Also graduate awards. By Feb. 1. Download application from Web site, www.pdkintl.org.

Engineering

General Motors. GM contributes to a variety of organizations to pay for scholarships for students pursuing engineering careers. For information, GM Scholarship Administration Center, 700 W. 5th Ave., Naperville, IL 60563, 888/377-5233, www.gm.com/corporate/careers/student_center.jsp.

Engineering (Civil/Construction)

Associated General Contractors (AGC) Education & Research Foundation. Over 100 renewable undergrad awards of $2,500/yr. Graduate awards of up to $7,500. By Nov. 1. Program Coordinator, AGC Education & Research Foundation, 2300 Wilson Blvd., #400, Arlington, VA 22201, 703/837-5342, www.agcfoundation.org.

Engineering (Materials)

ASM. 37 annual awards ranging from $500 - $10,000. Undergrads majoring in materials science and engineering (metallurgy, ceramics, polymers, and composites). By June 15. Citizen of US, Canada, or Mexico. ASM, Scholarship Program, 9639 Kinsman Rd., Materials Park, OH 44073, www.asminternational.org.

Engineering (Mining)

Society for Mining, Metallurgy, and Exploration. 25+ scholarships of $1,000 to $2,000. One Ph.D. fellowship ($30,000) as well. 8307 Shaffer Parkway, Littleton, CO 80127, www.smenet.org.

Enology & Viticulture

American Society for Enology and Viticulture. Several awards to graduate students and undergrads majoring in enology or other science basic to the wine and grape industry. Applicants must be at least a Junior and meet minimum GPA requirements. By 1 Mar. American Society for Enology and Viticulture, PO Box 1855, Davis, CA 95617, www.asev.org.

Entomology

Entomology Society of America. Several undergrad scholarships, up to $2,000. Major in biology, entomology, zoology, or related science at recognized school in U. S., Canada, Mexico. By May 31. Send SASE to

Undergraduate Scholarship Application, ESA, 10001 Derekwood Lane, #100, Lanham, MD 20706, www.entsoc.org.

Food (Management)

International Food Service Executives. $500-$1,500 grants totalling $100,000/ year. By Feb. 1. IFSEA, 8155 Briar Cliff Drive, Castle Pines North, CO 80108. Download application from www.ifsea.com.

Food (Management, Dietetics, Culinary Arts, etc.)

National Restaurant Assoc. $2,000 awards for students accepted to a foodservice-related program. Up tp $2,500. The Scholarship Foundation of the National Restaurant Association, 175 W. Jackson Blvd., #1500, Chicago, IL 60604, 800/765-2122, www.nraef.org/scholarships.

Food (Science and Technology)

Institute of Food Technologists. Over 110 undergrad and grad scholarships. $1,000-$5,000. By Feb. 1 for juniors, seniors and grad students, by Feb. 15 for freshmen, and March 1 for sophomores. Scholarship Dept., Institute of Food Technologists, 525 W. Van Buren, #1000, Chicago, IL 60607, www.ift.org.

Foreign Study

The Rotary Foundation offers Ambassadorial Scholarships to further international understanding among people of different countries. During the study period, scholars must be outstanding ambassadors of goodwill through appearances before Rotary clubs and other forums. Upon completion of the scholarship, scholars must share their experiences with the people of their home countries. Apply through local Rotary Club (deadlines may be as early as March 1) or write: The Rotary Foundation, One Rotary Center, 1560 Sherman Ave., Evanston, IL, 60201, www.rotary.org.

Three types of awards:

1. Academic-Year Ambassadorial Scholarships of up to $24,000 for one year of study in another country (undergrad, graduate or vocational study).

2. Multi-Year Ambassadorial Scholarships of $12,000 per year for two years.

3. Cultural Ambassadorial Scholarships for intensive language study (3 to 6 months, $11,000 and $16,000 respectively).

Geophysics

Society of Exploration Geophysicists (SEG). Academic ability. 170+ awards/year. $500 to $14,000 per year (averaging $2,600). Students working toward career in Geophysics. By Feb. 1. Scholarship Committee, SEG Foundation, 8801 S. Yale, Tulsa, OK 74137, www.seg.org.

Graphic Arts

Print and Graphics Scholarship Foundation. Over 350 scholarships from $500-$1,500. HS seniors by March 1, college students by April 1. GATF, 200 Deer Run Rd., Sewickley, PA 15143, 800-910-GATF, www.gain.org.

History

Daughters of the American Revolution. $2,000/year. Renewable. HS senior. Top third of class. Major in American History. All students are judged on the basis of academic excellence, commitment to the field of study and financial need. All applications must be sponsored by the local DAR Chapter. Send applications to the DAR Scholarship Committee State Chair by 1 Feb. Two winners from each state are submitted to the Division Level Chair. For more information, send SASE to: NSDAR, Scholarship Committee, 1776 D St., NW, Washington, DC 20006, www.dar.org.

Horticulture

American Orchid Society. Grants for orchid research in areas such as biological research, conservation, ecology. Up to $9,000 per year for up to 3 years working on orchid-related dissertation projects that lead to the Ph.D. Must be enrolled full-time in an accredited doctoral program. Application by Jan. 1 or July 1. American Orchid Society, 16700 AOS Lane, Del Ray Beach, FL 33446, 561/404-2050, www.orchidweb.org.

International Education

1. *National Security Education Program.* Federal scholarships for foreign languages and international affairs. Nearly 500 scholarships for undergrads and graduate students (800/498-9360).
2. *International Education Finance Corporation.* Loans to international students (including Canadians) studying in the US, or to US students studying abroad. IEFC, 781/843-5334, www.IEFC.com.

Journalism

The Journalist's Road to Success: A Career and Scholarship Guide is available online, www.dj.com/newsfund. It lists several million in print journalism scholarships. Includes a minority section. In addition, you can receive a (free) booklet on journalism careers from Dow Jones Newspaper Fund, Inc., PO Box 300, Princeton, NJ 08543-0300. 800/DOW-FUND, View it free online, www.newspaperfund.org.

Librarianship

American Library Association. The ALA lists numerous scholarships available for Technical Assistants and Librarians on its web site, ALA, 50 E. Huron St., Chicago, IL 60611, 800/545-2433, www.ala.org.

Merchant Marine

Maritime Academies. Up to $3,000 per year subsistence allowance for students at CA, ME, MA, NY, TX, and Great Lakes Maritime Academies. Service obligation. U.S. Department of Transportation, Academies Program Officer, Maritime Administration, West Building, Southeast Federal Center, 1200 New Jersey Ave., SE, Washington, DC 20590, www.marad.dot.gov/ Programs/state_aca.html.

Naval Architecture

Webb Institute. Ship design. All tuition paid. Top students. High SAT. 298 Crescent Beach Rd., Glen Cove, NY 11542, www.webb-institute.edu.

Real Estate Appraisers

Appraisal Institute Education Trust, 50 scholarships. $3,000 for graduate students, $2,000 for undergrads. By March 15, Appraisal Institute Education Trust, 550 W. Van Buren St., #1000, Chicago, IL 60607, 312/335-4100, www.appraisalinstitute.org.

Science

American Association for the Advancement of Science sponsors GrantsNet to help students find funds for training in the sciences and undergraduate science education, www.grantsnet.org.

Science

1. *Intel Science and Engineering Fair.* Finalists compete in 15 categories for $4 million in awards, ranging from $500 to $50,000. To enter, HS seniors submit a science, math or engineering project report. By late November, www.intel.com/education/ISEF.
2. *Siemens Competition in Math, Science and Technology.* Finalists compete for $1,000 to $100,000 in top scholarship prizes, Siemens Foundation, 170 Wood Avenue South, Iselin, NJ 08830, 877/822-5233, www.siemens-foundation.org.

Teaching

TeachingTips.com includes an extensive listing of scholarships for teachers-to-be, as well as a wealth of other information to help those pursuing a career in education, www.teachingtips.com.

Travel and Tourism

American Society of Travel Agents (ASTA) Foundation. Travel, tourism and hospitality majors, undergrad and graduate level, 2.5 GPA, Over 20 scholarships, $250-$3,000. By August 29. ASTA Foundation, 1101 King Street, Suite 200, Alexandria, VA 22314, 703/739-8721, www.astanet.com.

CHAPTER 22

■■■■■■■■■■■■■■■■■■■■

MONEY FOR MINORITIES
AND WOMEN

Most financial aid is based on need—not race or gender—which means many of you have an edge in the competition for aid. Why? Because, statistically, the income of minorities is lower than that of their majority peers, and because women earn less than men who hold equal positions.

Also, as part of their effort to retain more students, many schools give minorities and women more favorable aid packages (e.g., more grants than loans). The General Accounting Office has shown that grant money has a strong effect on low-income student persistence. Translation: An additional $1,000 in grant funds means a 14% decrease in dropout rates while a $1,000 increase in loan aid means a 3% increase in dropout rates.

Resource List

What these numbers say is that for once you have a leg up. You are a stride ahead. So take advantage of that lead, and then, only after you have navigated the traditional, need-based route with savvy, should you look for the icing, found in this chapter, or from the following scholarship sources. Before you decide to purchase these guides, look for them in your guidance office or public library:

1. *Higher Education Opportunities for Minorities and Women,* free from the Dept. of Education, Higher Education Programs, 400 Maryland Avenue, SW, Portals C-80, Washington DC 20202.

2. Books from Reference Service Press, 5000 Windplay Drive #4, El Dorado Hills, CA 95762, www.rspfunding.com: *Directory of Financial Aids for Women* ($45), *Financial Aid for African-Americans* ($40), *Financial Aid for Asian-Americans* ($37.50), *Financial Aid for Hispanic-Americans* ($40), *Financial Aid for Native-Americans* ($42.50).

3. Books from Garrett Park Press, PO Box 190, Garrett Park, MD 20896: *The Big Book of Minority Opportunities* ($35), *The Big Book of Opportunities for Women* ($35). Also, a six-part pamphlet series ($5.95 each, $30 per set) on career-related scholarships for minority students.

4. *Online Scholarship Gateways,* Black Excel (www.blackexcel.org) and the United Negro College Fund (www.uncf.org).

The Latest Twists on Affirmative Action

The over-use of test scores in college admission has been in the news, and in the courts. Rejected-white applicants claim bias when public universities admit minority students with lower test scores; rejected-minority applicants claim bias when public schools make admission (or financial aid) decisions based on racially-disparate "high-stakes" testing. Over the years, some federal courts upheld policies that allowed schools to consider race as a factor in admissions, while other federal courts struck down this practice.

So is diversity on campus a compelling government interest? And, if it is, may colleges consider race in achieving this diversity? In 2003, the Supreme Court has answered "yes" to both these questions in its rulings on two cases filed against the University of Michigan. But it was a qualified "yes." The Court ruled *against* the undergraduate admission policy which used statistical formulas and a numerical point system to give favor to certain groups as a whole, like minorities or athletes or alumni kids, but it *upheld* the Law School's admission policy which considered race as one factor in an individual, holistic review of each applicant.

According to the Court's majority opinion, student body diversity *is* of compelling interest—it enriches everyone's education and "better prepares students for an increasingly diverse workforce and society" (an opinion echoed in 'amici' briefs filed by many businesses, as well as the U.S. military). Furthermore, the Law School's policy is deemed an acceptable way to achieve this diversity because it:

"... requires admission officers to evaluate each applicant based on all the information in the file" and assess "academic ability, experiences and potential to contribute to the learning of those around them."

"... does not define diversity solely in terms of racial and ethnic status."

"... does not seek to admit any particular number or percentage of minority students."

"... frequently accepts nonminority applicants with grades and test scores lower than minority applicants who are rejected."

So for now, it looks like colleges can consider race as one factor in the admission process. But be warned. A few states have now passed legislation outlawing the practice, including Michigan (as well as California and Washington).

Percentage Plans

Prior to this Supreme Court ruling, California, Florida and Texas had already taken actions to prohibit their public university systems from using race, gender or ethnicity as factors in admission decisions. Previously, these state university systems relied on a mechanistic combination of grades and test scores to admit students, and sometimes gave qualified minorities an extra edge in the calculation. Then, in a scramble to preserve campus diversity, they began experimenting with an alternative: guaranteeing admission to the top 4% (CA), 10% (TX) or 20% (FL) of every high school graduating class in the state regardless of test scores or other factors.

Is this system perfect? Far from it. Privacy laws and bureaucratic difficulties can make it hard to identify top-ranked students. Also, some worry that high schoolers in these states will start taking easier courses just to boost their GPAs (and class rank). And others note that it introduces a whole new set of inequities into the higher education selection system, and many deserving students will still miss the cut. Furthermore, preserving diversity at the collegiate level using these types of quotas is dependent on the continued segregation of our neighborhoods and our public high schools.

Percentage plans (with their promise of automatic admission) can ensure geographic diversity as well, even if they sometimes limit the number of slots a college has for other applicants.

Holistic Remedies

The good news is that most colleges do place a premium on diversity. They know the quality of a student's educational experience depends on a balanced incoming class—one with athletes, singers, mathematicians, and poets, and one which values a diverse, inclusive campus.

Many schools, especially smaller, private colleges, already take a holistic approach to admissions. Other schools will likely work hard to expand their recruitment efforts and bring their admission processes in line, hiring additional staff to travel the country and evaluate applications. They will now have to examine academic achievement as well as recommendations, extra-curricular activities, socio-economic status and race. They will consider criteria ranging from the quality of your essays to your work experience to your ability to speak more than one language. What obstacles have you overcome? Are you the first in your family to attend college? Have you had to work harder as a result of your home life? In other words, your perseverance and tenacity will not go unnoticed!

Impact on Financial Aid

As a result of the Supreme Court ruling, some schools argued that financial aid can influence where students enroll, so race-exclusive scholarships could be used as a (legal) tool in improving campus diversity.

More schools, however, have taken the opposite approach. Concerned over possible lawsuits, they are re-thinking (and re-naming) race-exclusive programs, and opening them up to non-minority students, especially those from economically-disadvantaged backgrounds—look for terms like "multicultural award" or "diversity award" or "first-generation scholarship." It's too soon to weigh the impact of these changes, but most experts expect minority students to remain the primary beneficiary.

Summer Workshops

If you are overwhelmed by the admission and financial aid process, you might consider a college-transition program during the summer before your Senior year of high school. Sessions include help with test-prep, admission essays, and financial aid forms. Here are two national programs:

College Horizons. For Native-American students only. Five-day crash course on preparing for college. Co-sponsored by the American Indian Graduate Center, www.wcollegehorizons.org.

College Summit. Over 30 sites around the country sponsor nearly 70 four-day summer workshops (aka "college application boot camps"), www.collegesummit.org.

Federal Assistance for Minorities

All Minorities

Minority Participation in Graduate Education Programs. $6 million program funded through 73 colleges. For school list: Office of Higher Education Program Services, Dept. of Education, 400 Maryland Ave., SW, Washington DC, 20202.

Office of Minority Health Resource Center. A central resource for minorities interested in the health professions. The Resource Center does not offer scholarships, but its trained information specialists will be glad to help you search its database of funding opportunities—via the Web, www.omhrc.gov or phone, 800/444-6472.

Native Americans

Native American Higher Education Grants. Need-based awards for undergrads. Apply through your tribe or area Bureau of Indian Education. For more information, contact the Bureau of Indian Education, 866/703-7100, www.oiep.bia.edu.

Indian Health Service. Five programs: (1) Preparatory Scholarship Program for students enrolled in prep courses leading to entry in health professions schools (medicine, nursing, pharmacy, etc.). Two years. (2) Pre-Graduate Scholarship Program for students enrolled in pre-med (or pre-dentistry) bachelor degree programs. Four years. (3) Health Professions Scholarship Program. Tuition plus stipend. Four years. Service obligation. (4) Loan repayment program and (5) Extern (student) employment program. By May 1. Apply to Indian Health Service, Scholarship Program, 801 Thompson Avenue, #400, Rockville, MD 20852, www.ihs.gov.

Catching the Dream. (1) MESBEC is for high-achieving Native American students in math, engineering, science (including all medical fields), business, education, computers. (2) NALE (Native American

Leadership in Education) is for Native American paraprofessionals who plan to obtain credentials as teachers, counselors or administrators, and teach in Indian schools. (3) Tribal Business Management Program for students in business-related fields who plan to work in economic development for tribes. Contact: Scholarship Affairs Office, 8200 Mountain Rd NE #203, Albuquerque, NM 87110. 505/262-2351, www.catchingthedream.org.

Private Assistance for Minorities

In addition to "transportable" scholarships, you should consider schools geared entirely to your ethnic group. They often attract large foundation grants which they use to expand their financial aid offerings. For example, the Lily Endowment distributed $112 million via the Hispanic Scholarship Fund, the American Indian College Fund and United Negro College Fund.

- *Tribal Colleges*: (1) The American Indian College Fund, 8333 Greenwood Blvd., Denver, CO 80221, www.collegefund.org; (2) American Indian Higher Education Consortium, 121 Oronoco Street, Alexandria, VA 22314, www.aihec.org
- *Hispanic Serving Institutions*: Hispanic Association of Colleges and Universities, 8415 Datapoint Dr., #400, San Antonio, TX 78229, www.hacu.net
- *Historically Black Colleges and Universities*: Gateway to HBCUs (sponsored by Howard University), www.dll.org/hbcus.

All Minorities

Accounting. Approximately 400 awards for undergrad and graduate students. Up to $5,000. Apply by July 1. Manager, Minority Recruitment, American Institute of Certified Public Accountants, 1211 Avenue of the Americas, New York, 10036-8775, www.aicpa.org.

Architecture. 20 awards, $500-$2,500. Nomination by HS counselor, college, professional architect by Dec 1. Open to HS seniors and college freshmen. Nomination forms from American Architectural Foundation Scholarship Program, 1799 New York Avenue, NW, Washington, DC 20006, www.archfoundation.org.

Chemistry. 100 renewable awards of up to $3,000 for students majoring in the chemical sciences. Students planning careers in medicine or pharmacy are not eligible. By March 31. American Chemical Society, Scholars Programs, 1155 16th Street NW, Washington, DC 20036, www.chemistry.org/scholars.

Dental Hygienists. Up to $1,500. By May 1. American Dental Hygienists Assoc., 444 N. Michigan #3400, Chicago, IL 60611, www.adha.org.

Dentistry. 20 scholarships of $2,500 for first year in dental school. By May 1 to American Dental Association, www.ada.org.

Engineering. Awards of up to $20,000. By early February. The National Action Council for Minorities in Engineering, www.nacme.org.

Engineering. Tuition plus $10,000 stipend for students working towards a master's in engineering programs at a GEM Member University; must intern for a Member Employer during summer. Also, tuition plus $14,000 stipends for students enrolled in Ph.D programs. By Nov. 1. National GEM Consortium, GEM Fellowship, 1800 K St., NW, #900, Washington, DC 20006, www.gemfellowship.org.

General Studies. Over 1,000 awards, $500-$5,000, for minority and low-income students. The Sallie Mae Fund, www.thesalliemaefund.org.

General Studies. Minority members of the United Methodist Church. $100-$1,000. Contact your church for more information.

General Studies. Gates Millennium Scholars Program. $50 million/year need-based grant program funded by Bill Gates (Microsoft). Applicants must have at least a 3.3 GPA, and demonstrated leadership ability. By December 31, www.gmsp.org.

General Studies. (1) Student Opportunity Scholarships, $200-$3,000. By April 1. (2) Native American Education Grant Program for Indians, Aleuts, and Eskimos pursuing postsecondary education. $200-$1,500. By June 1. Financial Aid for Studies, Presbyterian Church, 100 Witherspoon St., Louisville, KY 40202, www.pcusa.org/financial aid.

General Studies. Ford Foundation Fellowships. 60 3-year predoctoral fellowships (of $20,000), 35 1-year dissertation fellowships (of $21,000), and 20 1-year postdoctoral fellowships (of $40,000). The Fellowship Office, National Research Council, 500 Fifth Street, NW, Washington, DC 20001, www7.nationalacademies.org/fellowships.

Geosciences. $500-$3,000/yr. By Mar. 1. American Geological Institute, 4220 King St., Alexandria, VA 22302, www.agiweb.org/mpp.

Graduate Studies. The Committee on Institutional Cooperation (CIC) offers funding opportunities to students attending member institutions (primarily large, Midwestern research universities). CIC, 1819 S. Neil Street, #D, Champaign, IL 61820, www.cic.uiuc.edu.

Legal Training for the Disadvantaged. Free pre-law summer workshops. Council on Legal Education Opportunity, ABA, 740 15th St. NW, 9th fl., Washington, DC 20005, cleoscholars.com.

African American

Engineering. National Society of Black Engineers, $500-$7,500, national.nsbe.org.

General Studies. For Washington DC-area students; based on academic merit, leadership, service. Must be nominated by your school. Washington Metropolitan Scholars, 1220 L St., NW, Box 202, Washington DC 20015, 202/270-1762, www.wmscholars.org.

General Studies. The United Negro College Fund administers over 450 scholarship programs. UNCF, 8260 Willow Oaks Corporate Drive, Fairfax, VA 22031, 800/331-2244, www.uncf.org.

General Studies. National Achievement Scholarship Program. For African-American students who take the PSAT/NMSQT (no later than their Jr. year of HS). Finalists compete for 700 nonrenewable $2,500 National Achievement scholarships, and about 100 corporate-sponsored awards, most of which are renewable (and worth $500-$2,000/year). National Merit Scholarship Corp., 1560 Sherman Ave., #200, Evanston, IL 60201, www.nationalmerit.org.

General Studies. Ron Brown Scholarship. $10,000 renewable awards based on merit, need, leadership and public service. Highly competitive. Early January. www.RonBrown.org.

General Studies. Jackie Robinson Foundation Scholarship. 100 awards, $7,200/year. By March 31, 75 Varick St., 2nd fl., New York, NY 10013, 212/290-8600, www.JackieRobinson.org.

Law. 10-20 $3000 awards for use at any ABA-approved law school. Based on academic achievement and financial need. By March 15. Earl Warren Legal Training Program, 99 Hudson Street, #1600, New York, 10013, www.naacpldf.org.

Latino

Communications and Law. For graduate students in journalism or communications and law students who plan to serve the Latino community. Financial and academic criteria. By June 30. MALDEF, 634 S. Spring St., 11th Fl., Los Angeles, CA 90014, www.maldef.org.

Engineering. (1) General Motors/LULAC award. 20 $2,000 awards to engineering majors with at least a 3.25 GPA. (2) General Electric/LULAC award. 2 $5,000 awards for engineering and business majors with at least a 3.25 GPA. LULAC Educational Service Centers, 2000 "L" St., NW #610, Washington, DC 20036, www.LNESC.org.

General Studies. Hispanic College Fund. Over $1 million in need-based awards ranging from $500-$5,000. By March 15, hispanicfund.org.

General Studies. LULAC National Scholarship Fund. $250-$2000. By March 31 from LULAC council in your community. For list of councils, send a SASE to LULAC Educational Service Centers, 2000 "L" St., NW #610, Washington, DC 20036, www.LNESC.org.

General Studies. National Hispanic Recognition Program. Provides names of academically-talented (self-identified) Latino students to colleges based on PSAT results, www.collegeboard.com.

General Studies. Hispanic Scholarship Fund. $1,000 - $5,000 awards. Deadlines vary. SASE to Hispanic Scholarship Fund, 55 2nd St., #1500, San Francisco, CA 94105, 877/HSF-INFO, www.hsf.net.

Native American
General Study. Misc. awards. By June 1. American Indian Graduate Center., 4520 Montgomery Blvd., NE, #1-B, Albuquerque, NM 87109. 800/628-1920, www.aigc.com.

Private Assistance for Women
Tip: If you have child care expenses, let the college know. The school can increase your expense budget, thus qualifying you for more aid.

Aerospace Science or Engineering
Amelia Earhart Fellowship Awards, 35 $6,000 grants for graduate students. By Nov. 15. Zonta International Foundation, www.zonta.org.

Engineering
Society of Women Engineers, 130 awards, $1,000-$10,000. By Mar. 31, 230 E. Ohio St., #400, Chicago, IL 60611, societyofwomenengineers.swe.org.

General
Junior Miss. $5 million in local, state, and national awards. Another $75 million in college-granted scholarships. Contestants are judged on scholastics (20%), fitness (15%), self-expression (15%), talent (25%), and interview (25%). For your local comptetition, America's Jr. Miss, www.ajm.org.

General
American Association of University Women. Over 250 graduate fellowships. By Nov. 15. AAUW Educational Foundation 1111 16th Street NW, Washington DC 20036, 800/326-AAUW, www.aauw.org.

General
Executive Women International. 225 awards, $1,000- $10,000 from Exec. Women International, 515 South, 700 East, #2A, Salt Lake City, UT 84102, www.executivewomen.org.

General
Kappa Kappa Gamma. For members only. By February 1. Apply online, www.kappakappagamma.org.

Golf
Women's Western Golf Foundation. $2,000 awards for undergrads. Golf involvement is required, skill not a criterion. Selected based on academic achievement, need, character. By March 1. WWGF Scholarships, 393 Ramsay Road, Deerfield, IL 60015, www.wwga.org.

Older Women
BPW Career Advancement Scholarship for women age 25+. By April 15. 1620 Eye St. NW, #210, Washington DC, 20006, www.bpwusa.org.

CHAPTER 23

■■■■■■■■■■■■■■■■■■■■■■

SPECIAL SITUATIONS:
NON-TRADITIONAL STUDENTS

Physically-Disabled

Physically-disabled students frequently incur special expenses while attending college. Make sure these expenses are reflected in your student budget. This, in turn, will increase your need and you'll qualify for more aid. Your best source of information on special student aid is the Office of Vocational Rehabilitation, or the Office of Special Education Programs in your home state's education department. Here are some additional sources:

1. *HEATH Resource Center,* George Washington U., 2134 G St NW, Washington, DC 20052. www.HEATH.gwu.edu, TTY 202/973-0904. HEATH is the national clearinghouse on postsecondary education for individuals with disabilities. Be specific about your situation to make certain you receive the correct materials. As a start, request *Financial Aid for Students with Disabilities.* HEATH also compiles a list of summer pre-college programs that help students with disabilities jump-start their college careers and offers an online toolkit for counselors, *Advising High School Students with Disabilities on Postsecondary Options.*

2. *National Dissemination Center for Children with Disabilities.* Another information clearinghouse. Copies of their publications are available for free on their Web site, www.nichcy.org, or you can contact them at PO Box 1492, Washington DC, 20013, 800/695-0285.

3. *Financial Aid for the Disabled and Their Families,* Reference Service Press, 5000 Windplay Drive #4, El Dorado Hills, CA 95762, www.rspfunding.com. Check your library or guidance office, first. The directory costs around $40 and lists about 1,200 aid sources available to people with disabilities, including a list of state sources of benefits.

Here are some national programs that provide good work and assistance:

The Alexander Graham Bell Association for the Deaf and Hard of Hearing. Scholarship program for profoundly or severely deaf students who plan to attend a college that primarily enrolls students with normal hearing. $500 to $5,000. By March 1. 3417 Volta Place, NW, Washington, DC 20007, www.agbell.org.

American Council of the Blind offers 25 scholarships ($500 to $4,000). By March 1. Must be legally blind in both eyes. Contact Scholarship Administrator, ACB, 1155 15th St. NW, Suite 1004, Washington, DC 20005, 202/467-5081, www.acb.org.

National Association of the Deaf. Their scholarship program has closed, but they can help you find other resources, www.nad.org.

National Federation of the Blind offers 30 scholarships ranging from $3,000 to $12,000 to high-achieving legally blind students. National Federation of the Blind, 1800 Johnson Street, Baltimore, MD 21230, 410/659-9314, www.nfb.org. By March 31.

Recording for the Blind & Dyslexic. Marion Huber Learning Through Listening Awards for HS seniors with specific learning disabilities who plan to continue their education. Three awards of $6,000; three awards of $2,000. Must have B average or better and be registered with Recording for the Blind and Dyslexic for at least one year prior to the March 1 deadline. Public Affairs Dept., Recording for the Blind and Dyslexic, 20 Roszel Rd., Princeton, NJ 08540, www.rfbd.org.

Sertoma International. $1,000 awards. Applicants must have documented hearing loss and be a full-time student in a four-year institution. By May 1. SASE to Scholarships, Sertoma International, 1912 East Meyer Blvd., Kansas City, MO 64132, www.sertoma.org.

Special Accomodations

To maximize your SAT/ACT scores (and improve your chances for merit-based awards), ask about special accommodations, for example, taking the test in Braille, using a tape recorder, or simply receiving extra time.

- ACT Services for Students with Disabilities, www.act.org/aap/disab
- College Board Services for Students with Disabilities, www.collegeboard.com/ssd/student

Part-Timers

Most financial aid is reserved for students who attend college at least half-time. But take heart. Uncle's definition of "half-time" is pretty generous—six credits per term, which translates to about two courses—so apply for federal student aid even if you aren't sure of your status. Besides, colleges must set aside some of their SEOG and Work-study fund for part-timers. And thanks to the new Lifetime Learning Credit, part-timers are eligible for education tax credits.

Finally, TERI will be happy to lend a hand, and some money (up to $15,000), using TERI's Continuing Education Loan (800/255-TERI, www.teri.org).

Our Suggestion: Take another course, and boost your status to half-time.

Are You 50, 60 or Older?

If you plan to study at least half-time, most financial aid is awarded on the basis of need and not age. Hence, you can freely compete with those who are just out of high school and anybody else for all available aid.

If you plan to take just a few courses, many schools will let you attend for free or on a space available basis. Check with your local college.

Similarly, many states reduce (or waive) tuition for older citizens. Eligibility varies from state to state, but generally, students must be state residents age 60+ and attend state schools. Sometimes the discount is given to students only on a space-available basis. Contact your state higher education agency (addresses in Chapter 11).

Are You Only 25? 30?

Nearly half of all college students are 25 or older. Your best bet for financial aid (assuming you aren't a zillionaire) is that you will be filing your FAFSA as an independent student, thus only your own income and assets are assessed in calculating expected family contribution. This "independent" status will probably increase your eligibility for the need-based federal, state and collegiate resources described earlier in this book.

Many colleges view "older" students in the community as a potential boon to their enrollment base, and have special awards to attract these adult learners. They're also providing extras like commuter lounges and free (or low-cost) on-campus child care centers. Check with the financial aid offices at nearby schools.

International Students

International students are generally not eligible for U.S. government-sponsored student aid and, in the past, were usually only granted admission to U.S. colleges if they had the resources to pay full tab. Now, however, the competition for the best and the brightest has gone global, and more and more colleges are making their own aid resources available to geniuses from abroad. In fact, some of our top schools now have need-blind admission for international students, accepting them without regard to their ability to pay, and promising to meet their full financial need.

In the wake of 9/11, the U.S. developed a new system to track international students which caused some students to have a more difiult time obtaining a visa and contributed to several years of declining international enrollments. But the visa process has now improved, schools have stepped up their international recruiting efforts, and enrollment has risen to near-record levels

Of the 582,984 international students studying in the U.S., nearly 60% come from Asian nations; the majority study business, math, engineering or science.

CHAPTER 24

■■■■■■■■■■■■■■■■■■■■■

A FEW WORDS ABOUT
GRADUATE SCHOOL

Graduate student aid falls into three main categories: Fellowships, assistantships and loans (including loan cancellation for students who work in certain low-paying, public-interest jobs after getting their pricy-degrees). Neither fellowships nor assistantships need to be repaid, however both usually require some sort of service (e.g., conducting research, working with faculty or teaching undergraduates). Most students rely on a combination of these three aid sources, however, Doctoral candidates are most likely to receive fellowships and assistantships, Master's students are most likely to receive a balance of assistantships and loans, and professional students are most likely to receive loans.

Further analysis of graduate student aid shows that of non-doctoral students, those in law, medicine and business have the largest loans. Those in engineering and the natural sciences receive the largest assistantships, and those in the natural sciences, medicine and the social sciences receive the largest fellowships.

Similarly, of Doctoral students, those in medicine have the largest loans, those in engineering and the natural sciences receive the largest assistantships, and those in the natural sciences and the humanities receive the largest fellowships.

Tax Considerations

Tuition discounts (or tuition payments) received in exchange for services is considered taxable income. The University of Wisconsin (as reported by Jane Bryant Quinn) sums up graduate aid nicely: Stipends for teaching assistantships are taxable because the work helps the school without being central to a student's studies. Stipends for research assistants are tax free because the research, while of interest to the student and the teacher, isn't necessary to the school. Fellowships are clean—no work, no tax.

70% of All Graduate Aid

To learn where 70% of all graduate aid is, re-read Chapters 2 through 9. These lessons found there are as applicable to graduate students as they are to undergrads. Tuition discounts are especially common.

Second, review Chapter 10 and become familiar with tuition tax credits (and deductions) and federal sources of aid: Stafford Loans, Perkins Loans and Work-Study. (Graduate students are not eligible for Pell Grants or SEOGs.) If your future is in a medical field, add Chapter 20 to your reading.

And, if all else fails, investigate the commercial loans listed in Chapter 7.

3% of All Graduate Aid

For 3% of all graduate aid, check your home state. Last year, states spent $60 million on need-based grant aid for grad students and $32.9 million on merit-based aid. In addition, states give money for loans, work-study and loan forgiveness. Many opportunities are restricted to specific study fields (e.g., teaching, medicine, law) or population groups (e.g., minorities or veterans). Furthermore, students must usually enroll at in-state schools.

10% of All Graduate Aid

About 10% of all graduate aid is dispersed throughout this book. For instance, if you get a commission in the military and are willing to extend your period of service, you may qualify for graduate training. Employer-paid tuition and cooperative education (Chapter 12) are also rich in graduate opportunities. And you'll find more in Chapters 21 and 22.

12% of All Graduate Aid

For 12% of all graduate aid, talk to your department chair. Here is how these people can help you:

- *With departmental fellowships and grants.* These are the most prestigious forms of aid and require very little from you in return.
- *With graduate assistantships.* Consider this an apprenticeship. While you have to work (quite a bit) for your money, the experience will look wonderful on your Curriculum Vitae (the academic version of a resume), and help you bond with more senior faculty members, leading to better recommendations when you finally hit the job trail. More than 60% of all doctoral students have paid assistantships.
- *With internships and summer jobs.* With any luck, you may even find work you can turn into your thesis or dissertation.
- *With employment funded by a research grant.* The professor usually gets the grant, but will need help to count chromosomes, wash test tubes, show slides, or lead discussion groups. Private industry doles out over $23 billion each year for science and technology research. The federal government kicks in another $27 billion. For example, the National Institutes of Health and the National Science Foundation give $12 billion to university scientists each year, while lawmaker-directed research grants (aka "academic pork") top $2.25 billion, spread out over 2,300 research projects at 920 institutions.

In grad school, the committee that decides on admission also decides on departmental awards. To better your chances for both, get to know the faculty. After you apply for admission, make appointments to meet professors in your area of interest. Send them a copy of your undergraduate thesis or a research paper. Visit their classrooms. Observe their teaching styles. Be humble. And remember, unless you're applying to professional schools (law, medicine, business, engineering), your most important consideration is to find a professor with whom you want to work. The reputation of the univeristy can be secondary to the reputation of an individual department. And top name professors attract the largest grants, no matter where they teach.

You might also consider going to work for a university. Many schools discount tuition for full-time employees, and while it may take a few extra years to get through the program, you won't have a huge debt burden when you're through.

And check the placement office. If you're going to leave school with large loans, you should know more about your job prospects.

1% of All Graduate Aid

Private foundations may award funds for projects in your area of interest. These you have to discover yourself. The best bet starting points: two publications put out by the Foundation Center and one by the Oryx Press. We don't recommend you buy these references. They are expensive. But do locate them online, or in the reference room of your library and spend some time looking through them.

1. The Foundation Center's current *Foundation Directory* and *Foundation Grants to Individuals* (www.FoundationCenter.org).

2. The Oryx Press' current *Directory of Grants in the Humanities*.

4% of All Graduate Aid

All Disciplines

You're a graduate student. You should be good at research. So spend some time surfing government resources. Even as Uncle shrinks his budget, hundreds of little grant programs remain. The White House site will link you to every federal agency and commission (www.whitehouse.gov/government/independent-agencies.html).

You should also click through the 200+ programs funded by the Department of Education. There's an index of programs (by title and category) at www.ed.gov/programs/gtep.

All Disciplines

NCAA Postgraduate Awards. Nearly 175 postgrad scholarships (non-renewable grants of up to $7,500 each) to student-athletes who compete on a varsity team at an NCAA member school and excel academically and athletically. www.ncaa.org.

All Disciplines

Jack Kent Cooke Scholars. 30 awards of up to $50,000 per year. Must be nominated by your institution by March 15. For more information, contact the foundation at 800/498-6478, www.jackkentcookefoundation.org.

Arts, Humanities and Social Sciences

Javits Fellowships. Over 220 awards/year for graduate students in the arts, humanities and social sciences. $3,000 to $42,627 (depending on need). Early October. Dept. of Education, Jacob Javits Fellowship Program, 1990 K St., NW, 6th fl., Washington, DC 20006, www.ed.gov/programs/jacobjavits.

Communicative Disorders

Sertoma. For students pursuing master's degrees in audiology or speech pathology. 30 awards of $2,500 per year. For more information, send SASE to Sertoma World Headquarters, Communicative Disorders Scholarship, 1912 East Meyer Blvd., Kansas City, MO 64132, www.sertoma.org.

Engineering, Math and Science

National Defense Science and Engineering Graduate Fellowship Program. Three-year fellowships leading to graduate degree in science or engineering. 200 new awards each year. Full tuition plus $30,500 stipend. No service obligation. NDSEG Fellowship Program, 1818 N Street NW, #600, Washington, DC 20036, www.asee.org/ndseg. By early-January.

Family and Consumer Sciences

AAFCS. $3,000-$5,000 fellowships. Early January. For information, write AAFCS, 400 N. Columbus St., #202, Alexandria, VA 22314, 703/706-4600, www.aafcs.org.

Geology

Geological Society of America. Nearly $450,000 in annual grants to 225 students doing masters/doctoral thesis research in earth sciences. By Feb. 1. Contact Research Grants Administrator, Geological Soc. of America, PO Box 9140, Boulder, CO 80301, www.geosociety.org.

International Education and Business

International Education and Graduate Programs Service. Fifty-one funded projects. Some fellowships. For school list, write: IEGP, US Dept. of Education, 500 Independence Ave., SW, Washington, DC 20202.

International Exchange

Fulbright Fellowships. Live and study abroad as a Fulbright fellow. 1500 students go to over 140 nations. Fulbright Student Programs, 809 United Nations Plaza, New York, NY 10017, www.iie.org/fulbright.

Languages and Teaching

Foreign Language and Area Studies (FLAS). Graduate fellowships for foreign language and international studies. Funded through schools. Schools select students. For information and school list write: International Education and Graduate Program Service, FLAS Fellowships, 1990 K Street NW, 6th floor, US Department of Education, Washington, DC 20006.

Law (including Bar Review)

LawAchiever (Key Bank) and SallieMae offer law school loans of up to $150,000 as well as bar exam loans of up to $15,000 to help pay for law school and living expenses while you study for the Bar. Rates can be high, but students who can't get a loan from their parents or a future employer often have no other choice. After all, what bank is going to lend $150,000 to a person with no income or assets?

- LawAchiever, 800/KEY-LEND, www.key.com/educate
- SallieMae, www.salliemae.com

Law

Loan Repayment Assistance Programs. 16 states and more than 100 of our top law schools forgive loans for students who bypass high-paying law firms and go on to practice public interest law or become public defenders or government prosecutors. Fellowship information as well, www.equaljusticeworks.org.

Marine Sciences

John A. Knauss Marine Policy Fellowship Program for graduate students. Late Feb. National Sea Grant College Program, Knauss Program Manager, 1315 East West Highway, NOAA/SeaGrant R/SG, room 11718, Silver Spring, MD 20910, www.nsgo.seagrant.org/knauss.html.

Miscellaneous

Woodrow Wilson National Fellowship Foundation has created a suite of fellowships to achieve its mission of "identifying and developing the best minds for the nations most important challenges." Sample fields include: teaching, foreign affairs, conservation, women's studies and religion. Woodrow Wilson National Fellowship Foundation, Box 5281, Princeton, NJ 08543, 609/452-7007. www.woodrow.org.

Music

The American Musicological Society offers 50 doctoral dissertation fellowships per year. By January 15. Applications must be submitted online, www.ams-net.org/awards.

National Needs Areas

National Needs. Need-based stipends to enhance teaching in designated academic needs areas. Funding is tenuous. For school list, write Div. of Higher Educational Incentive Programs, OPE, Dept. of Education, Rm. 3022, 400 Maryland Ave. SW, Washington, DC 20202.

New Americans

Paul and Daisy Soros Fellowships. 30 awards/year to students who are holders of Green Cards, naturalized citizens or children of two naturalized citizens. $20,000 plus 1/2 tuition for up to two years, by November 1, www.pdsoros.org.

Professional Students

Assorted Loans. Most financial aid for professional students takes the form of loans. Student loan recipients who attend professional schools graduate with an average debt over $60,000 (compared to $26,500 for those pursuing masters degrees). Quite a few schools (and states) offer loan forgiveness for students who enter low-paying, public service fields, in hopes their job choice won't be influenced by the size of their repayments.

If you would rather not borrow under the Federal PLUS program (Chapter 10), many private lenders will let you borrow enough to cover the cost of your education with 20-30 years to repay. Interest is tied to the Prime or LIBOR plus 2%-3.5% with a 7-13% fee (based on credit history). For more information, contact the commercial loan sources listed in Chapter 7.

Science, Math, Engineering

Graduate Research Fellowship Program. Up to 1,600 fellowships/year for graduate study in science, mathematics and engineering. Three years of support. $30,000 annual stipend plus $10,500 for tuition. Early Nov. National Science Foundation, 4201 Wilson Blvd., Arlington, VA 22230, 866/NSF-GRFP, www.nsf.gov/grfp.

Space-Related Science, Math and Engineering

NASA. Summer programs and renewable graduate school awards of up to $30,000. By Feb. 1. For more information: Graduate Student Researchers Program, Education Division, NASA Headquarters, Mail Code FE, 300 E St., SW, Washington, DC 20546, education.nasa.gov/gsrp.

Additional Resources

The National Association of Graduate and Professional Students has an active and extensive web site: www.nagps.org.

CHAPTER 25

■■■■■■■■■■■■■■■■■■■■■■

A TREASURE CHEST OF TIPS

Students today must cope with aid funding that doesn't keep pace with rising tuition. But to get all the money due you (from your college, state and Uncle), you must know more about every aspect of financial aid or dig deeper. To save you the cost of a new shovel, here is a summary of the skills you, as a student, must master.

1. When picking a college, go beyond the normal search criteria. Don't just look at majors, academic reputation, and distance from home. Also inquire about innovative tuition aid features; matching scholarships, sibling scholarships, installment plans, middle income assistance programs, tuition remission, etc. **See Chapter 9.**

2. All factors being equal, pick colleges most likely to offer you an aid package rich in grants you don't have to repay. Such a package is a lot better than one made up of loans which will saddle you with a repayment burden for many years after graduation. Best bet: Any school in which your academic record places you in the upper 25% of the profile of the incoming freshman class. **See Chapters 7 and 9.**

3. Send applications to competing colleges of equal merit. If you get accepted by both, you might be able to use their rivalry to secure a more favorable package. **See Chapters 7 and 9.**

4. Try the online degree route. Win a sheepskin without leaving home or job. Such a diploma will cost less in money and time than if it had been earned through campus attendance. And don't forget, you can get additional academic credit for learning you've already acquired, through real-life experience. **See Chapter 7.**

5. Do four years work in three. You attend summer school, but the compressed time saves you the inflationary increase of the fourth year. Also, avoid taking extra years to get through college. Fewer and fewer students are graduating in four years, costing them a whole extra year's tuition. **See Chapter 7.**

6. Start at a community college. Work hard. Get good grades. Transfer to a solid four-year institution and pick up a prestige diploma at half the cost. **See Chapter 7.**

7. Accelerate your degree. Get credit for a semester or year of college work through the Advanced Placement Program or by enrolling in college courses in high school. When tuition credits cost as much as $500 each, receiving credit for high school work leaves money in the bank. **See Chapters 7.**

8. Understand how need analysis works. By knowing the formulas, the shrewd family obtains more need-based aid—sort of like presenting one's financial picture to the IRS to as to qualify for the smallest possible tax liability. **See Chapters 6 and 7.**

9. Try some "what if?" calculations. But first, learn how need analysis works. You'll be surprised at the dollar figures generated by "what if" drills. **See Chapter 7.**

10. Search for scholarships. Test the (free) Web-based searches. **See Chapter 3.**

202 • Don't Miss Out

11. Don't pass up entitlement programs. Billions in low-interest, subsidized federal student loans go unused each year because students think they are ineligible, or don't bother with the paper work hassle. **See Chapter 10.**

12. Go to college on the house. Many home owners have accumulated large amounts of equity in their houses. Your strategy: Releasing this equity through a line of credit or through refinancing the first mortgage. **See Chapters 7 and 9.**

13. Improve your aid package. The FAA will present you with an aid package to cover the difference between what college costs and what your family can pay. If you feel the college really wants you, because you are a brain or an athlete or the child of an alum or you help it meet a geographic or minority quota, ask about improving the package. Your objective: To increase the grant component (money you don't have to repay) and reduce the loan component. **See Chapters 6, 7, and 9.**

14. Try for an academic scholarship. Over 1,200 colleges offer academic scholarships to students with B averages and SAT scores of 900 or more. Moreover, most of these scholarships are not based on financial need. If you are just outside the SAT eligibility range for one of these awards, take a good SAT prep course. It may raise your scores enough to enter the winner's circle. **See Chapter 18.**

15. Go the cooperative education route. Over 500 colleges offer co-op education programs. Alternate formal study with periods of career-related work. Earn up to $15,000 per year during the work phase. It may take an extra year to win the degree, but it will be easier on the pocketbook. **See Chapter 12.**

16. Try for athletic student aid. We aren't talking about the "Body by Nautilus, Mind by Mattel" tackle who can do 40 yards in 4 seconds. Husky U. will find that person. We're talking about students who are better than average in a variety of sports, from swimming to soccer to crew. The rewards come in two forms: outright scholarships or "improved" financial aid packages. **See Chapter 19.**

17. Be an accurate, early bird. Be accurate in filling out financial aid forms. Submit them as early as you can. When resources are tight, it's first-come, first-served. Those who must resubmit their forms and those who are slow in applying go to the end of the line. By then, all the money is gone. **See Chapters 6 and 7.**

18. Check the military offerings. For a hitch in the National Guard you pick up a state benefit, a federal bonus, loan forgiveness, drill pay, and sometimes, tuition remission at the State U. Or, go on active duty, take courses while off duty (the military will pay most of your tuition) and participate in the GI Bill. When you get your degree, you will be a few years older than your non-saluting contemporaries, but you will also be more mature, self-confident, and debt-free. **See Chapter 13.**

19. Take advantage of teacher mania. Most states forgive loans for prospective teachers. You teach Ohm's law for four years to pay off the obligation. You pick up a little maturity, a lot of patience. You contribute to the well-being of hundreds of scholars-to-be. And you're young enough to begin a new career if teaching is not for you. **See Chapter 11.**

20. Sacrifice. You may have to give up a few luxuries, like swapping Lobster-tail for McFish Filet, and grande-triple-mochas for home-brewed joe.

■ ■ ■ ■ ■ ■ ■ ■ ■ ■ ■ ■ ■ ■ ■ ■ ■ ■

Dependent Students
(2009/2010 Academic Year)

Parent's Contribution from Income

1. Parents' Adjusted Gross Income .... $_____
2. Parents' Tax-exempt Interest Income .... $_____
3. Veteran's Non-educational Benefits .... $_____
4. Parents' Other Untaxed Income and Benefits.
   This may include child support received, untaxed portions of pensions and
   IRA distributions, workers' compensation, disability payments, housing,
   food and living allowances for military, clergy or others .... $_____
5. Deductible IRA, Keogh, SEP, 403 (b), 401(k) pymnts made by parents .. $_____
6. **Total Income.** Add Lines 1 through 5 .... $_____
7. US Income Taxes paid .... $_____
8. State Income Taxes paid.. $_____
9. Social Security/Medicare Taxes paid .... $_____
10. Child Support paid by you for another child .... $_____
11. Hope credit and/or Lifetime Learning credit, AmeriCorps awards, taxable
    earnings from Federal Work-Study (or other need-based work program)
    and other student financial aid that may have been included in Line 6. ... $_____
12. Income Protection Allowance from Table A .... $_____
13. Employment Expense Allowance. If both parents work, enter 35% of
    the lower income or $3,500, whichever is less. If your family has a
    single head of household, enter 35% of that income or $3,500, whichever
    is less. Otherwise, enter $0 .... $_____
14. **Total Allowances.** Add Lines 7 through 13 .... $_____
15. **Parents' Available Income.** Line 6 minus Line 14. If negative, subtract
    from Line 30 .... $_____

Parents Contribution from Assets[1]

16. Cash, savings and checking accounts .... $_____
17. Net Worth of real estate (excluding primary residence), investments, stocks,
    CDs, bonds, trusts, commodities, precious metals, college savings plans $_____
18. Business and/or Commercial Farm Net Worth (excluding family farms
    and family-controlled small businesses) from Table B .... $_____
19. **Total Assets.** Add Lines 16 through 18 .... $_____
20. Asset Protection Allowance. From Table C .... $_____
21. Discretionary Net Worth. Line 19 minus Line 20 .... $_____
22. **CONTRIBUTION FROM ASSETS.** Multiply Line 21 by 12%.
    If negative, enter $0 .... $_____

Parental Contribution

23. Adjusted Available Income. Add Lines 15 and 22 .... $_____
24. **PARENT CONTRIBUTION.** From Table D. If negative, enter 0. .... $_____
25. Number in College Adjustment. Divide Line 24 by the number in college at
    least half-time (excluding parents). Quotient is the contribution/student . $_____

Student's Contribution from Income

26. Student's Adjusted Gross Income .... $_____

27. Student's Tax-exempt Interest Income .... $_____

28. Student's Other Untaxed income and benefits. See Line 4.
Also include any cash support paid on your behalf which was not
reported elsewhere .... $_____

29. Deductible IRA payments made by student .... $_____

30. Total Income. Add lines 26 through 29 .... $_____

31. US Income Taxes paid .... $_____

32. State Income Taxes paid .... $_____

33. Social Security/Medicare Taxes paid .... $_____

34. AmeriCorps awards, student financial aid that may have been included
in Line 30, taxable earnings from Federal Work-Study or other
need-based work programs .... $_____

35. Income Protection Allowance. Enter $3,750 .... $_____

36. Total Allowances. Add Lines 31 through 35 .... $_____

37. Students Available Income. Line 30 minus Line 36 .... $_____

38. **STUDENT'S CONTRIBUTION FROM INCOME**
Multiply Line 37 by 50%. If negative, enter $0 .... $_____

Student's Contribution from Assets[1]

39. Add net worth of all of student's assets—cash, savings, trusts,
investments, real estate .... $_____

40. **STUDENT'S CONTRIBUTION FROM ASSETS**
Take 20% of Line 39 .... $_____

Family Contribution

41. If one student is in college, add lines 24, 38, and 40. .... $_____

42. If two or more students are in college at the same time,
add for each, Lines 25, 38, and 40. .... $_____

Notes to Appendices

[1] Contribution from student and parent assets will equal $0 if Parents' AGI (Line 1) is less than $50,000 and the parents are eligible to file a 1040A, 1040 EZ, or no tax return at all.

[2] Contribution from assets will equal $0 if student (and spouse) AGI (Line 1) is less than $50,000 and the student (and spouse) are eligible to file a 1040A or 1040EZ or no tax return at all.

■■■■■■■■■■■■■■■■■■■■■■■■■■■■■■■■■■

Independent Students with Dependents (2009/2010 Academic Year)

Contribution from Income (Student's and Spouse's)

1. Student's (and Spouse's) Adjusted Gross Income .... $_____
2. Student's (and Spouse's) Tax-exempt Interest Income .... $_____
3. Student's (and Spouse's) Veteran's Non-educational Benefits .... $_____
4. Student's (and Spouse's) Other Untaxed Income and Benefits.
   This may include child support received,untaxed portions of pensions and
   IRA distributions, workers' compensation, disability payments, housing,
   food and living allowances for military, clergy or others .... $_____
5. Deductible IRA, KEOGH, 403 (b) and 401(k) payments made by
   student (and spouse) .... $_____
6. **Total Income.** Add Lines 1 through 5 .... $_____
7. US Income Taxes paid .... $_____
8. State Income Taxes paid... $_____
9. Social Security/Medicare Taxes paid .... $_____
10. Child Support paid by you for another child .... $_____
11. Hope credit, Lifetime Learning credit, AmeriCorps awards, taxable
    earnings from Federal Work-Study (or other need-based work program)
    and other student financial aid that may have been included in Line 6. ... $_____
12. Income Protection Allowance from Table A .... $_____
13. Employment Expense Allowance. If both student and spouse work, enter
    35% of the lower income or $3,500, whichever is less. If student qualifies
    as a single head of household, enter 35% of that income or $3,500,
    whichever is less. Otherwise, enter $0 .... $_____
14. **Total Allowances.** Add Lines 7 through 13 .... $_____
15. **Student's (and Spouse's) Available Income.** Line 6 minus Line 14 .... $_____

Contribution from Assets (Student's and Spouse's)[2]

16. Cash, savings and checking accounts .... $_____
17. Net Worth of real estate (excluding primary residence), investments, stocks,
    bonds, trusts, commodities, precious metals, college savings plans .... $_____
18. Business and/or Commercial Farm Net Worth (excluding family farms
    and family-controlled small businesses) from Table B .... $_____
19. **Total Assets.** Add Lines 16 through 18 .... $_____
20. Asset Protection Allowance. From Table E .... $_____
21. Discretionary Net Worth. Line 19 minus Line 20 .... $_____
22. **CONTRIBUTION FROM ASSETS.** Multiply Line 21 by 7%. .... $_____
23. Adjusted Available Income. Add Line 15 and Line 22. .... $_____
24. **TOTAL CONTRIBUTION.** From Table D. If negative, enter 0. .... $_____
25. Number in College Adjustment. Divide Line 24 by the number in college
    at least half-time at the same time. Quotient is the contribution/student .. $_____

■■■■■■■■■■■■■■■■■■■■■■■■■■■

Independent Students without Dependents (2009/2010 Academic Year)

Contribution from Income (Student's and Spouse's)

1. Student's (and Spouse's) Adjusted Gross Income .... $_____
2. Student's (and Spouse's) Tax-exempt Interest Income .... $_____
3. Student's (and Spouse's) Earned Income Credit .... $_____
4. Student's (and Spouse's) Other Untaxed Income and Benefits.
   This may include child support received, untaxed portions of pensions and
   IRA distributions, workers' compensation, disability payments, housing,
   food and living allowances for military, clergy or others .... $_____
5. Deductible IRA, KEOGH, 403 (b) and 401(k) payments made by
   student (and spouse) .... $_____
6. **Total Income.** Add Lines 1 through 5 .... $_____
7. US Income Taxes paid .... $_____
8. State Income Taxes paid .... $_____
9. Social Security/Medicare Taxes paid .... $_____
10. Income Protection Allowance of $7,000 for single student or
    married student if spouse is also+ enrolled in college at least half time;
    $11,220 for married student if spouse is not enrolled at least half-time ... $_____
11. Child Support paid by you for another child .... $_____
11. Hope Tax credit, Lifetime Learning credit, AmeriCorps awards, taxable
    earnings from Federal Work-Study (or other need-based work program)
    and other student financial aid that may have been included in Line 6. ... $_____
13. Employment Expense Allowance. If the student is single, enter $0. If the
    student is married and both the student and spouse are working, enter 35%
    of the lower income or $3,500, whichever is less. Otherwise, enter $0 .... $_____
14. **Total Allowances.** Add Lines 7 through 13 .... $_____
15. **Available Income.** Line 6 minus Line 14 .... $_____
16. **Contribution from Income.** Take 50% of Line 15 .... $_____

Contribution from Assets (Student's and Spouse's)[2]

17. Cash, savings and checking accounts .... $_____
18. Net Worth of real estate (excluding primary residence), investments, stocks,
    bonds, trusts, commodities, precious metals, college savings plans .... $_____
19. Business and/or Commercial Farm Net Worth (excluding family farms
    and family-controlled small businesses) from Table B .... $_____
20. **Total Assets.** Add lines 17 through 19 .... $_____
21. Asset Protection Allowance. From Table E .... $_____
22. Discretionary Net Worth. Line 20 minus Line 21 .... $_____
23. **CONTRIBUTION FROM ASSETS.** Multiply Line 22 by 20%.
    If negative, enter $0 .... $_____
24. **TOTAL CONTRIBUTION.** Add Line 16 and Line 23 .... $_____
25. Number in College Adjustment. Divide Line 24 by the number in college
    at least half-time at the same time. Quotient is the contribution/ student . $_____

Table A—Income Protection Allowance

Family Members (Incl. Student)	Dep. Student Allowance	Indep. Stdnt Allowance
2	$15,840	$17,720
3	$19,730	$22,060
4	$24,370	$27,250
5	$28,750	$32,150
6	$33,630	$37,600
Each Addit'l	$3,800	$4,240

Note: *For each student over one in college, subtract $2,700 from the appropriate maintenance allowance (for dependent students) or $3,020 from the appropriate maintenance allowance (for independent students).*

Table B—Adjustment of Business/Farm Net Worth

Net Worth of Business/Farm	Adjustment
To $115,000	40% of Net Worth
$115,001 to $340,000	$46,000, plus 50% of NW over $115,000
$340,001 to $565,000	$158,500, plus 60% of NW over $340,000
$560,501 or more	$293,500 plus 100% of NW over $565,000

Table C—Asset Protection Allowance, Dependent Student

Age of Older Parent	Two-Parent Family	One Parent Family
40-44	$45,300	$18,600
45-49	51,200	20,900
50-54	58,000	23,500
55-59	66,400	26,500
60-64	76,600	30,300
65 +	84,000	32,800

Table D—Parent and Independent Student Contribution

Adjusted Available Income (AAI)	Parent Contribution
To minus $3,409	-$750 (negative figure)
Minus $3,409 to plus $14,200	22% of AAI
$14,201 to $17,800	$3,124 plus 25% of AAI over $14,200
$17,801 to $21,400	$4,024 plus 29% of AAI over $17,800
$21,401 to $25,000	$5,068 plus 34% of AAI over $21,400
$25,001 to $28,600	$6,292 plus 40% of AAI over $25,000
$28,601 or more	$7,732 plus 47% of AAI over $28,600

Table E—Asset Protection Allowance, Independent Student

Age	Single	Married
25 & Under	$ 0	$ 0
26	1,200	2,900
29	4,800	11,600
32	8,400	20,300
35	11,900	28,900
38	15,500	37,600
45	19,900	48,700
50	22,400	55,300
65+	32,800	84,000

College Planning Guides from Octameron

Don't Miss Out: The Ambitious Student's Guide to Financial Aid **$13.00**
Hailed as the top consumer guide to student aid, *Don't Miss Out* covers scholarships, loans, and personal finance strategies. It will save readers hundreds, if not thousands of dollars in college costs.

The A's and B's of Academic Scholarships **$13.00**
Money for being bright! This book describes 100,000 awards offered by nearly 1200 colleges. Best of all, most of these (which must be used at the sponsoring school) are not based on financial need.

Loans and Grants from Uncle Sam **$8.00**
Increase your eligibility for federal student aid. This guide describes it all—the aid application process as well as loans and grants for students, parents and health professionals.

Financial Aid FinAncer: Expert Answers to College Financing Questions **$8.00**
Learn how special family circumstances impact on student aid.

The Winning Edge: The Student-Athlete's Guide to College Sports **$9.00**
It's all here. Scholarship opportunities. NCAA rules and regulations. Advice from coaches. Sample athletic resumes. Strategies, timetables, and worksheets—all to help you take your sport to college!

Financial Aid Officers: What They Do—To You and For You **$5.00**
Should you accept your award package as offered? Can you request it be changed, or increased? Knowledgeable dealings with FAOs can result in more money. This book shows you how.

Behind the Scenes: An Inside Look at the College Admission Process **$8.00**
Ed Wall, former Dean of Admission at Amherst College, offers sage advice and detailed profiles of successful applicants. An invaluable view from inside on how the selection process really works.

Do It Write: How to Prepare a Great College Application **$7.00**
Personalize your essays so they stand out from the crowd. Author Gary Ripple is the former Admission Director at Lafayette College and the College of William and Mary

College Match: A Blueprint for Choosing the Best School for You **$11.00**
Author Steve Antonoff combines dozens of easy-to-use worksheets with lots of practical advice to make sure you find schools that meet your needs and your preferences.

Campus Pursuit: Making the Most of the Visit and Interview **$6.00**
Nervous about your interview? In his companion book to *Do-It Write*, Gary Ripple gives advice that will help you shine, as well as show you how to maximize the benefits of a campus visit.

College.edu: On-Line Resources for the Cyber-Savvy Student **$12.00**
Lost in Cyberspace? *College.edu* takes you to hundreds of useful sites on admission and financial aid, giving you Internet tips and warnings along the way.

Campus Daze: Easing the Transition from High School to College **$8.00**
Learn what to expect during your first year of college and how to succeed starting on Day One. Author George Gibbs is the former Dean of Admission and Freshmen at Muhlenberg College.

College Majors That Work **$10.00**
Get in. Get out. Get a job. Worksheets help match a student's goals and expectations with the right college major and explores how that choice plays out in the real world—influencing both career and lifestyle options. Written by Michael P. Viollt, President of Robert Morris College (IL),

Calculating Expected Family Contribution (EFC) Software **$45.00**
Estimate how much you will be expected to pay for college. This Windows-compatible CD-Rom software holds data on hundreds of families and let's you analyze different income and asset scenarios.

Ordering Information

Send Orders to: Octameron Associates, PO Box 2748, Alexandria, VA 22301, or contact us at: 703-836-5480 (voice), 703-836-5650 (fax), octameron@aol.com (e-mail).

Order Online: www.octameron.com.

Postage and Handling: Please include $3.00 for one publication, $5.00 for two publications $6.00 for three publications and $7.00 for four or more publications.

Method of Payment: Payment must accompany order. We accept checks, money orders, American Express, Visa and MasterCard.

If ordering by credit card, please include the card number and its expiration date.

HEALTH AND SAFETY ASPECTS IN THE LIVE MUSIC INDUSTRY

Chris Kemp
Iain Hill

**ENTERTAINMENT
TECHNOLOGY PRESS**

Safety Series

To Ian Thomson, whose sharp wit and editing skills will be sorely missed. Good luck in your retirement.

HEALTH AND SAFETY ASPECTS IN THE LIVE MUSIC INDUSTRY

Chris Kemp, Iain Hill

Entertainment Technology Press

Health And Safety Aspects in the Live Music Industry

© Chris Kemp, Iain Hill

First edition Published January 2004 by
Entertainment Technology Press Ltd
The Studio, High Green, Great Shelford, Cambridge, CB22 5EG
Internet: www.etnow.com

ISBN 1 904031 22 6

A title within the
Entertainment Technology Press Safety Series
Series editor: John Offord
in association with Buckinghamshire New University

CODE / LHS-002_03-04